Building a
TypePad
BLOG
People Want to Read

Scott McNulty

Building a TypePad Blog People Want to Read

Scott McNulty

Peachpit Press
1249 Eighth Street
Berkeley, CA 94710
510/524-2178
510/524-2221 (fax)

Find us on the Web at: www.peachpit.com
To report errors, please send a note to errata@peachpit.com.

Peachpit Press is a division of Pearson Education.
Copyright © 2010 by Scott McNulty

Executive editor: Clifford Colby
Editor: Kathy Simpson
Production editor: Danielle Foster
Compositor: Danielle Foster
Indexer: Valerie Haynes Perry
Cover design: Charlene Charles-Will
Interior design: Peachpit Press

ISBN-13 978-0-321-62451-2
ISBN-10   0-321-62451-3

9 8 7 6 5 4 3 2 1

Printed and bound in the United States of America

About the Author

Scott McNulty has been blogging for ten years, seven of those on TypePad. He owns more e-readers than one man should and several times more books than are sensible.

Scott lives in Philadelphia with his wife, Marisa. By day, he's the mild-mannered chief blogger at Comcast. By night, he blogs about whatever strikes his fancy at http://blog.blankbaby.com. He has also been known to tweet once or twice under the handle @blankbaby.

Acknowledgments

Most folks have no idea how many people it takes to produce a good book (and I take all the help I can get). My thanks to Cliff Colby, for once again persuading me to feel the joys of tech authorship; to Kathy Simpson, who proves that it takes more than one bad tooth to keep a good editor down; and to all the people at Peachpit Press who made this book a reality, including Danielle Foster and Charlene Charles-Will.

I'd also like to thank Jenn and Kate for encouraging my moonlighting.

To Sean, my brother, for helping tend to practical matters during our childhood (while I didn't).

Contents

Preface

Because you picked up this book (and perhaps even bought it), I assume that you're interested in learning more about TypePad (www.typepad.com; **Figure P.1**) and, by logical extension, about blogging. This book is mainly a TypePad primer, but it also covers how best to leverage your blog for your business.

Figure P.1 The TypePad logo.

Before I get into the meat of TypePad, however, I need to cover some blogging basics.

note If you want even more basics, you can find a glossary of blogging terms in the back of this book.

What Is a Blog?

The answer to this question is very important, don't you agree? At its most basic level, a *blog* is a Web site that's frequently updated and usually displays the most recent content first, with the older content listed in reverse chronological order. To that basic structure, a variety of things can be added—comments, videos, and pictures, to name just a few.

By contrast, here are a few things that a blog *isn't*:

- A static Web site
- A get-rich scheme
- The solution to all your problems
- For every business

note It might be a little odd for someone who's writing a book about blogging to start by saying that blogs aren't for every business, but they're not. During a job interview for a corporate blogging position, I was asked whether I think that all companies should start blogs. I responded, "The only thing worse than not having a blog at this point is having one that isn't updated or engaging."

Is Blogging for You?

I'm sure you've heard from your more social-media-savvy friends that blogs are dead and that all the cool kids are Tweetbooking or something. It's true that today, people have more outlets to express their opinions, share ideas, or just talk about their cats. Blogging is just one part of a varied and magical social-media landscape.

Lest you think I'm advising you to shun blogs in favor of social media (see the sidebar "What Makes Social Media Social?" later in this section), let me point out one of the biggest benefits of having a blog: It's your launching pad into the rest of social media.

A dirty little secret of social media is that it's tough to come up with content to post/tweet/share across numerous sites. Luckily, a TypePad blog provides an even bigger benefit: TypePad automatically shares your content across all the social networks that your customers are participating in. (I cover this subject in full in Chapter 5.)

Also, a blog gives you lots of things that other forms of social media don't:

- A central location where your customers can find out about your business and opinions

- A forum that you control

- More than 140 characters to express yourself, talk about the latest industry trends, or post a few pictures of your latest widget in a gallery

- A place for your customers to post experiences, questions, and general feedback directly to you

What Makes Social Media Social?

Aren't all media social? Not necessarily. Once, you had to invest in expensive equipment such as printing presses or television studios to be part of the media. In the 1980s, however, desktop publishing ushered in an era of poorly produced family newsletters and festive banners for all occasions. (I still remember tearing the edges off dot-matrix-printer paper in grade school.) Those newsletters had much in common with newspapers because they represented one central source distributing information to many people.

Social media—which includes sites such as Twitter, Facebook, and Flickr—flips that setup on its side. Today, many people can share information with many people at the same time. Centralization falls to the side, and the result is a free-flowing virtual conversation.

Is Blogging a Waste of Time?

Here's the deal: Keeping your blog interesting and fresh is a lot of work. So is thinking up great content for Facebook, Twitter, and all the rest. Also, you need to respond to comments, think of witty titles for your posts, and (unless you use TypePad) make sure that your blogging software is up to date. I can just feel a few of you more numbers-oriented folks out there thinking, "Isn't my time better spent focusing on doing things that create some income flow...you know, like working on my business?"

That's a fair question. But let me give you the scoop: Your customers are talking about you (kind of feels like high school, doesn't it?) through social media, whether it be on their blogs or elsewhere. That's right—people on the Internet are talking about your goods and services without your consent. The nerve! Isn't it a better idea for you to participate in that conversation and give your customers a deeper look at your business than to stick your head in the sand like an ostrich? (Yes, I know that ostriches don't actually do that, but I was brought up on Warner Bros. cartoons.) I would say so. A blog not only gives you a great opportunity to share your passion with the world, but also helps more people find out about you.

What to Expect in This Book

First off, who is this book for? Anyone who's interested in TypePad, of course! More specifically, this book concentrates on two different kinds of bloggers: individuals and business users. If you want to use TypePad just to blog about your day, this book will help you do it. This book is also useful if you have a business of any size that would benefit from having a blog.

For a while, I've been thinking about launching a blog devoted to tech tutorials, and I want to use TypePad to host it. Therefore, starting in Chapter 2, I'm going to use this new blog—called Scott Explains—as a running example. By the end of the book, you'll know all that you need to know about TypePad, and I'll have created, set up, and populated a new blog. Everybody wins!

Why TypePad?

When it comes right down to it, your choice of blogging tool won't help or hinder the success of your blog. Blogging is all about having a strong voice, being an expert, and sharing what you love. TypePad won't make you a better blogger, just as a fancy camera won't make you a better photographer. (Check out my Flickr account for proof of that!) But TypePad greases the rails of your creativity by making it super-simple to maintain, update, and customize your blog.

TypePad officially launched in October 2003 (**Figure 1.1**, on the next page), targeting people who were looking for a more professional-looking blog without the hassles that come with self-hosting. I signed up quickly because Six Apart is the company behind TypePad, and it knows blogging (see the "Movable Type" sidebar in this chapter).

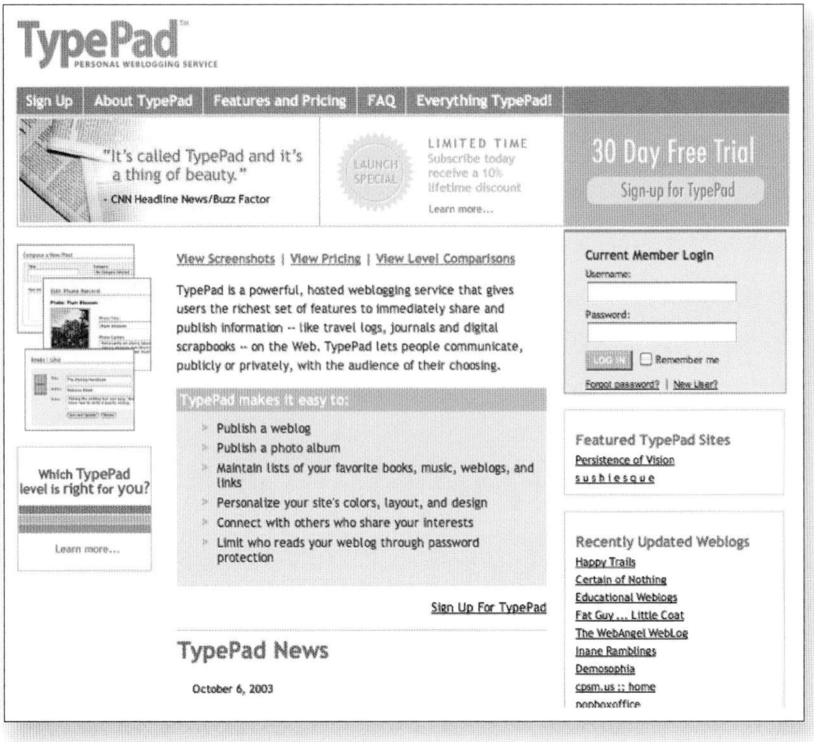

TypePad™
PERSONAL WEBLOGGING SERVICE

Sign Up | About TypePad | Features and Pricing | FAQ | Everything TypePad!

"It's called TypePad and it's a thing of beauty."
- CNN Headline News/Buzz Factor

LAUNCH SPECIAL

LIMITED TIME
Subscribe today, receive a 10% lifetime discount
Learn more...

30 Day Free Trial
Sign-up for TypePad

View Screenshots | View Pricing | View Level Comparisons

TypePad is a powerful, hosted weblogging service that gives users the richest set of features to immediately share and publish information -- like travel logs, journals and digital scrapbooks -- on the Web. TypePad lets people communicate, publicly or privately, with the audience of their choosing.

Which TypePad level is right for you?

Learn more...

TypePad makes it easy to:

> Publish a weblog
> Publish a photo album
> Maintain lists of your favorite books, music, weblogs, and links
> Personalize your site's colors, layout, and design
> Connect with others who share your interests
> Limit who reads your weblog through password protection

Sign Up For TypePad

TypePad News

October 6, 2003

Current Member Login

Username:

Password:

LOG IN   ☐ Remember me

Forgot password? | New User?

Featured TypePad Sites
Persistence of Vision
sushiesque

Recently Updated Weblogs
Happy Trails
Certain of Nothing
Educational Weblogs
Fat Guy ... Little Coat
The WebAngel WebLog
Inane Ramblings
Demosophia
cpsm.us :: home
nonboxoffice

Figure 1.1 TypePad.com, circa October 3, 2003.

Today, many major companies—including Rubbermaid, General Electric, and Coca-Cola—use TypePad as their blogging platform. They chose TypePad for a variety of reasons, including the fact that it takes no investment of time to set up (no need to buy servers, pay people to deploy them, and so on). Also, TypePad is very easy to use.

What TypePad Offers You

I'm going to cover TypePad's features in depth throughout the book, but in this section, I give you a high-level idea of what you get with your TypePad service.

Visibility

You wouldn't be interested in blogging if you didn't want to get the word out about something: a product, your business, or even yourself. (You may be familiar with the phrase *personal brand*. I abhor the term, but the idea is sound; you should be using all the tools in your arsenal to sell yourself and your services.)

Movable Type

If you're not familiar with Six Apart, I can guarantee that you've read blogs created with its best-known product: Movable Type (www.movabletype.org; **Figure 1.2**). Widely regarded as being the great-grandfather of blogging platforms, Movable Type is powerful and extensible, giving the blog administrator a great deal of power over settings, templates, and the like—but it's also a pain to install and keep up to date.

MOVABLE TYPE™   **Figure 1.2** Movable Type is the Six Apart product on which TypePad is based.

TypePad has many of the same features as Movable Type, but it also has a couple of important differences:

- TypePad is geared toward people who are interested in blogging, not people who are interested in blogging engines.

- TypePad is a hosted solution (see "Hosting" later in this chapter).

Now think about how you find stuff on the Internet these days: You use a search engine. Your customers are just like you. When they want to find out about a product or topic, they do one of two things:

1. Ask their friends.

2. Search for information online.

Search-engine optimization (SEO) is a technique that makes your content search-engine-friendly. I can't promise you that I know any secrets, but I do know that TypePad is set up to leverage SEO without your having to do a thing. (Isn't that the best way?)

I cover SEO settings for your blog in Chapter 5. In the meantime, rest assured that Google, Bing, and Yahoo will be able to find it.

Community

Social media is all about people, and people want to connect with one another. TypePad gives users several ways to do just that, ranging from *TypePad Profiles*, which TypePad users create and connect to their blogs, to automatic posts of blog entries on a variety of social-networking sites. TypePad also features the best blogs and communities at http://featured. typepad.com (**Figure 1.3**).

Figure 1.3 TypePad's Featured Blogs and Communities page.

TypePad not only allows you to interact with a community, but also enables you to create a community of your very own in your blog. No, I'm not talking about setting up a full-fledged social network. Rather, your TypePad blog allows your readers to interact via comments. They can reply to one another, enable their own TypePad Profiles, and create lasting relationships while spending time at your blog. (True story: One of my friends met his wife in the comments section of my TypePad blog.)

 tip   **If you're interested in setting up a highly specialized social network for your blog, check out Ning (www.ning.com).**

Hosting

I've mentioned *self-hosted* and *hosted* a couple of times already, so now is a good time to explain what the heck I'm talking about.

Self-hosted blogs

You probably have some geeky friends to whom you turn with all your technological questions, such as "What phone should I get?" (I can answer that: an iPhone) or "Mac or PC?" When you started thinking about starting your own blog, you probably told one of these friends, "I wanna start a blog. What should I do?" I'll bet that your friend suggested getting a Web-hosting account, registering a domain, and installing some sort of blogging software in your newly purchased Web space. Heck, I bet she even offered to install the software for you.

This sort of arrangement is a *self-hosted* solution. You're responsible for everything from hosting to keeping your blogging software up to date. Self-hosting does have several benefits:

- It gives you a lot of control. You can install any number of *plug-ins* (functional additions to software), modify code, and generally do what you want.

- Web-hosting accounts are dirt cheap.

- Most self-hosted blogging packages are open-source and free to install.

- All your nerdy friends will be impressed.

Hosted blogs

By contrast, tools such as TypePad are known as *hosted* (or *turnkey*) solutions. The fine people at TypePad take care of running the servers, updating the software, and generally keeping your blog ticking. You just concentrate on creating fantastic content for your blog (which is tough enough, let me tell you) and growing your business.

You're probably thinking, "Scott, you strike me as being a fairly big geek. You're a tech author, for goodness sake! Why are you running your personal blog on a hosted service?" That's an easy question to answer (which is why I'm so glad that I had you ask it). I had several reasons for choosing TypePad:

- **Ease of use.** I just want my blog to work. I don't want to think about updating it with the latest security patch or try to figure out why my blog won't load. (Is it my Internet connection? Is my host having an issue?) TypePad lets me focus on all the fun parts of blogging without having to get my hands dirty with day-to-day technical administration.

- **Access to expertise.** There's wisdom in the chestnut "There's strength in numbers." TypePad hosts a large number of blogs, so the company is a blog-hosting expert. I'm not. Thanks to the TypePad team's expertise, I can sleep soundly at night, knowing that if my blog strikes it big and tons of people start linking to it, sending traffic my way, I won't have to worry about my server melting under the strain.

- **Overall cost.** On the surface, self-hosting seems cheaper; a Web-hosting plan costs less than $20 a year nowadays, and the software itself is free. But this cost doesn't include personal time. As I get older, I realize that it's wise to spend a little more money up front to save some time down the road. I'll bet that you agree with me on this point, which is why you've spent some money (and time) getting this book. You want to know the best way to do something; you aren't interested in tinkering.

A hosted solution isn't all unicorns and candy canes, however. It has some drawbacks, such as these:

- You don't have complete control of all aspects of your blog.

- You can't install cool random plug-ins that you find on the Internet.

Bottom line, if you're a small-business owner (or a writer) who doesn't want to worry about setting up databases, keeping software up to date, and making sure that the blog is actually working, a hosted solution is perfect for you. If you're more into tweaking settings, fiddling with code, and generally being a technical control freak (not that there's anything wrong with that!), you're probably self-hosting your blog—and you aren't reading this book.

Comparing the TypePad Plans

TypePad offers four plans: a free Micro plan and three Pro plans (Plus, Unlimited, and Business Class). Each plan has the same basic functionality, allowing you to create a blog that supports posts with images, video, and links to other sites.

Table 1.1 provides a quick overview of the four TypePad plans. (You can find a detailed chart at www.typepad.com/micro/compare.) In the following sections, I take a deeper look at each plan in turn.

Table 1.1   TypePad Plans

Plan	Cost per Month	Features	Target Audience
Micro	Free	Support for posting links, videos, and pictures	People looking for a super-easy way to share things with their friends
Plus	$8.95	All the features of Micro, plus custom domain names, support for up to three blogs, and 150 MB in uploads per month	One-man shops looking to set up a blog quickly without a custom design
Unlimited	$14.95	All the features of Micro and Plus, plus support for unlimited blogs and authors, 1 GB in uploads per month, and totally customized design	Businesses that want a custom look, that want their blogs to match the rest of their designs, or that want to host more than three blogs in one TypePad account
Business Class	$89.95 and up	All the features of Micro, Plus, and Unlimited, plus priority support, additional administrators, and annual invoicing	Large companies looking to outsource blog hosting

TypePad Micro

TypePad Micro, which is free, is the most limited version of TypePad. It's best suited for people who want to create *microblogs* (also known as *tumbleblogs*), which are limited blogs designed for sharing links, images, and video with friends. Microblogs aren't supposed to be full-fledged blogs, so TypePad Micro isn't a good choice if you're looking to run a business blog.

The Micro plan has several limitations:

- You have to use one of the three available designs.

- You can create only posts in a TypePad Micro blog; pages aren't supported. (For details on posts and pages, see Chapter 7.)

- You can't use your own *domain* (Web address) with a TypePad Micro blog. Your blog's URL will be http://*yourusername*.typepad.com, where *yourusername* is the user name you chose when signing up for TypePad Micro.

- As you might expect, you can upload only a small amount of files to your TypePad Micro site—100 MB per month—so you can't use the site to host large videos or lots of pictures of your products. TypePad Micro limits you to 3 GB worth of files (though it would take you a while to get to that limit, with the small amount of files you can upload).

If TypePad Micro isn't a great choice for a business or a serious blogger, why do I even bother mentioning it? Besides the fact that Micro is one of the four TypePad plans, you can use Micro to create a microblog in addition to your more serious blog in another TypePad plan.

TypePad Pro

TypePad Micro is cool and all, but you need more power for your blog. The remaining TypePad plans all fall into the category *TypePad Pro* because they're aimed at professionals who want to set up a blog quickly and easily.

The three TypePad Pro plans are Plus, Unlimited, and Business Class. Think of Plus as being the starter-level Pro blogging platform; each subsequent level includes the features of the preceding level and adds some features.

What makes all three of these plans so Pro? They share a few important features:

- **Unlimited storage** for all your blog-file needs. Shoot HD video to your heart's content, and don't worry about storage!

- **Support for multiple blogs.** You can create more than one blog with your TypePad account—a great benefit if you want to set up a network of blogs, or if you want to create separate business and personal blogs.

- **Tech support.** Stuff may break, or a particular feature may not work the way you think it should. You can turn to TypePad support (see Chapter 11 for details), which will have an answer for you. (You can also keep this book handy.)

- **Customized designs.** Two of the three Pro plans—Unlimited and Business Class—allow you to customize your design. TypePad Pro Plus allows you only to tweak the thousands of included TypePad designs.

- **Personalized URL.** To me, nothing says *amateur* more clearly than a blog running in someone else's domain. It's very cheap—and easy—to register a domain name these days, and if you want to look like a pro, you really need to get yourself a domain. If you already have a Web site (and domain) for your business and simply want to add a blog to your existing site, you can do so by mapping a subdomain to your TypePad blog.

  Suppose that you have a business called Scott's Awesome Books and the Web site www.scottsawesomebooks.com. Because you already have a great Web site, you don't want that URL to take people to a blog, but you do want to add a blog to your site. You can use a subdomain such as http://blog.scottsawesomebooks.com and point it to your TypePad blog by using domain mapping. (See Chapter 3 for more details about domain mapping and TypePad.) That way, you get the best of both worlds: Your business Web site doesn't change, and you get an easy-to-update blog.

- **Monthly cost.** Any of the Pro plans will cost you money each month. (The best things in life may be free, but the best features of TypePad aren't.) TypePad does offer a free 14-day trial for all three Pro plans, however. Take a plan for a spin, and figure out whether you like TypePad.

 If you don't mind shelling out more money initially, TypePad offers a nice discount for paying in yearly installments. If you can't lay out that much cash all at once, though, monthly payments are accepted.

In the following sections, I delve into what each Pro plan offers and discuss why you might pick one plan over another.

Plus

The entry-level Pro plan costs $8.95 a month. It allows you to upload 150 MB of files to your TypePad account each month and to host up to three separate blogs, each with its own URL and each with its own domain. (I discuss how to manage multiple blogs in one TypePad account in Chapter 4.)

This plan is great if you're looking for a super-simple, though flexible, blogging solution. But it has a few drawbacks, such as the fact that it lets you have only one author. You can have three blogs, but only one person (whom I assume is you) will be able to post to them. If you hope to have a group blog, you'll want to look at the Unlimited and Business Class plans. Also, you're limited to using one of the built-in designs for your blog, but that's fine if you don't have an existing Web design that you want to use for your blog. (You can make small changes in the stock designs, such as adding your logo.)

The perfect customer for TypePad Pro Plus is a one-person shop that wants one to three blogs and isn't interested in customizing the heck out of the blog.

> **tip** **TypePad makes it very easy to upgrade or downgrade a Pro plan. It may make sense to start with the Plus plan and see how you like it. If you find yourself itching to change the design, the Unlimited plan is just a click away.**

Unlimited

As the name implies, this plan is all about being unlimited, and it'll set you back $14.95 a month. For that extra money, you can host as many blogs as you like and have as many authors writing for those blogs as you like. (Each author gets his own login for the blog, and you can set how much control every author has over the blog itself.)

This plan allows you to have multiple authors for your TypePad blog, but only one account can be the blog administrator, who has access to every setting, including payment information and the ability to delete the entire blog.

The Unlimited plan lets you control the look and feel of your blog by implementing a custom design. You can use one of TypePad's included designs as a jumping-off point or create a new design for your blog—perhaps one that matches your current Web site.

One thing that *isn't* unlimited is the amount of files you can upload to TypePad a month; you're limited to 1,000 MB (or 1 GB). Chances are that you won't hit this limit unless you're uploading large photos—if, say, you're a photographer, and you want to upload lots of RAW images. I've been using the TypePad Pro Unlimited plan for a couple of blogs for more than six years, though, and I've never hit this limit.

This plan is the one that I recommend for most people who are reading this book (including you!). You'll really appreciate the ability to have total control of the way your blog looks, even if you aren't a designer. At some point in time, you'll want to tweak something, and if you're on the Plus plan, you may not be able to change it. The Unlimited plan, however, lets you change whatever you like. Also, you can host a large number of blogs right from one TypePad account and invite your friends, co-workers, or fans to blog with you.

Business Class

You're probably thinking, "Hey, I run a business! Clearly, I should pony up the dough for TypePad Pro Business Class." Sure, you could do that, though at $89.95 a month per blog (or more), it isn't priced for small businesses. Notice that this price is *per blog*. Much like the Unlimited plan, TypePad Pro Business Class allows you to host a large number of blogs, but you're charged a monthly fee based on the number of blogs you have.

Why is that? Well, Business Class is aimed at large enterprises, like the *Los Angeles Times,* that need enterprise-level features. This means that Business Class users get priority support, annual invoicing (a feature that accounts-payable departments like), 40 GB worth of uploads a month, and multiple blog administrators.

Generally, it's safe to assume that you aren't going to go with TypePad Pro Business Class unless you're in charge of finding a blogging solution for a large company that's interested in starting several blogs. Visit www.typepad.com/business for more information.

TypePad for Journalists

If you're a journalist, TypePad has a great deal for you. How great a deal? How about a free TypePad Pro account? The program is called TypePad for Journalists, and you can get all the details at www.typepad.com/about/bailout.html. All you have to do is email a link to a piece of reporting that you did for a Web, print, or broadcast outlet. The good folks at TypePad will review it and get back to you with a free code for a blog. Neat, huh?

Getting Started with TypePad

Choosing a TypePad plan (see Chapter 1) may be hard, but setting up your TypePad account couldn't be much easier. It's almost as though Six Apart wants people to sign up for its services!

In this chapter, I cover the process of signing up for a TypePad Pro account, because you'll need the extra features for your blog, but keep in mind that you can cancel within 14 days and incur no charges or penalties.

note If you decide that a Pro plan isn't for you and cancel your account, your blog isn't gone; it's downgraded to a Micro-plan blog. Many of the Pro features, such as domain mapping, will no longer work.

Setting up Your TypePad Account

If you already have a TypePad account, feel free to skip the rest of this chapter. Otherwise, follow these steps to set up an account:

1. Point your browser to www.typepad.com (**Figure 2.1**), and click the yellowish Get a Pro Blog button.

Click this button to go Pro.

Figure 2.1 The main page of TypePad.com.

2. In the resulting Choose Blog page, click the radio button for the plan you want to purchase: Plus or Unlimited (**Figure 2.2**).

note **If you're interested in Business Class, you have to click a link to contact TypePad directly, because Business Class accounts are special (in a good way).**

I suggest that you go with Unlimited, which also happens to be the default choice. You can always downgrade your account later if you find that you aren't using all the features.

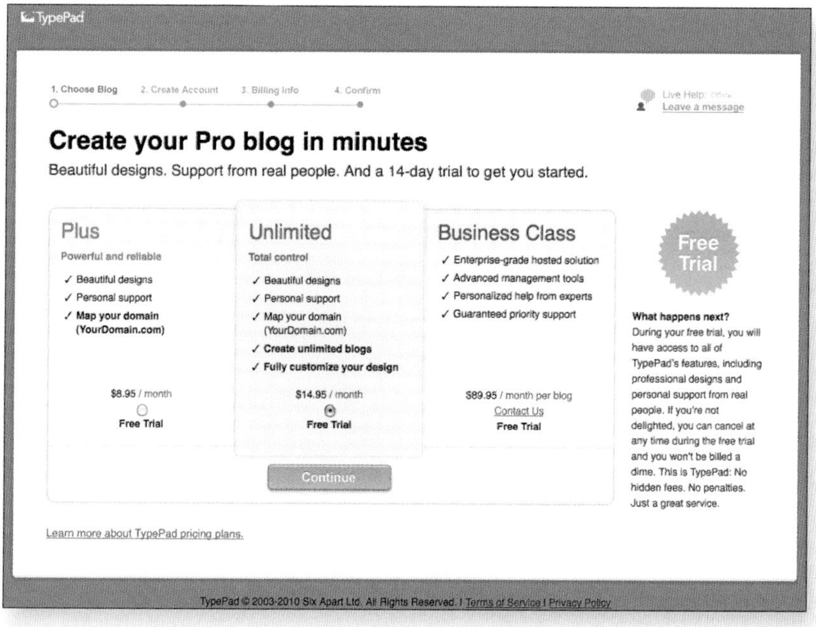

Figure 2.2 Choose the TypePad plan that's right for you.

3. Click the yellowish Continue button to…well, continue to the Create Account page (**Figure 2.3**).

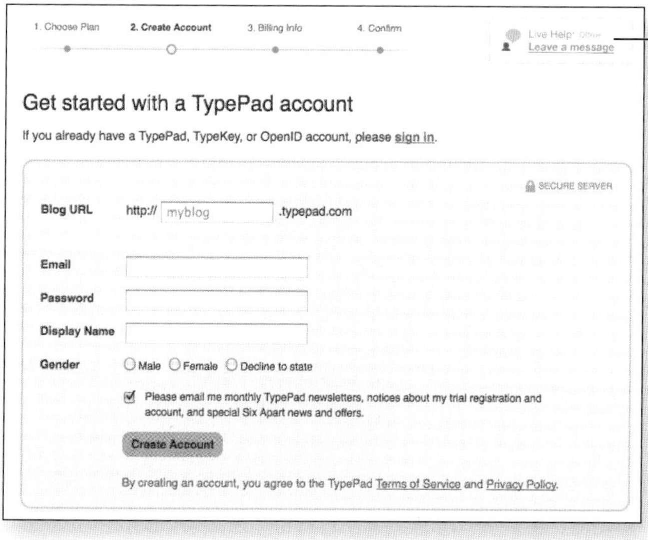

Get help here if you need it.

Figure 2.3 Claim your blog URL in the Create Account page.

tip Don't overlook the Live Help link in the top-right corner of the Create Account page. If you encounter any issues, don't be afraid to ask for help. During normal business hours, live chat is available; otherwise, click the Leave a Message link, and someone will get back to you.

4. Enter your blog URL in the top field.

   The blog URL isn't the actual name of your blog; you'll get to that in a little bit. This entry is important, however, because whatever you choose becomes your TypePad login and is the basis of your TypePad URL, which your customers/readers will see. Choose a combination of letters and numbers that you'll remember and that makes sense in the context of your blog. (For suggestions, see the sidebar "What's in a Name?" in this section.)

   After you enter a blog URL, the form checks to see whether the name you entered has been taken (**Figure 2.4**). As you see in the figure, http://typepadbook.typepad.com is available.

Availability status

Figure 2.4 The Blog URL field helpfully checks to see whether the URL you entered is available.

5. In the Email field, enter an email address.

   Make sure to use an email address that you check regularly, because TypePad will use this address to send you information about your account and various alerts about your blog.

6. In the Password field, enter the password you want to use.

note Be sure to use a strong password that consists of numbers, letters, and symbols. You wouldn't want anyone guessing your TypePad credentials.

What's in a Name?

TypePad allows you to create several blogs in just one TypePad account, which is great because it makes managing all those blogs easy, but each blog's URL is based on the blog URL you enter in the Create Account page. (Domain mapping allows you to mask this URL, however, and I explain how to do that in Chapter 3.)

As you may remember from the preface, I'm setting up a blog called Scott Explains, so I might enter **scottexplains**, which would make my TypePad URL http://scottexplains.typepad.com. This URL is my *base URL* for all the blogs I might set up in that TypePad account. If I set up the blog called Scott Explains, the URL of that blog would be http://scottexplains.typepad.com/ scottexplains; another blog, called Lame Example Name, would be located at http://scottexplains.typepad.com/lameexamplename, and so on.

You might be wondering, "What happens when someone visits http://scottexplains.typepad.com, then?" That base URL points to the default blog in my TypePad account. If you have only one blog, the base URL is your default; if you have several blogs, you can set the default to whichever blog you want to use. (I show you how to do this in Chapter 3.)

7. Enter a display name in the Display Name field.

   This name is what will show up in your TypePad Profile, which I cover in depth in Chapter 3. Generally, I recommend that you use your own name here, not the name of your business. One thing that people love about small businesses is the fact that they're run by regular people, not by faceless entities. Having your name show up in your TypePad Profile allows your readers to associate a name with your business, which is a good thing.

8. Select your gender or (if you aren't into sharing your gender with anyone) the Decline to State radio button.

9. Select the check box at the bottom of the page if you want to sign up for TypePad's email newsletter.

10. Click the Create Account button to proceed to the Billing Information page (**Figure 2.5**, on the next page).

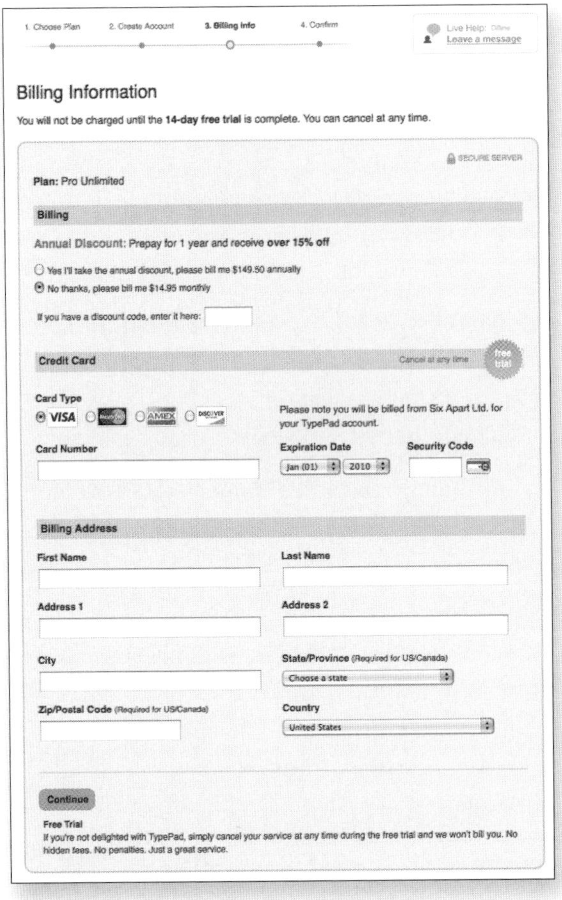

Figure 2.5 TypePad offers a 14-day free trial but requires you to enter your billing information to start that trial.

11. Enter your billing information, and click the Continue button when you finish.

    Notice that the Billing section gives you a choice of monthly or annual billing. The annual price is discounted, but you'll have to pay it in a lump sum (obviously).

12. In the Confirm Your Information page (**Figure 2.6**), verify what you've entered.

    If you notice a mistake, just click one of the edit links on the right edge of the page and make your correction.

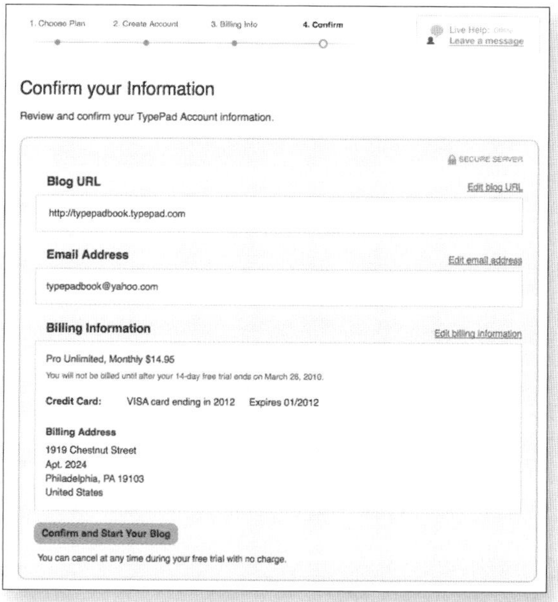

Figure 2.6 Confirming your information is fun, of course, but the best thing about this page is that it puts you one click away from starting your blog.

13. When you're ready to jump into the world of TypePad, click the Confirm and Start Your Blog button.

Setting up Your First Blog

If you followed all the steps in the preceding section, TypePad has already set up your first blog for you and is displaying the Congratulations, You Have a TypePad Blog! page (**Figure 2.7**).

Figure 2.7 Congratulations— you've created a TypePad blog.

Now all you have to do is follow these few steps:

1. Enter a title for your blog in the top field.

   The title is the name that everyone will know your blog by; more important, it's what search engines will index and display when people
   search for something. I'm going with Scott Explains; you can use it,
   too (and change it later), or enter your own blog's title.

2. Accept the selected check box (**Figure 2.8**).

   Generally, you want to leave this option checked because it means that
   your blog will be indexed by search engines and linked to from your
   TypePad Profile (which I cover in Chapter 3). If you clear this box,
   your blog will be invisible from search engines and won't show up
   in your TypePad Profile.

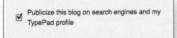

Figure 2.8 If you want your blog to be
successful, you have to get the word
out, so leave this option selected.

tip   If you want some time to make sure that your blog is set up and
ready for launch, you may want to clear this check box. That way, the
chance that someone will stumble upon your blog is pretty slim. You
can always re-enable this option in your blog's Notifications page,
which I cover in "Notifications" later in this chapter.

No Second Chance for a First Impression

It's a good idea to create some content on your blog before you start telling
everyone about it, for a couple of reasons:

- When you share a blog that has content, people are likely to subscribe to it
  and come back for more.

- The only thing worse than not having a blog is having a blog that's either
  abandoned or seldom updated. You don't have to update your blog five
  times a day, but people expect to see fresh content at regular intervals.
  Creating some content for your blog before you unveil it to an adoring
  public will help you gauge the amount of time you'll need to invest in the
  care, watering, and maintenance of your blog.

3. You may be tempted to click either Write Your First Post or Design Your Blog, but if you want to follow along with this book, click the link titled Skip This and Head to the Dashboard.

Touring the TypePad Dashboard

I cover the Dashboard (**Figure 2.9**) in full in Chapter 4, but because you just entered your billing information, now is a good time to show you how to configure it and how to upgrade, downgrade, or cancel a TypePad Pro plan at any time.

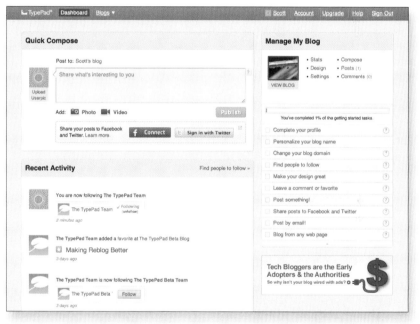

Figure 2.9 The TypePad Dashboard.

note The Dashboard is always one click away no matter where you are in your TypePad account. Just click the Dashboard link in the green navigation bar at the top of every TypePad page.

The right end of the navigation bar at the top of the Dashboard shows your display name (which should be your full name; see step 7 of "Setting up Your TypePad Account" earlier in this chapter). Next to your display name, you'll see a link called Account (**Figure 2.10**). Click it to go to your Account Summary page, which I cover in depth in the next section.

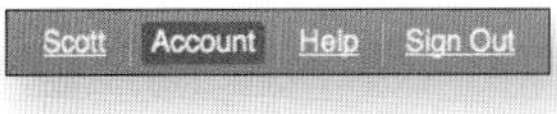

Figure 2.10 This link takes you to your TypePad Account Summary page.

On the left side of the Account Summary page is a blue navigation menu, which includes a Billing Info option (**Figure 2.11**).

Figure 2.11 The Account Summary page's navigation menu, with Billing Info selected.

When you choose Billing Info, TypePad opens the Billing Info page, which has two sections: Billing Summary and Transaction History (**Figure 2.12**). Because you've just signed up for TypePad, you should see only one transaction listed; I'm a longtime TypePad user, so I have several entries.

> **note** Should you require invoices for your records (or accountants), click the View Invoice link in the Invoice column of any transaction in which money changed hands.

Your current plan is listed in the Billing Summary section, followed by two links: Upgrade or Downgrade and Cancel Pro Plan. Upgrading and downgrading are easy and available at any time. Click the Upgrade or Downgrade link, and you'll be given the option to choose a new TypePad Pro plan (**Figure 2.13**). Make your choice and then click the Change My Plan button. If you downgrade to a less costly plan, your account will be credited the difference, and that credit will be applied during your next payment period. If you upgrade to a more expensive plan, you'll be charged a prorated fee.

Billing Summary

Current Plan: **Pro Unlimited**
Upgrade or Downgrade | Cancel Pro Plan

Billing Cycle: **Yearly** Change

Payment Method: ▓▓▓▓▓ Update

Billing Rate: **$127.08 Yearly**

Next Billing: **November 1, 2010**

Member Since: **August 2003**

Discount Code: **15.00% lifetime discount**

Transaction History

Date	Credit Card	Description	Charge	Invoice
November 2, 2009	▓▓▓▓▓	Membership fee	$127.07	View Invoice
November 6, 2008	▓▓▓▓▓	Changed credit card to Visa-2012		
November 6, 2008		Changed billing address ▓▓▓▓▓ ▓▓▓▓▓ ▓▓▓▓▓		
November 2, 2008	▓▓▓▓▓	Membership fee	$127.08	View Invoice

Figure 2.12
The Billing Info page shows your current plan, upgrade/downgrade options, transaction history, and complete billing information.

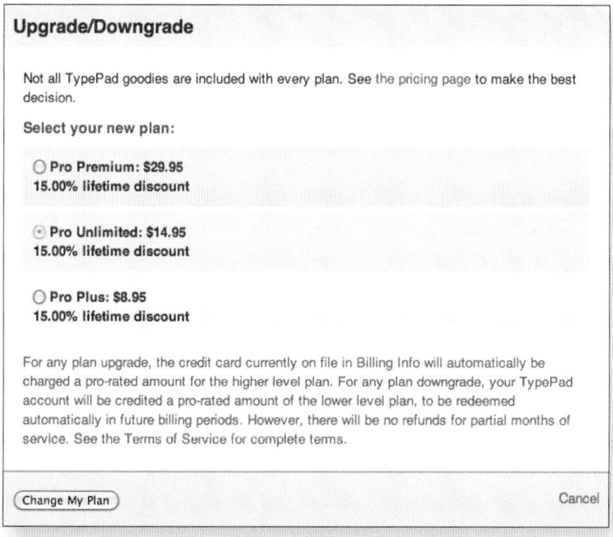

Upgrade/Downgrade

Not all TypePad goodies are included with every plan. See the pricing page to make the best decision.

Select your new plan:

○ **Pro Premium: $29.95**
15.00% lifetime discount

◉ **Pro Unlimited: $14.95**
15.00% lifetime discount

○ **Pro Plus: $8.95**
15.00% lifetime discount

For any plan upgrade, the credit card currently on file in Billing Info will automatically be charged a pro-rated amount for the higher level plan. For any plan downgrade, your TypePad account will be credited a pro-rated amount of the lower level plan, to be redeemed automatically in future billing periods. However, there will be no refunds for partial months of service. See the Terms of Service for complete terms.

(Change My Plan)   Cancel

Figure 2.13
Upgrading or downgrading your TypePad plan is easy. Just remember that different plans offer different options.

If you click the Cancel Pro Plan link because you've decided that TypePad isn't for you, you'll be taken to the Cancel Pro Plan page (**Figure 2.14**).

Cancel Pro Plan: Downgrade to free TypePad Micro

Payments
Your credit card will not be charged going forward. However there are no refunds for unused portions of the current billing cycle, and promotional codes or discounts will be discarded.

Changes to Your Account
By canceling your paid plan, your TypePad account will automatically be downgraded to the free TypePad Micro plan.

Your blog will remain available with access to the free TypePad Micro plan features only.

You'll also maintain access to your commenting and following history on the dashboard, and your profile will remain active.

This downgrade does not affect your guest status on other blogs.

Questions
If you have additional questions about the downgrade process, please contact our support team.

Confirmation
If you have an email on file with TypePad, you will receive an email to confirm the change in your account status. Otherwise, you can confirm by checking your billing status on the Billing Info page in the Account section.

☐ I agree to the terms of cancellation

(Cancel Pro Plan)   Return to Billing Info

Figure 2.14 When you cancel your Pro plan, your blog isn't deleted; it's just downgraded to a free TypePad Micro plan.

Your content isn't lost if you decide to cancel your Pro plan; rather, your blog is downgraded to a TypePad Micro blog. If you have more than one blog associated with this TypePad account, you'll have to pick only one to keep on the TypePad Micro account (**Figure 2.15**). The rest of your blogs, along with the files associated with them, are deleted.

Choose which blog you're going to keep ✓ Blankbaby
                                          Building a TypePad Blog People Want to Read
☐ I agree to the terms of cancellation   Scott Explains
                                          Stuff I want
                                          tweet
                                          TypePad, Defined

Figure 2.15 If you're hosting multiple blogs in TypePad and decide to cancel your Pro plan, you can keep only one blog as a TypePad Micro blog. The rest are deleted.

note Before you cancel your Pro plan, be sure that you've backed up all your TypePad blogs, just to be on the safe side.

Navigating Your Account

Because you're already in the account section of TypePad, you may as well check out the other sections. To start, click Summary in the blue navigation menu (refer to Figure 2.11) to see the Account Summary page of your TypePad account.

Account Summary

The Account Summary page has two parts: your account information and a utility that lets you change your TypePad password. I'll show you around the Account Information section first (**Figure 2.16**).

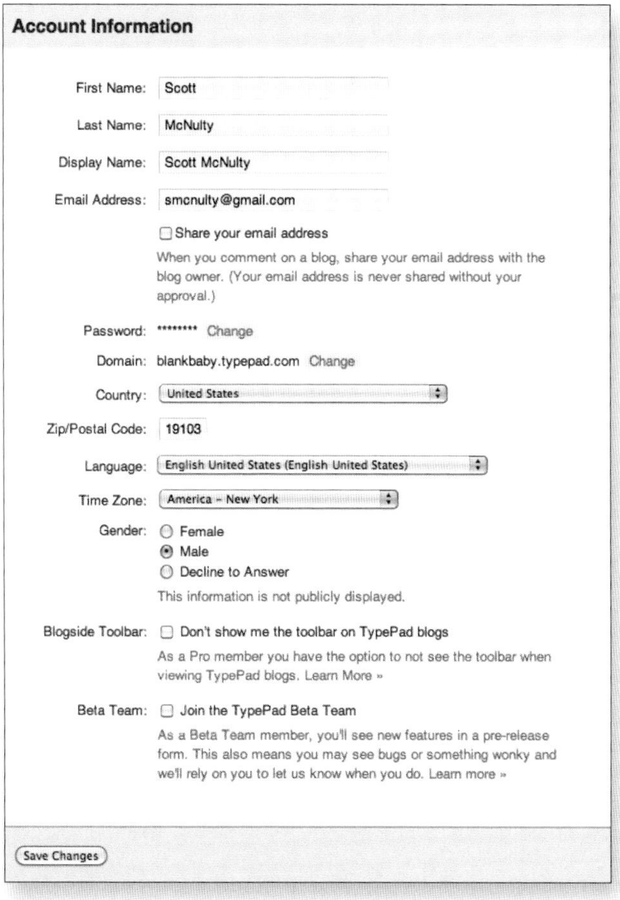

Figure 2.16 The Account Information section.

note All the settings in the Account Summary page are global, affecting all the blogs you have in your TypePad account. In "Password Protection" later in this chapter, I show you how to change settings on a per-blog basis.

Account Information

Most of this section doesn't require any explanation, with the exception of these items:

- **Domain.** When you signed up for your account (see "Setting up Your TypePad Account" earlier in this chapter), you picked a TypePad URL. This URL (http://*yourTypePadaccountname*.typepad.com) is your TypePad *domain.* All your blogs are hosted in this domain, though your blog readers may never know it if you use domain mapping (see Chapter 3). If you decide that you don't like the TypePad domain you created, you can change it here (for details, see Chapter 3).

- **Blogside Toolbar.** If you're a Pro member or higher, you can turn off this feature by selecting its check box. When you do, TypePad won't display the blogside toolbar on any blog page while you're signed in.

  What's the blogside toolbar? By default, TypePad automatically displays a little gearlike icon in the top-left corner of all blog pages (**Figure 2.17**). Clicking this icon reveals the toolbar's options.

Click to view toolbar options.

	Follow The TypePad Team	Reblog It	Start your free blog now	Sign In

Figure 2.17 Blogside-toolbar options available when you aren't logged in to TypePad.

- **Beta Team.** TypePad rolls out new features every now and again, and those features need to be tested in the wild before they're released to all TypePad users. Select the Beta Team check box to be part of the action. (Before you click, keep in mind that some of those beta features may not work as intended.)

Password Changes

If you want to change your password, click the Change link next to the Password field in the Account Information section. This link takes you to the Change Your Password page (**Figure 2.18**). As with most password-changing utilities, you'll need to know your old password in addition to whatever you want to change it to. Just fill in the fields and then click the Change Password button. If you decide not to change the password after all, click the Return to Account Summary link instead.

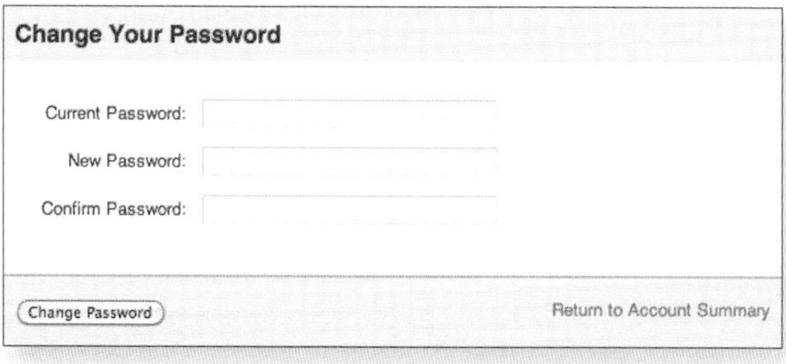

Change Your Password

Current Password:
New Password:
Confirm Password:

Change Password   Return to Account Summary

Figure 2.18 A good old-fashioned password-change form.

> **note** If you change any of the information in the Account Information section, make sure that you click the Save Changes button when you finish. Otherwise, all your changes will be discarded when you navigate to another section of TypePad.

Notifications

Choose Notifications in the blue navigation menu (refer to Figure 2.11) to access the Notifications page (**Figure 2.19**, on the next page).

TypePad uses your email address to send you a variety of notifications. Among the items that you can opt into by selecting the top check box (or out of by clearing that box) are the TypePad newsletter and special Six Apart news and offers.

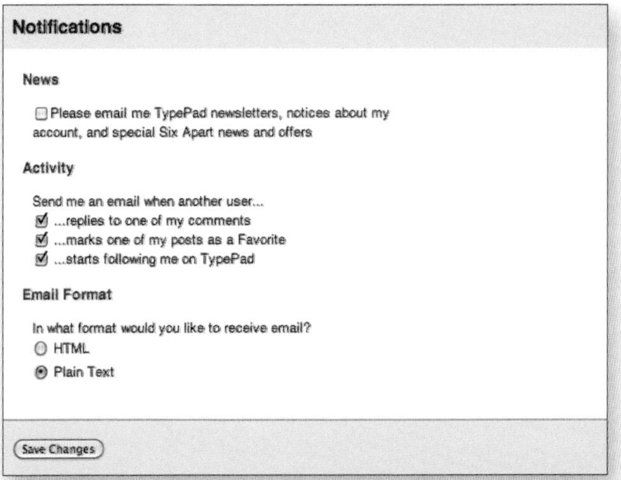

Figure 2.19 TypePad will send you email when you want it to, and you can even tell it to use HTML or plain-text emails.

The Activity section is the real meat of the Notifications page. Every time someone does one of these things to, or with, your blog, TypePad will happily send you an email alerting you to the fact that

- Someone replied to a comment you left on your blog or another TypePad blog

- Someone marked one of your posts as a favorite

- Someone started to follow you on TypePad

If you don't want to TypePad to email you when any of these events happens, just clear all the check boxes. Or mix and match, if you want to know when someone is following you on TypePad but don't care about replies to comments.

Finally, you can tell TypePad what format you want it to use to email you. If you like rich text and graphics in your email, go ahead and select HTML. If you're like me and hate HTML emails with a passion, you'll be happy to see the Plain Text option. Plain-text emails are only text—no fancy graphics— and are readable on a variety of devices.

When you're done configuring your notifications, be sure to click the Save Changes button.

About Me (well, about you, really)

Your readers want to know a little about the person or people behind the blog. It makes them feel more connected when they can put a face to the name and the text. To help them do that, introduce yourself in the About Me page (**Figure 2.20**), which you open by choosing About Me Page from the blue navigation menu (refer to Figure 2.11).

Because there's a lot more to working with this page than just entering a simple bio, I cover it in detail in Chapter 3.

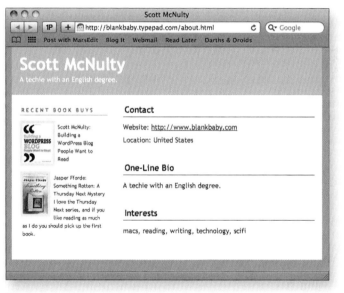

Figure 2.20 My About Me page.

Your Other Accounts

Wouldn't it be great if you could somehow automatically tweet new blog posts or post them to Facebook? A page called Your Other Accounts lets you do just that, in addition to listing all your accounts in one place so that you can display them on your blog.

Click Other Accounts in the blue navigation menu (refer to Figure 2.11), and you'll be able to add some accounts. As you can see in **Figure 2.21** on the next page, I already have my AIM, Flickr, and Twitter accounts linked to my TypePad account.

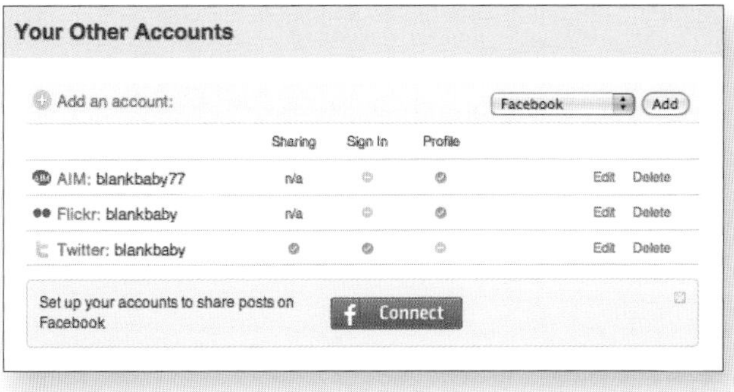

Figure 2.21
Your Other Accounts page. You can edit and delete accounts here.

Each account has three columns' worth of data:

- **Sharing.** The Sharing column lets you know whether you can post things from TypePad directly to that service. As you can see from the settings in Figure 2.21, you can't share posts from TypePad to an AIM or Flickr account, but you can tweet them to a Twitter account. (I talk more about sharing, including how to do it automatically, in Chapter 5.)

- **Sign In.** This column tells you at a glance whether you're signed in to that service via TypePad. As you may know, Twitter and Facebook allow third-party applications like TypePad to sign in and post things. Figure 2.21 shows that I'm signed in to Twitter because a green check is displayed in the Sign In column.

- **Profile.** Finally, the Profile column tells you whether this account is displayed on your TypePad Profile page. A green check means yes; a gray dash means no.

Editing accounts

You can edit an account by clicking its Edit link in the Your Other Accounts page. This link brings up the Set Preferences window for that account (**Figure 2.22**). If you want to share posts via this service, check the Sharing box. (If the Sharing box doesn't appear, TypePad doesn't support automated sharing to that service, so you'll have to share manually.)

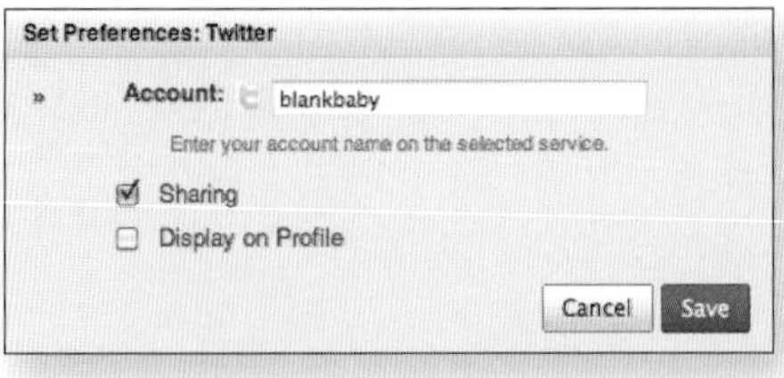

Figure 2.22 Click an account's Edit link to display the Set Preferences window for that account.

You can also decide whether you want to list this account in your TypePad Profile by selecting or clearing the bottom check box. As you can see in Figure 2.22, I'm not listing my Twitter account in my Profile (but feel free to say hi; I'm @blankbaby).

Click Save to save your preferences for that service.

Deleting accounts

Right next to an account's Edit link in the Your Other Accounts page is a Delete link. As you may have guessed, clicking this link deletes the selected account.

Adding accounts

Adding another account is easy as well. First, select the account type from the voluminous drop-down menu in the top-right corner of the Your Other Accounts page (**Figure 2.23**). Then click the Add button to open the Add Account window.

Figure 2.23 The account types that TypePad supports.

What happens next depends on the service that you're adding. If TypePad can't take advantage of sharing posts with the service, enter your user name or the URL of your account with that service (**Figure 2.24**) and then click Save.

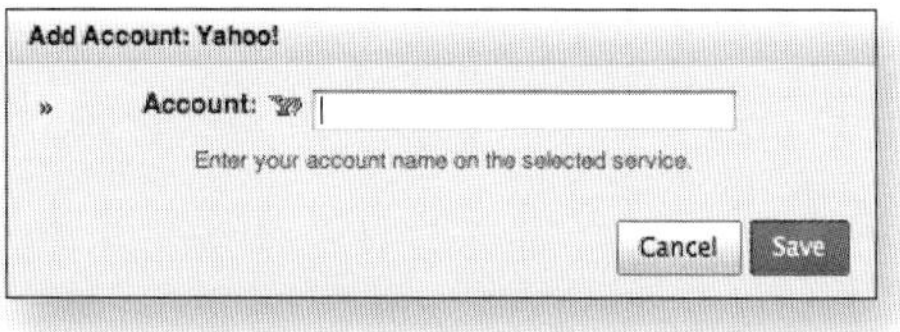

Figure 2.24 Enter your account name in the Add Account window (here, I'm adding a Yahoo account) and then click Save.

Things are different for Twitter and Facebook, which are the only two services that support posting at the moment. In each case, you have to approve posting from TypePad by signing in to your account and changing some settings. To see how the process works, try it with Facebook. (Make sure first that you don't have any pop-up blockers enabled.) Follow these steps:

1. Choose Facebook from the menu shown in Figure 2.23, or click the blue Facebook Connect button at the bottom of the Your Other Accounts page.

   A pop-up login window opens (**Figure 2.25**).

Figure 2.25 Log in to your Facebook account to allow TypePad access.

2. Log in to Facebook.

   A prompt asks you to grant TypePad constant authorization to your Facebook account (**Figure 2.26**).

Figure 2.26 TypePad requires constant authorization to Facebook. If you don't like the sound of that, click Don't Allow.

3. Click Allow.

   You move to the second authorization step: allowing TypePad to publish posts and comments on Facebook by using your account without prompting you (**Figure 2.27**).

Figure 2.27 If you want to have TypePad post things for you on Facebook automatically, you must grant it publishing rights.

4. Click Allow Publishing.

   This step authorizes TypePad to post to your Facebook account. (I cover how to actually do that in Chapter 5.)

5. Finally, click Save at the Add Account: Facebook prompt.

   You're all set.

note If you no longer want TypePad to have access to your Facebook account, go to www.facebook.com/editapps.php. That Web page allows you to edit the applications that have access to your information on Facebook itself.

tip The more accounts you feel comfortable adding to and displaying in your TypePad Profile, the better. That way, you give your readers additional ways to connect with you, and people are all about connecting these days.

Password Protection

Speaking of connecting with people, you'll find some creeps out there on the Internet. That's why TypePad allows you to password-protect some or all of your content.

Generally, people want to start a blog so that they can share their thoughts, products, and what-have-yous with the entire world, but it's not uncommon to restrict a blog to a limited number of people, for a couple of reasons:

- The blog isn't ready for public consumption, but you want to see how it looks in browsers (or you're working with a team of people and want to share the site with some members of the team, but not everyone).

- You're blogging about some very personal or top-secret subjects that are aimed at a particular audience.

Password protection allows you to have a blog but keep it private. A password-protected blog won't be indexed by search engines (so people need to know that it exists to find it) and can't be read by anyone who doesn't happen to have the password.

To set your password preferences, choose Password Protection from the blue navigation menu (refer to Figure 2.11). When you do, the Password Protection page opens (**Figure 2.28**).

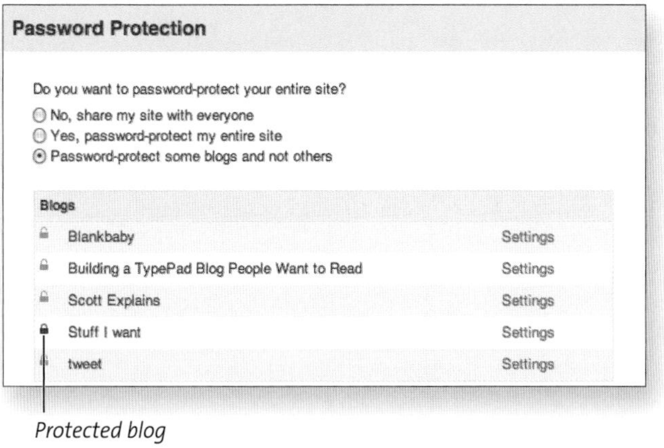

Protected blog

Figure 2.28 The blog with the black lock is password-protected.

You can set all your content to be publicly available, keep it all under lock and key, or password-protect only some blogs. When you select the third option, a list of all the blogs associated with your TypePad account becomes available. The icon to the left of a blog's name tells you whether the blog is protected. A light gray unlocked icon means that the blog doesn't have a password; a black locked icon means that it does.

To password-protect a blog from the Password Protection page, follow these steps:

1. Click the Settings link for the blog you're looking to protect.

   This link takes you to the Blog Settings page. (See Chapter 5 for full details on blog settings.)

2. At the bottom of the page, check the check box titled Protect This Blog with a Password.

   When you do, two new fields appear: Username and Password (**Figure 2.29**).

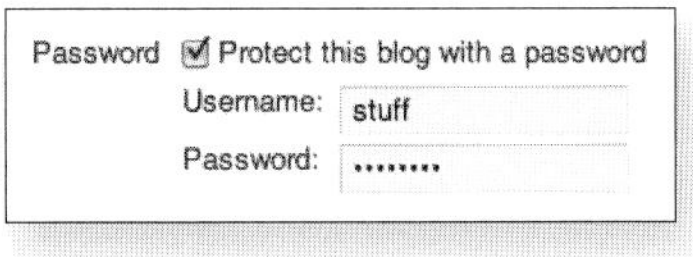

Password ☑ Protect this blog with a password
Username: stuff
Password: ••••••••

Figure 2.29 The per-blog password controls.

3. Enter a user name and password.

4. Click Save Changes.

   Now, when someone goes to that password-protected blog, she'll be prompted for the user-name/password combination. You'll need to provide the credentials to whomever you want to read the blog.

note **You can return to this page at any time to protect or unprotect any of your blogs.**

Domain Mapping

Domain mapping (the next option in the navigation menu; refer to Figure 2.11) is very important but a little complicated. Turn to Chapter 3 for full coverage.

Developer

The final section of your TypePad account is Developer, which you access by choosing that option from the blue navigation menu (refer to Figure 2.11). Unless you're a software developer, chances are that you'll never need to access this area for any reason, but if you *are* a developer, it should excite you.

First, what the heck is an API? *API* stands for *application programming inter-face*, which allows a developer to build applications that interact with the data of the API provider. The TypePad API allows you to create desktop applications to manage your TypePad account, for example, or to create a Web site that pulls data from one of TypePad's other, more developer-friendly services.

To access the TypePad API, you must apply for an API key. When you choose Developer from the navigation menu, TypePad opens the page shown in **Figure 2.30**. Click the green API: Apply Here button, and fill out the resulting form. TypePad will be in contact with you later if your application is approved.

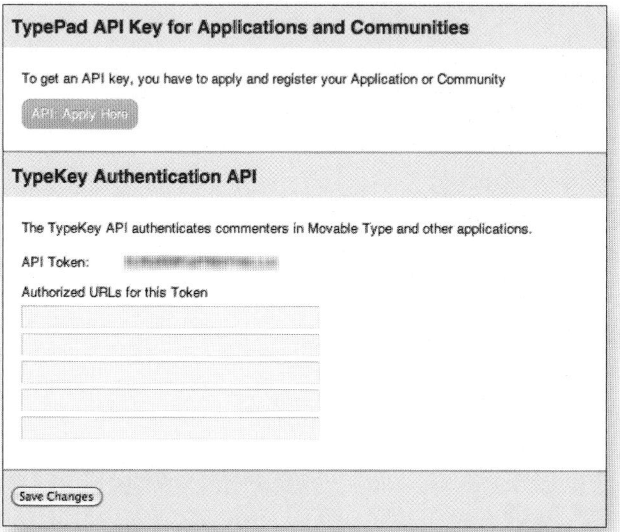

Figure 2.30 Apply for an API key here.

The ins and outs of the TypePad API are beyond the scope of this book, but feel free to check out TypePad's developer documentation at http://developer. typepad.com to get the skinny on the TypePad API and what you might be able to do with it.

Now that you've set up your account and laid the foundation of your first blog, you're ready to start configuring the blog. I show you how to do that in Chapter 3.

3

Personalizing All Your TypePad Blogs

You've set up your TypePad account, and it automatically created your very first blog. Aren't you excited? I'll bet that you want to jump right into it and start blogging.

Although starting now might seem like a good idea, I suggest that you read this chapter first. Here, I show you how to give your TypePad blog its own URL (or use a URL based on the one you already use for your business) and discuss some settings that you can enable to personalize your blog.

Working with Domains

What are domains, and why should you care about them? I'm glad you asked.

Knowing your domains from your subdomains

When you get right down to it, a *domain* is a Web address. Amazon.com is a domain, as is TypePad.com. When you sign up for TypePad, your blog is given a Web address based on TypePad.com. That address is known as a *subdomain*—a unique domain within a domain. In this case, the domain is TypePad.com, so the subdomain assigned to your blog is *yourTypePadaccount*.typepad.com. Whenever you create a new TypePad blog, it's created under this subdomain.

By default, your blog's URL is going to be your TypePad URL followed by the name of your blog. My Scott Explains blog, for example, has the URL http://blankbaby.typepad.com/scottexplains.

Wouldn't it be great, though, if I could use http://scottexplains.com instead of that TypePad URL? Domain mapping allows me to do just that, and you can do the same with your own blog.

 note   The definitions I'm using here are layman's terms, so please don't email me to point out that domains are technically x, y, and z. Domains (like networking in general) are rich technical topics that are outside the scope of this book. I'm just pointing out the basics so that you know what you need to know when dealing with your blog.

Registering your own domain

If you're running a business and want to have a recognizable presence on the Internet, it makes good sense to register your own domain. To start, just do a Google search for *domain registrar,* and you're sure to find a bunch of companies that can do the work for you.

tip   If you have an account for Web hosting, you should check with the service provider to see whether it also registers domains. Many companies offer both services because they go hand in hand.

Expect to pay about $10 a year for a .com Web address. Many companies offer special deals if you register a domain for multiple years at the same time.

> **note** Don't forget to jot down the date on which you need to renew your domain's registration; otherwise, when the domain expires, people won't be able to use that address to get to your site.

Because so many domains are already in use, you'll have to be pretty creative to come up with a domain name that hasn't been registered. All domain registrars provide tools that let you check whether the domain you want to register is available.

I'm going to assume from this point onward that you have a domain that you want to use for your TypePad blog.

Mapping a domain

After you've registered a domain, you have a bit of a dilemma: pointing it to your blog. That's where the TypePad feature known as *domain mapping* comes in. You can enable this feature with a little help from your domain registrar or your Web hosting company.

To *map* your domain (make it point to your blog), follow these steps:

1. Log in to TypePad, if you haven't already.

2. Click the Account link in the navigation bar at the top of the Dashboard (**Figure 3.1**).

   The blue navigation menu on the left side of the resulting screen includes a bunch of options, most of which I cover in Chapter 2.

Figure 3.1 The Account link in TypePad's global navigation bar.

3. Choose Domain Mapping from this menu.

   An information page opens (**Figure 3.2**, on the next page), displaying the big red warning *Important Requirements*. These requirements are serious stuff, but luckily, you're reading this book, which covers all of them.

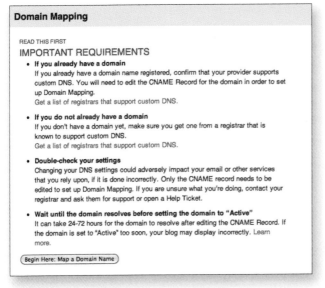

Figure 3.2 TypePad's requirements for using domain mapping.

4. Click the Begin Here: Map a Domain Name button.

The Domain Mapping page opens (**Figure 3.3**). Here, you can apply this domain to all your TypePad blogs or assign it on a per-blog basis.

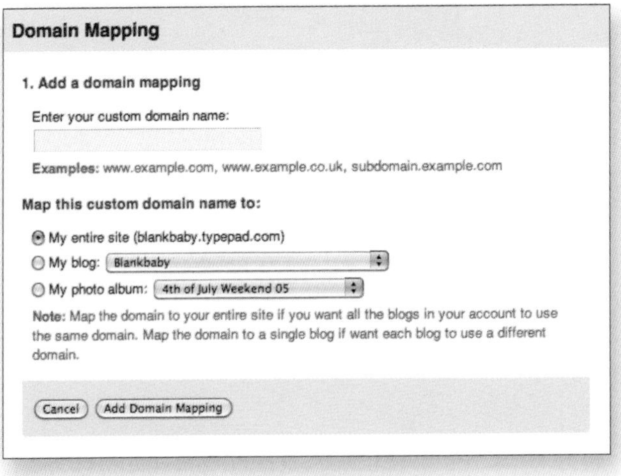

Figure 3.3 The Domain Mapping page lets you add domain mapping to your blog.

5. In the top text field, enter your custom domain name.

I want to map the domain scottexplains.com to http://blankbaby. typepad.com/scottexplains, so I'm entering **scottexplains.com** for this example.

6. Specify the content you want to map to this domain by choosing the appropriate option at the bottom of the page.

Generally speaking, you'll want to do one-to-one domain mapping— one domain to one blog—so you'll want to select the My Blog radio button and then choose that blog from the drop-down menu, which lists all the blogs that you've created in TypePad.

In **Figure 3.4**, I'm mapping the domain to my Scott Explains blog.

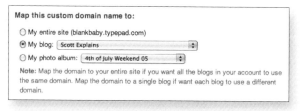

Figure 3.4 Mapping a domain to a specific blog.

If you want to map a domain to your entire TypePad site instead, select the My Entire Site radio button. Setting that option changes your base TypePad URL from *yourTypePadaccount*.typepad.com to *whateverdomain.com/BlogName*.

> **tip**
> If you're thinking about creating a network of blogs, you should map the entire site to a domain.

> **note**
> In addition to creating several blogs with one TypePad account, you can create photo albums (see Chapter 10), so you can map a domain to a particular photo album by selecting the My Photo Album radio button and then choosing that album from the drop-down menu.

7. Click the Add Domain Mapping button at the bottom of the page.

TypePad creates the domain mapping and adds a new section to the Domain Mapping page that lists all your domain mappings (**Figure 3.5**). A green check mark next to a mapping means that the mapping is active; a yellow triangle next to a mapping means that it isn't.

Domain Mapping

2. Configure your domain's DNS record

The next step is to configure the DNS record for your domain with the recommended DNS settings below. We've provided shortcuts to some common domain registrars below (you will have to sign in at their site if you haven't already).

CNAME Record
Domain: **www.testtypepad.com**
Points to: **blankbaby.typepad.com**

Here is a list of several popular registrars you may have registered with:
- pairNIC
- GoDaddy
- Network Solutions
- Dotster

Once you have configured the DNS record for your domain and your custom domain points to your site, blog, or album, return to this page and activate your domain mapping from the table below.

(Map Another Domain Name)

Domain Mappings

Note: Do not activate your domain until you are sure that the domain's DNS record has been updated.

⚑ Domain	Mapped To	Actions	
⊘ blog.blankbaby.com	blankbaby.typepad.com/blankbaby/	Deactivate	Remove
⊘ www.scottexplains.com	blankbaby.typepad.com/scott_explains/	Deactivate	Remove
⚠ www.testtypepad.com	blankbaby.typepad.com/photos/july42005/	Activate	Remove

Figure 3.5 This page lists all the domain mappings you have in TypePad.

As you can see in Figure 3.5, my account has two domain mappings at the moment: one that points to my personal blog and one that points to the Scott Explains blog. Notice the yellow triangle next to the last entry. That symbol means that this domain mapping has been created but isn't active. If you attempted to go to www.testtypepad.com at this point, you'd get a blank page.

8. To activate a dormant domain mapping, click the Activate link next to it; to deactivate an active domain mapping, click the Deactivate link next to it.

9. If you want to remove a domain mapping altogether, click its Remove link.

Domain Mapping Tutorials

For your domain mapping to work, you need to configure some settings with your domain registrar. TypePad offers a few provider-specific domain-mapping tutorials:

- Domain Mapping with Yahoo: http://help.sixapart.com/tp/us/yahoo.html

- Domain Mapping with Network Solutions: http://help.sixapart.com/tp/us/network_solutions.html

- Domain Mapping with GoDaddy: http://help.sixapart.com/tp/us/godaddy.html

If your registrar isn't listed here, don't worry. The tutorials can be generalized to fit just about any provider.

Changing your TypePad domain

As I explain earlier in this chapter, TypePad creates a main domain for all blogs created in your TypePad account, using the format http://*yourTypePadaccount*.typepad.com. You can change the domain whenever you like. This isn't something to do lightly, because it changes the URL for all your blogs (except those for which you're using domain mapping; see the preceding section). But if you really want to, you can. Here's how:

1. Click the Account link in the green navigation bar at the top of the Dashboard (refer to Figure 3.1).

   Your Account Summary page opens. As you can see in **Figure 3.6**, on the next page, the Account Information section lists my TypePad domain as blankbaby.typepad.com.

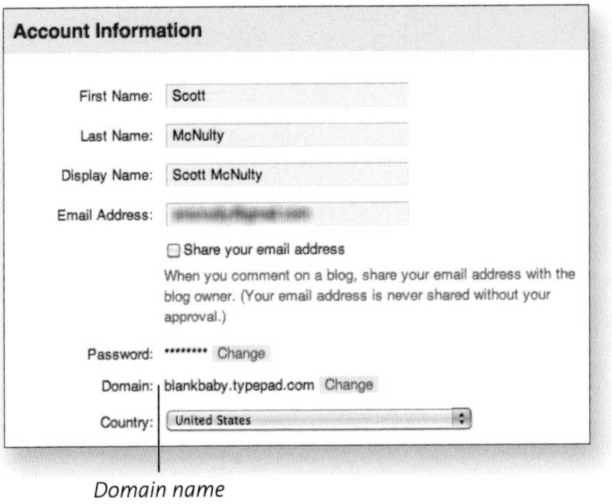

Figure 3.6 The Account Summary page lists your active domain.

Domain name

2. Click the Change link next to the domain name.

   The Change Your Domain page opens (**Figure 3.7**), displaying a bunch of warnings in a lot of red writing.

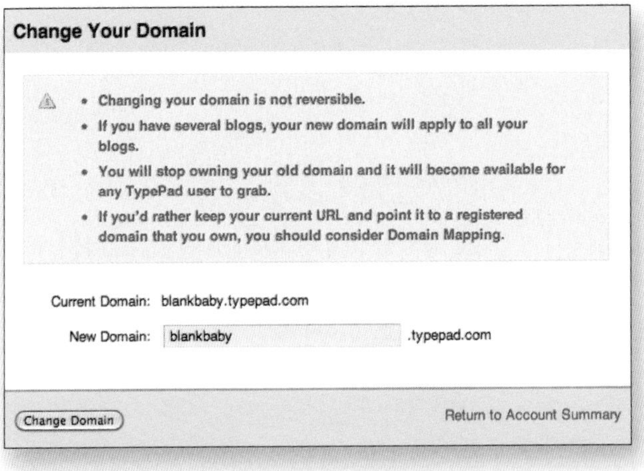

Figure 3.7 Read these warnings carefully before you proceed, because changing your domain will change all your blog URLs.

The warnings boil down to these points:

- This change will change the TypePad URLs of all your blogs and every one of your posts, so all links pointing to the old URL will break.

- You can't reverse this decision, so make sure that you *really* want to change your domain.

- After you change it, your old domain becomes available. Someone else who signs up for TypePad can nab your old domain, and you can't stop him.

3. If you're still itching to change your domain, type the new domain in the New Domain field.

   TypePad checks to see whether that domain is available. An error message appears if the domain you want is already taken.

4. If the new domain is available, click the Change Domain button; if you change your mind, click the Return to Account Summary link.

About Me Is All About You

In Chapter 2, I introduce the About Me page; in this section, I show you how to configure it for your blog by using either the default About Me template or custom HTML.

Working with the default About Me template

The strength of the default About Me template is that it lets you enter the information only once. You don't need to keep separate About Me pages for all your blogs, which can get a little annoying when you're running more than two or three. Also, the template makes it easy to add and subtract information; it even takes care of the design and layout of the page for you.

To configure your About Me page by using the default About Me template, click the Account link in the navigation bar at the top of the Dashboard. When the Account Summary page opens, choose About Me Page from the blue navigation menu on the left side of the page.

Now you can see the options available to you for your About Me page. To use the default template, select the check box titled Use the About Me Page Default Template (Recommended) (**Figure 3.8**, on the next page).

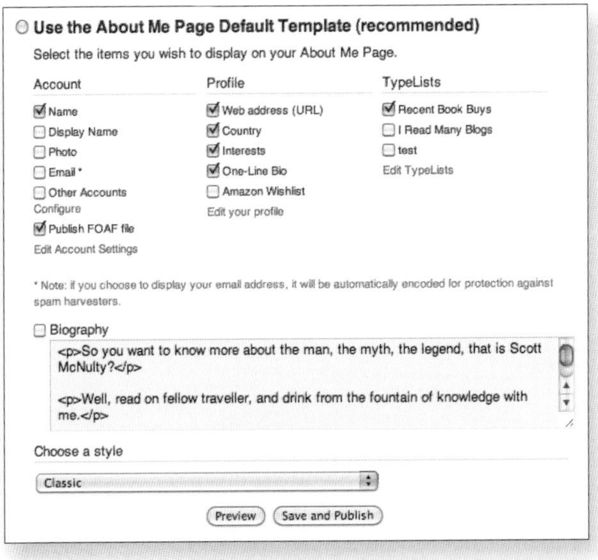

Figure 3.8 The configuration choices available in the default template for your About Me page.

As you can see in Figure 3.8, the default template makes creating an About Me page all about checking some boxes. Easy, right? You have three columns of check-box options to choose among, and I describe them all in the following sections.

Setting account options

You set most of this information in the Account Summary page when you set up your TypePad account (see Chapter 2). Simply check the boxes for the items that you want to display in your About Me page:

- **Name, Display Name,** and **Photo.** These options are pretty self-explanatory.

- **Email.** If you choose to include your email address on your About Me page, TypePad will encode it so that spammers won't be able to nab it.

- **Other Accounts.** The one piece of information in this column that you didn't set up when you set up your TypePad account is Other Accounts. If you click the Configure link below this option, the Other Accounts Module window opens (**Figure 3.9**). In this window, you can give your other accounts a new title—perhaps something like Find Me Elsewhere—and choose to display those accounts on your About Me page in a list or a grid of icons. Click OK to save your changes.

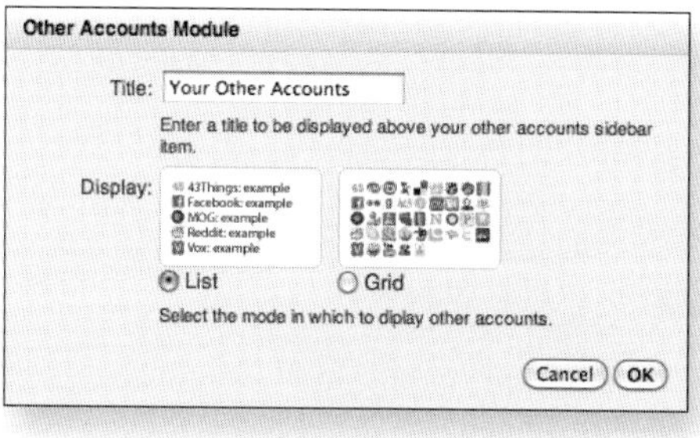

Figure 3.9 The Other Accounts Module window.

- **Publish FOAF File.** This option tells TypePad to create and share an *FOAF (friend of a friend) file* on your About Me page. This file is in a standard format that allows other Web sites and applications to consume the file and read the information that you've shared in the file.

At the bottom of the Account column, TypePad provides an Edit Account Settings link that takes you back to the Account Summary page.

Setting profile options

In addition to your TypePad account, you have a TypePad Profile, which contains more information about you. This profile shows up in other people's blogs when you comment on them (if you want), and it's what you use to interact with the rest of the TypePad community. These items are self-explanatory, so I won't cover them here. A link at the bottom of the column lets you edit your profile at any time.

Setting TypeLists options

TypeLists collect similar pieces of information—such as lists of links, books, and movies—and display them in your blogs. You can display TypeLists in one blog or in multiple blogs, and you have to update them in only one place.

After you've set up some TypeLists, you can display them in your About Me page by selecting the check boxes next to the ones that you want to use. To edit them later, click the Edit TypeLists link at the bottom of the column. I cover TypeLists in detail in Chapter 10.

Creating your biography

So far, all the information available for display in your About Me page has been pulled from other areas of TypePad. What if you want to display some text or use some HTML to point to your other Web sites? The Biography section (refer to Figure 3.8) is here to help.

The Biography text box can display anything that you can code in HTML. This box is designed to let you type a few autobiographical paragraphs, but you can also display a YouTube video by pasting its embed code here or create a list of all the other Web sites that you run. The sky's the limit. (Well, actually, HTML is the limit, but that still gives you a lot of leeway.)

Be sure to check the Biography check box to display the contents on your About Me page.

Choosing a style

Finally, the Choose a Style drop-down menu allows you to select a style for your About Me page. The styles in this menu are based on the themes you use in your blogs (I cover themes in Chapter 9), so your menu will likely look different from the one shown in **Figure 3.10**.

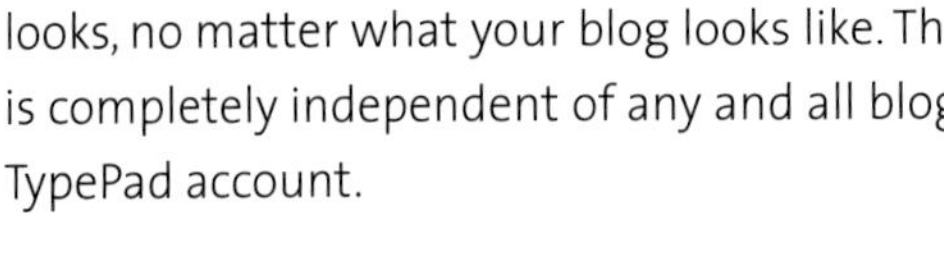

Figure 3.10 The style you choose for your About Me page can say something about you.

Keep in mind that the style you apply will dictate how your About Me page looks, no matter what your blog looks like. The About Me page's appearance is completely independent of any and all blogs associated with your TypePad account.

Previewing and publishing your page

When you're happy with the options you've picked, click the Preview button at the bottom of the configuration page (refer to Figure 3.8) to see what your About Me page will look like (**Figure 3.11**).

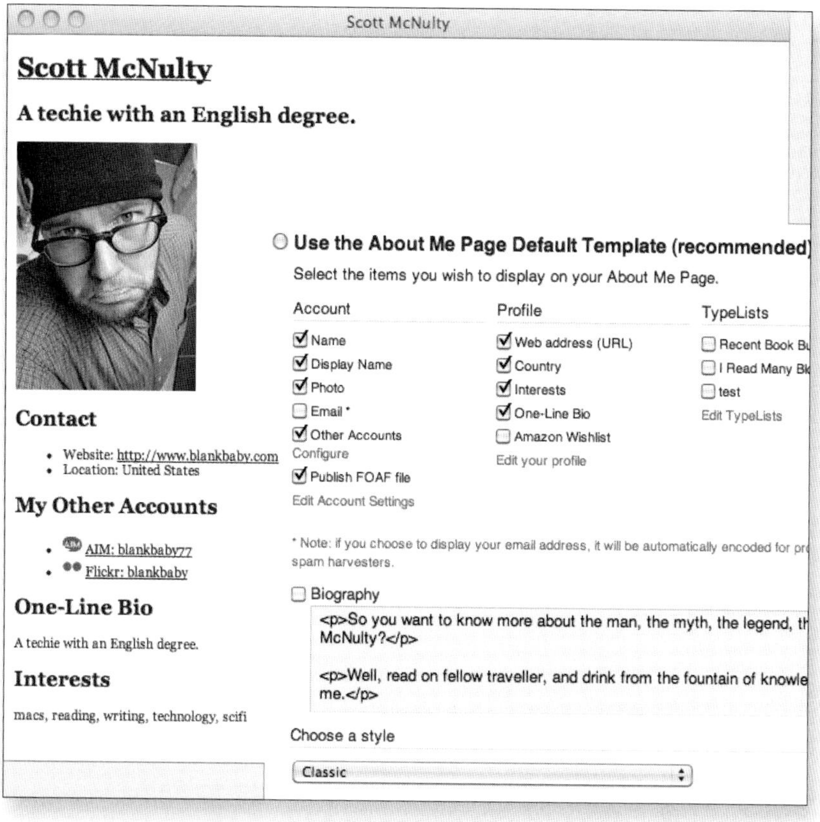

Figure 3.11 Here's a preview of my plain-Jane About Me page. Notice the selected options and how they display.

If you aren't happy with the way that the page looks, continue to tweak and preview it until you get everything just right.

When you've decided that your About Me page reflects well upon you, click the Save and Publish button to save all your settings, create the actual About Me page, and make that page available on the Internet.

Writing your own HTML page

The other option for creating an About Me page gives you more control of what TypePad displays but requires more knowledge to set up.

To enable this option, click the Account link in the navigation bar at the top of the Dashboard. When the Account Summary page opens, choose About

Me Page from the blue navigation menu on the left side of the page. Then select the Write Your Own HTML Page option to open the Write Your Own HTML Page. This page is so named for obvious reasons: Instead of choosing what to display in your About Me page by clicking check boxes, you create the page manually in HTML.

If you don't know what the heck HTML is, or if you know what it is but aren't interested in hand-coding anything, you should just stick with the default template (see the preceding section).

Keep in mind that when you choose the HTML option, you're creating an entire Web page by hand. You can use CSS (Cascading Style Sheets, a technique that allows you to control the design of your Web site) and any other HTML tricks you want.

note Covering HTML in full is far outside the scope of this book. If you want a handy quick reference, make sure to get a copy of *The HTML Pocket Guide*, by Bruce Hyslop (Peachpit Press).

Entering code gives you lots of freedom to do what you want, but what about all that information that you've entered in your TypePad account? Will you have to re-enter it into this custom About Me page? No. You can take advantage of a feature called *template tags* to get easy access to that information. For the full list of TypePad template tags, visit http://developer. typepad.com/tags. (This page displays different categories of template tags; for the About Me page, you're interested in User tags.)

As you can when you use the default template, you can preview and save your custom About Me page by clicking the appropriate button at the bottom of the configuration page.

4

Managing Blogs from the Dashboard

Now that you're familiar with the global TypePad settings, I'll show you how you'll be getting around TypePad on a day-to-day basis, as well as how to create, delete, and manage blogs in your TypePad account.

Think of the TypePad Dashboard as being command central (or your captain's chair, if you're a "Star Trek" geek like me). From this vantage point, you can overlook your TypePad kingdom: see your blog stats at a glance, look at what the people you follow on TypePad are up to, and see whether anyone left a comment or trackback on your blog. You can even post right from the Dashboard.

tip **TypePad actually has two different types of command consoles. One is the TypePad Dashboard, which is the subject of this chapter; the other is an individual blog dashboard for each blog you create. I cover blog dashboards in Chapter 6.**

Working with the Dashboard

How do you get to this wondrous place called the Dashboard? Simple:

- **Log in to TypePad.** After you log in, you're automatically whisked away to the Dashboard.

- **Click the Dashboard link.** A green navigation bar runs across the top of every page in TypePad. If you look at the left end of that bar, you'll see a Dashboard link (**Figure 4.1**). You can get to the Dashboard from anywhere in TypePad by clicking this link.

Figure 4.1 Clicking Dashboard in TypePad's global navigation bar always returns you to your TypePad Dashboard.

Figure 4.2 shows the Dashboard, which is divided into five sections:

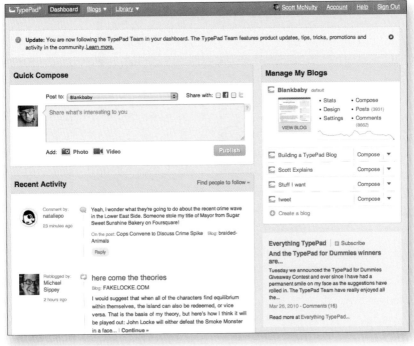

Figure 4.2 The TypePad Dashboard.

- Update

- Quick Compose

- Manage My Blogs

- Recent Activity

- Everything TypePad

In the following sections, I show you each part of the Dashboard in turn.

Update

From time to time, a light blue box appears at the top of the Dashboard, as shown in **Figure 4.3**. This Update box, which is displayed only on the Dashboard, is how the folks behind TypePad alert you to new features and announcements that they want to share with you.

Click to close.

Update: You are now following the TypePad Team in your dashboard. The TypePad Team features product updates, tips, tricks, promotions and activity in the community. Learn more.

Figure 4.3 An alert from the TypePad team.

This box stays on the Dashboard until you banish it by clicking the little red X in the top-right corner. After you close the Update box, there's no way to bring it back, so make sure that you've read its contents before you close it.

Quick Compose

It stands to reason that if you're looking at your Dashboard, you probably want to post something to your blog. The Quick Compose module (**Figure 4.4**, on the next page) is just what it sounds like: a quick way to dash off a blog post. This module doesn't offer all the features of the full-fledged entry page (which I talk about in Chapter 7), but it's great for posting a video from YouTube or a short text update.

tip   To get some help with the Quick Compose module, just click the little question mark.

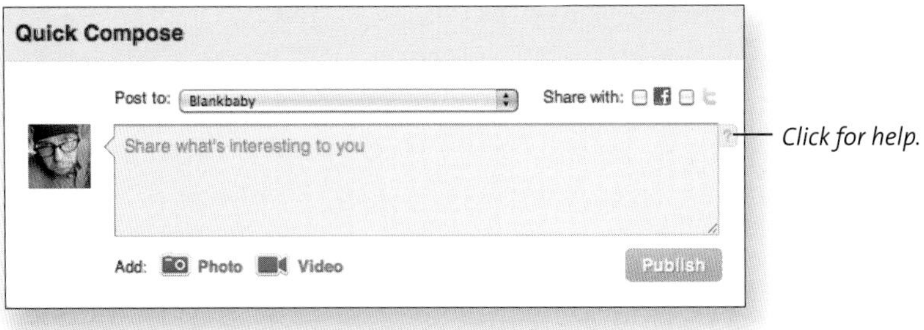

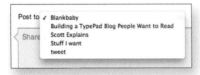

Figure 4.4 The Quick Compose module, featuring my TypePad Profile picture. (Your picture will be displayed on your own Dashboard.)

Creating text posts

If you have multiple blogs, you can use Quick Compose to post to any of them. By default, your default blog is selected. (In "Linking to your other blogs" later in this chapter, I show you how to set your default blog.) If you want to post elsewhere, choose it from the Post To drop-down menu, which lists all the blogs you can post to (**Figure 4.5**). Then whatever you enter in the text box will end up in that blog.

Figure 4.5 You can post to any blog from the Quick Compose module by choosing it from this menu.

 **If you have only one blog, you won't see this menu.**

To the right of the Post To drop-down menu, you may see check boxes next to the icons of familiar social-networking sites (**Figure 4.6**). The options presented here depend on what you entered in the Your Other Accounts page of your TypePad account. (See Chapter 5 for more information on associating social-networking sites with TypePad.)

Figure 4.6 Sharing your posts is easy: Click the check box for each site you want to post to.

tip TypePad makes it so easy to share your blogs with a variety of social networks that it's tempting to post a link to every entry you ever write in all your social networks. Be judicious in what you share, though, because people value their time and attention. If you push a constant stream of blog posts to a variety of social networks without context, or without a motive other than building traffic to your site, people will become irritated with you. Always remember that the unfollow/unfriend button is just a click away.

The meat of the Quick Compose module is the text box (**Figure 4.7**), where you type whatever you want to post on your blog.

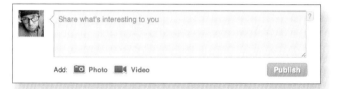

Figure 4.7 The text box is where all the action happens in the Quick Compose module.

Posting photos

In addition to posting just plain old text (boring!), you can post pictures to your blog from the Quick Compose module. Just follow these steps:

1. Click the Photo icon below the text box (**Figure 4.8**).

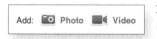

Figure 4.8 You can add photos to a post by clicking the Photo icon.

Clicking this icon opens a set of controls that lets you upload a photo to display with your post (**Figure 4.9**). In keeping with the simplicity of the Quick Compose module, you can't fiddle with any of the image settings associated with the file you upload here, as you can do in the full-blown post editor (see Chapter 7).

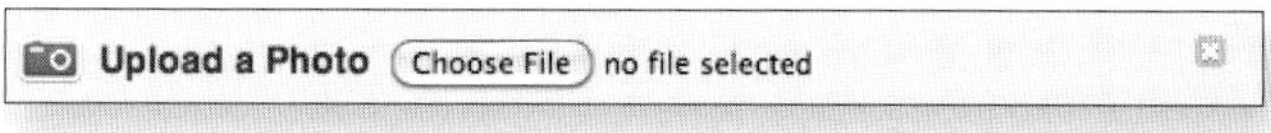

Upload a Photo (Choose File) no file selected

Figure 4.9 Click Choose File to select a picture on your computer.

2. Click the Choose File button.

A file browser pops up.

3. Locate and select the photo on your computer that you want to insert.

4. Click the appropriate command button: Choose (Mac) or Browse (Windows).

TypePad uploads the picture (**Figure 4.10**).

Figure 4.10 Your photo is uploading, as you can tell by the little swirling circle.

As the upload progresses, you'll see a little swirling circle, which will be replaced by a small thumbnail of the image when it's completely uploaded (**Figure 4.11**). (Don't worry because the thumbnail is a square; the image you uploaded still has the proper dimensions.)

Figure 4.11 The thumbnail lets you know that the picture was uploaded successfully.

If you decide against using the picture, click the little gray-and-white X next to the thumbnail.

Posting video

Video has become a huge part of the Web, and the Quick Compose module has you covered. If you want to embed some video from a video Web site such as YouTube, Hulu, or Vimeo, all you need is the URL for that video. Click the Video icon below the text box (refer to Figure 4.8), and a text field appears, ready for you to paste that URL into it (**Figure 4.12**). When you click the Publish button, TypePad embeds the video in your post for you. How nice!

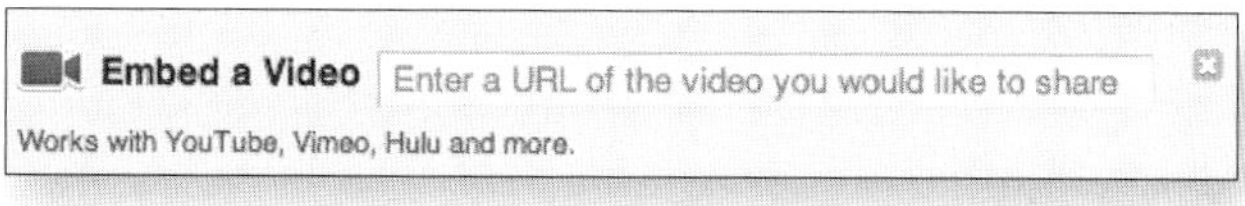

Figure 4.12 You can embed a video by pasting a URL from a video sharing service.

When you use this method, you can insert only one video per post.

> **tip** To embed multiple videos via Quick Compose, just paste the URLs of the videos directly in the text field. You can even mix and match services, posting Hulu videos alongside YouTube videos, for example.

Quick Compose Caveats

You should remember a few things about the Quick Compose module:

- You can't set the title of a post with the Quick Compose module, which isn't ideal, because search engines really like to index titles. (As I discuss in Chapter 7, the title of your post also becomes the title of that post's page, which is a sort of search-engine double whammy.)

- You can't use HTML in the Quick Compose module. You can try to hand-code links, enter images, and the like, but when you click Publish, you'll notice that TypePad ignores all the code you entered. You have to stick with plain text.

- Any URLs that you type in the Quick Compose module are automatically turned into clickable links, which is kind of neat. The text of the link is the URL that you typed, and the automatically created link points to that same URL.

Bottom line, the Quick Compose module is very easy to use but also quite limited. If I were a wagering man, I'd bet that you won't be spending too much time with it, but when you need to post something in a hurry, you'll appreciate Quick Compose.

Publishing your content

When you're ready to publish your post, just click the green Publish button. Just like that, you've created a blog entry.

When TypePad has posted your entry, the text box in the Quick Compose module is overlaid with a confirmation message (**Figure 4.13**), which includes a link to the entry you just posted.

Figure 4.13 After you publish your post, an alert congratulates you and allows you to view the post or compose another.

Manage My Blogs

The Manage My Blogs module (**Figure 4.14**) is a one-stop shop for all your blog-management needs. You can't do much management directly from the module itself, but it allows you to get to your management tools quickly. You can also create a new blog right from this module.

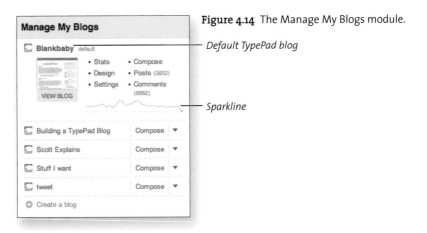

Figure 4.14 The Manage My Blogs module.

Default TypePad blog

Sparkline

Viewing your default blog

At the moment, you probably have only one blog listed: the default blog in your TypePad account. As you can see in Figure 4.14, the Manage My Blogs module gives you an overview of your default blog, starting with a thumbnail image of it. This image gives you a good idea of what your blog looks like at the moment, and if you click it, your blog opens in a new browser window.

To the right of the thumbnail image are links to various administrative sections of your blog:

- **Stats.** This link takes you to the statistics-tracking page of your blog (see Chapter 6). Check it out to see your blog's traffic.

- **Design.** You can change your blog's design here. (For more on design, see Chapter 9.)

- **Settings.** Each blog has several blog-specific settings, which I go over in Chapter 5.

- **Compose.** The Quick Compose module is great for quickie posts, but this link takes you to the full-featured entry page (see Chapter 7).

- **Posts.** This link takes you to the post management page (again, covered in Chapter 7). The number in parentheses is the number of posts in your blog.

- **Comments.** Click this link to manage the comments on your blog (see Chapter 8). As with the Posts link, the number in parentheses is the number of comments your blog has received.

Below all those links is an odd little line that looks like some sort of graph. Information-graphic nerds know that this line is a *sparkline*, which is a fancy name for a small graphic that shows you a trend in a concise way. In TypePad, that trend is your blog's traffic for the past 30 days. The graphic doesn't include any numbers, but it gives you a sense of how much traffic your blog is getting.

 tip   Clicking the sparkline takes you to that blog's dashboard; clicking the blog's name does the same thing.

Linking to your other blogs

If you have more than one blog, as I do, the Manage My Blogs module lists all your blogs at the bottom of the page in alphabetical order (**Figure 4.15**). Each blog name is actually a link that takes you to that blog's dashboard. Also, each blog in this list has a prominent Compose link, so you can jump into writing an entry for any of your blogs right from the Dashboard. Pretty nice, huh?

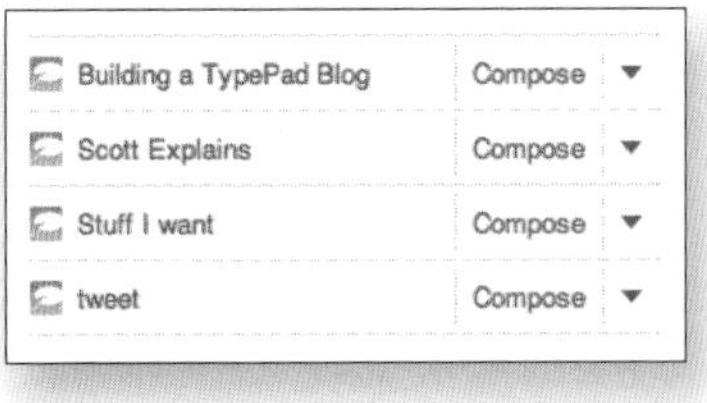

Figure 4.15 The rest of your blogs are listed below the default blog's thumbnail.

If you click the down arrow to the right of any Compose link, you get a menu of options (**Figure 4.16**).

Figure 4.16 Clicking the arrow to the right of each blog entry brings up a menu of management links.

These options pretty much mirror the links that are listed for the default blog, with a couple of notable differences:

- **Overview/Stats.** This link takes you to that blog's dashboard.

- **Posts** and **Pages.** Posts takes you to the post management screen, and Pages takes you to the page management screen.

- **Make This the Default Blog?** This link allows you to change the default blog in TypePad—the one that the Quick Compose module posts to and the one that gets the most information displayed in the TypePad Dashboard. Think of the default blog as being your main blog. You can change it as often as you like without suffering any consequences.

Creating a blog

The final item in the Manage My Blogs module is an unassuming link at the bottom of the page called Create a Blog (**Figure 4.17**).

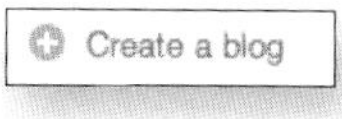

Figure 4.17 Click this link to start creating a new blog.

When you click this link, you're taken to the Add a Blog page (**Figure 4.18**).

Figure 4.18 Adding a blog is as simple as filling out this form.

Give the new blog a name, decide what you want the TypePad URL to be (you can use domain mapping to map this URL to another, more professional URL, as I explain in Chapter 3), and tell TypePad whether you want to have this blog indexed by search engines. Then click Create Blog. You've just created your second blog. How does it feel?

note If you clicked Create a Blog by accident, just go to another section of TypePad. The creation process will be canceled.

tip You can also switch from one blog to another or create a new blog no matter where you are in the TypePad interface, thanks to the Blogs link in the global navigation bar. Click that link to display your list of blogs and an Add a Blog link (**Figure 4.19**, on the next page).

Figure 4.19 Access and create blogs via the Blogs link in the TypePad navigation bar.

Recent Activity

The Recent Activity module (**Figure 4.20**) displays the most recent activity on your blog. If someone leaves a comment, sends a trackback, starts to follow your TypePad Profile, or *reblogs* one of your posts (posting it on his own blog with a link back to your post; see Chapter 8), that activity shows up in this module. The activities of people you follow in TypePad are also displayed here.

Figure 4.20 The Recent Activity module shows your blog's (and your own) recent activities in the TypePad universe.

The right side of the module displays the TypePad Profile picture (also known as an *avatar*) of whoever was responsible for the activity being displayed. As you can see in Figure 4.20, I posted an entry on my blog, so my picture shows up along with some information about the blog post. If you click the title of the post, you're taken to the post itself. Clicking the Edit button takes you to the post composition page (available only for posts that you created). Finally, you can see how many favorites, comments, and reblogs a post has received. (Clearly, no one cares about my new haircut.) The buttons are also links, so you can easily favorite, reblog, or comment on a post that intrigues you.

Tracking comments

The Recent Activity module is great for keeping track of who is commenting on your blog. Every time a comment is left—including a comment that you leave yourself—it shows up in the module (**Figure 4.21**), which displays the name of the commenter, a picture, and the title of the post in question.

Figure 4.21 Comments displayed in the Recent Activity module.

> **note** If the commenter has a TypePad account, the picture is her TypePad Profile picture. If not, TypePad generates a picture for that person.

A green check mark below a comment indicates that it has been approved and is being displayed in your blog. If you want to remove or edit the comment, just click the Manage button, and you'll be taken to the Comments page (see Chapter 8).

You can also reply to a comment by clicking the Reply button, which opens a new browser window and loads the appropriate page of your blog. Then you can leave your reply via your blog's comment form.

Following and unfollowing people

At the moment, you're probably seeing updates only from yourself and the TypePad team in the Recent Activity module, because you aren't following anyone at the moment. You may be asking, "How do I find people to follow on TypePad, Scott?" I'm so glad you asked, reader!

Right at the top of the Recent Activity module is a link called Find People to Follow (**Figure 4.22**). Click that link, and you're greeted by the people finder (**Figure 4.23**).

Figure 4.22 You have to find people before you can follow them in TypePad. This link will help.

Figure 4.23 Bloggers are categorized for ease of following.

The menu on the left side of the people finder lists different categories of TypePad users or communities that may be of interest to you. Click a category to see a list of users you can follow, click the Follow button next to each user you want to follow, and that's it.

If you want to follow everyone in a certain category, click the Follow All button at the bottom of the people finder. If someone you're already following is listed, TypePad lets you know by displaying a green Following link next to that user's name. To stop following him, click the gray Unfollow link.

When you're done with the people finder, click the X in the top-right corner, and you're back in the TypePad Dashboard.

Now that you're following people, you'll get information about them automatically. When someone you follow posts an entry to his blog, for example, you'll see an alert similar to the one shown in **Figure 4.24**. This alert includes the title of the post, an excerpt, and a Continue link. Clicking Continue opens the post in a new browser window where you can read it, comment on it, reblog it, or favorite it. The alert has no Edit button; because you didn't create this post, you can't change it unless you have administrative rights to that person's blog.

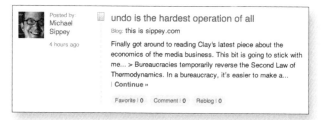

Figure 4.24 A post by someone you follow in TypePad.

Also, if you place your mouse over an avatar in the Recent Activity module, some information about that person pops up (**Figure 4.25**). You see his name, where he is (if he's filled in that information), how many people he's following in TypePad, and how many people are following him in return. Because this person shows up in your Recent Activity module, it makes sense that you're following him, which is confirmed by the Following link below his name. Right below that is a Unfollow link, which you can click if you've had enough of this person's updates.

Figure 4.25 When you mouse over an avatar, you see more information about the TypePad user you're following.

| tip | Following others in TypePad gives you a glimpse of what they're enjoying in other TypePad blogs. You can check out the posts that people are favoriting and reblogging for inspiration and pointers that you can apply to your own blog. Think of following people as being a form of free market research—available right from your TypePad Dashboard. |

Managing alerts

The Recent Activity module can become a busy place after you start following a few people and building your own blog audience. Posts and comments will start coming in, and because you want to stay on top of things, you get a little alert whenever new content is available (**Figure 4.26**). This alert tells you the quantity and type of new content that's ready to be displayed and includes a link that refreshes the module without refreshing the entire browser window. This feature is handy if you're working on a post in the Quick Compose module and someone leaves a comment, because clicking the Refresh link in the alert will keep you from losing the post you're working on.

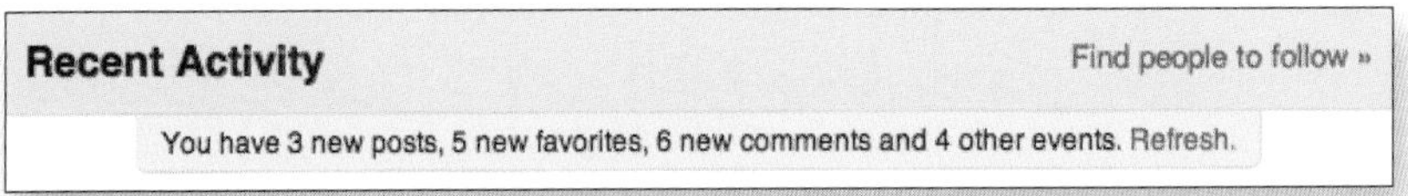

Recent Activity   Find people to follow »

You have 3 new posts, 5 new favorites, 6 new comments and 4 other events. Refresh.

Figure 4.26 The Recent Activity module doesn't autorefresh, but you'll see this yellow notice whenever new content is available.

Viewing less-recent activity

Given the nature of the Recent Activity module, you may see a lot of new entries when you log into TypePad after a little while. If you scroll all the way to the bottom of the TypePad Dashboard, you'll see the navigation options for the Recent Activity module (**Figure 4.27**). If you want to see older activity, click the Older link. When you want to see the newer stuff, click the Newer link.

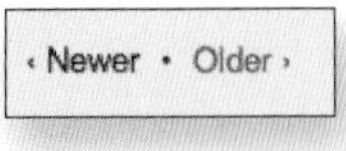

‹ Newer • Older ›

Figure 4.27 The Recent Activity module's navigation links.

> **note** The Older link is available only when you're viewing the most recent entries, such as the first page of entries in the Recent Activity module.

Everything TypePad

The final section of your TypePad Dashboard is also the simplest, but I want to highlight it because it offers a wealth of information. I'm talking, of course, about the Everything TypePad module (**Figure 4.28**).

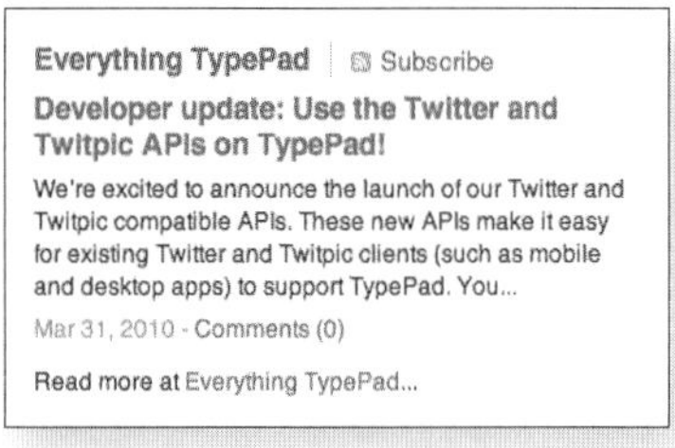

Figure 4.28 You can subscribe to Everything TypePad right from your Dashboard, as well as read an excerpt of the most recent post.

This module displays the most recent entry from the Everything TypePad blog (http://everything.typepad.com/blog). It's a great way to keep up with the latest TypePad news, straight from the horse's mouth.

You can go to the blog directly to read the entire post by clicking the post's title. (In Figure 4.28, that would be "Developer update: Use the Twitter and Twitpic APIs on TypePad!") The red *Everything TypePad* text is a link to the blog too, as is the blue *Everything TypePad* text.

If you use a newsreader, you can subscribe to the Everything TypePad blog by clicking the orange Subscribe icon or the Subscribe link. That way, the news comes to you, not the other way around.

Be sure to visit and subscribe to the blog. It's a great resource.

5

Working with Blog-Specific Settings

Chapter 3 covers a bunch of global settings that apply to all your blogs equally. Each blog, however, also has settings that affect it separately. In this chapter, I show you how to get to those blog settings and explain what each setting does.

Getting to Your Blog Settings

To get to a blog's specific settings from your TypePad Dashboard, you have to return to your old friend the Manage My Blogs module (see Chapter 4). If you want to access your default blog's settings, or if you have only one blog, just click the Settings link to the right of the blog's name (**Figure 5.1**). If you have more than one blog, click the blue triangle next to the name of blog you're interested in working on and then choose Settings from the resulting drop-down menu.

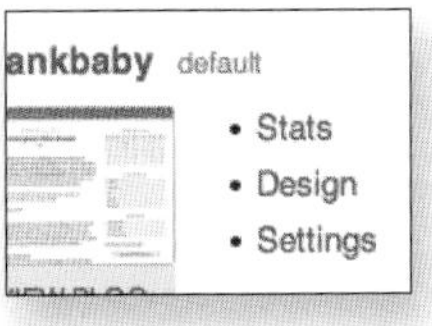

Figure 5.1 The Settings link takes you to blog-specific settings.

No matter which method you use to get there, your settings page looks like **Figure 5.2**.

Figure 5.2 A blog's Basics settings page. Here, you can change your blog's name, description, and URL, as well as password-protect it.

The navigation is just like that of your TypePad Account Summary page. The blue navigation menu on the left side of the page takes you from section to section; the body of the page displays the actual settings.

In the following sections, I take a look at each group of settings.

Basics Settings

The settings in the Basics page are pretty...well, basic.

Blog Name

This setting is the title of the blog (**Figure 5.3**). You can change it at any time, but doing that would be akin to the Coca-Cola Co.'s changing the name of its flagship product to something else. (If you're old enough to remember New Coke, you know how well that worked out.) Make sure that you pick a good name to start with.

Blog Name:	Scott Explains
	Example: The Backpacking Fool

Figure 5.3 Your blog name. Remember to pick a good one!

Because the blog in this example is all about me explaining technical issues to people, Scott Explains is a great name (and it goes with the URL—www.scottexplains.com—quite nicely).

Blog Description

This description (**Figure 5.4**) can be displayed in the blog itself. In fact, many of TypePad's built-in themes display the description by default. Make sure that the description isn't too long and gives a new reader a good idea of what to expect from your blog. Think pithy and helpful (which is actually a pretty good description for a blog).

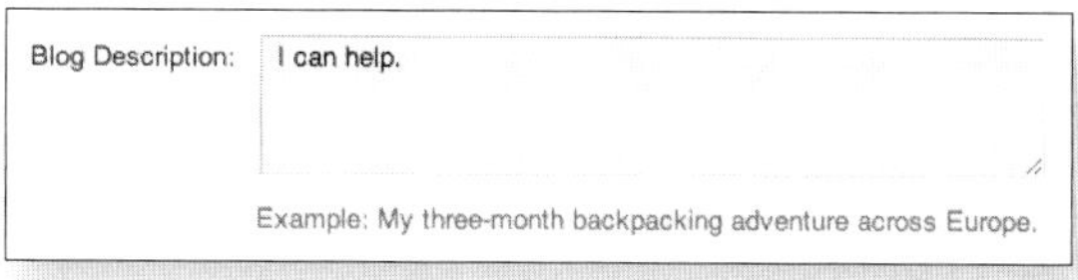

Blog Description:	I can help.
	Example: My three-month backpacking adventure across Europe.

Figure 5.4 The description is often displayed in your blog's header by the built-in TypePad themes. Keep it short.

Blog Folder

Your blog's folder setting (**Figure 5.5**, on the next page) determines what the TypePad URL of your blog is. TypePad uses this URL for all images that are uploaded to your blog, and people might use it to access your blog (though you really should use domain mapping, which I discuss in Chapter 3).

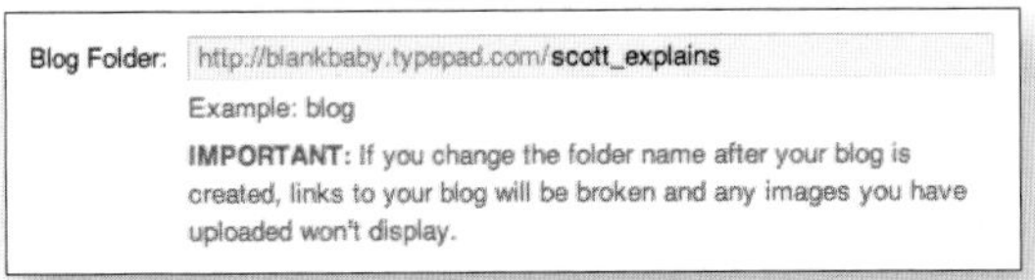

Blog Folder: http://blankbaby.typepad.com/**scott_explains**

Example: blog

IMPORTANT: If you change the folder name after your blog is
created, links to your blog will be broken and any images you have
uploaded won't display.

Figure 5.5 The Blog Folder
setting is your blog's URL.

Technically, you can change this folder after your blog has been set up, but
I strongly recommend against it; doing that would be like changing the
name of Coke. A better idea is to start with a good name.

note

**Remember that all your TypePad blogs have the same root URL
(in Figure 5.5, http://blankbaby.typepad.com).**

Password

There are many reasons why you might want to password-protect your
blog. When you enable this feature (**Figure 5.6**), only people who have the
user name and password will be able to read your blog. Search engines and
your average Web surfers won't be able to access its contents.

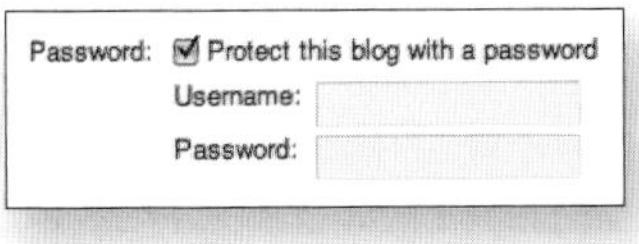

Password: ☑ Protect this blog with a password
Username:
Password:

Figure 5.6 Password-protect your blog if you
don't want prying eyes seeing what you're up to.

Password protection is a great option to enable while you're working on
your blog and don't want people to see any wacky formatting. Or perhaps
you've shuttered your business (I hope not!) and don't want people to place
orders or find out anything about the former business. You can toggle this
setting on and off whenever you like.

Delete This Blog

This unobtrusive link is at the bottom of the Basics page, right across from
the Save Changes button (**Figure 5.7**). I suggest that you *not* click this link
unless you've thought long and hard about it first, because doing so will
delete all traces of your blog from TypePad's servers. Nothing is backed up
(unless you've been backing up your content yourself), and you don't have
an Undo button. When a blog is deleted, it's gone, as are all the comments,
images, and posts related to it.

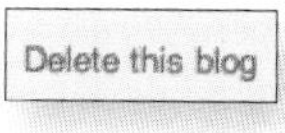

Delete this blog

Figure 5.7 The Delete This Blog link is small and tucked out of the way because you never want to click it by accident.

If you've mulled it over and decided that you really do want to delete the blog, click the link. A pop-up dialog box asks you whether you're sure (**Figure 5.8**). This is your only chance to back out. Click Cancel, and the selected blog won't be deleted. If you click OK, the blog is deleted, and you're taken to your TypePad Dashboard, which displays an alert to tell you that the deleted blog is gone (**Figure 5.9**).

http://www.typepad.com

Are you sure you want to permanently delete this blog? (All posts, comments, images and other information associated with the blog will be deleted and cannot be restored.)

Cancel   OK

Figure 5.8 This dialog box is a last way out in case you don't really want to delete the blog.

The selected blog has been deleted.

Figure 5.9 You deleted your blog, and all you got was this simple alert.

Save Changes

When you're happy with your settings in this page, click the Save Changes button. TypePad displays the confirmation shown in **Figure 5.10**.

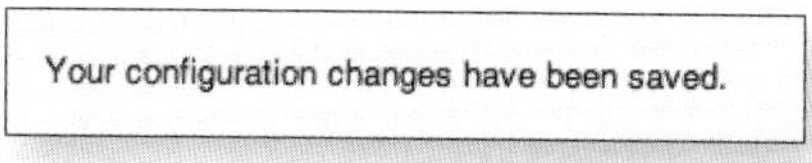

Your configuration changes have been saved.

Figure 5.10 Whenever you click Save Changes, a yellow alert lets you know that your changes were saved successfully.

SEO Settings

SEO stands for *search-engine optimization,* which is a bunch of best practices that help search engines index your blog better. SEO means that your blog will show up higher in search results, which means that more people will discover your blog.

There's no easy way to get lots of traffic, but applying some of the following SEO settings can only help you.

When you have all your SEO settings to your liking, remember to click the Save Changes button. Otherwise, your changes will be discarded when you leave the page.

Publicity

Publicity (**Figure 5.11**) is the most basic of all the SEO settings. Selecting the Yes, Publicize This Blog check box does a couple of things for your blog: It allows your blog to be indexed by search engines, and it puts your blog in the Six Apart Update Stream so that all your content gets indexed by search engines quickly.

 You can find out more about the Six Apart Update Stream at www.sixapart.com/labs/update.

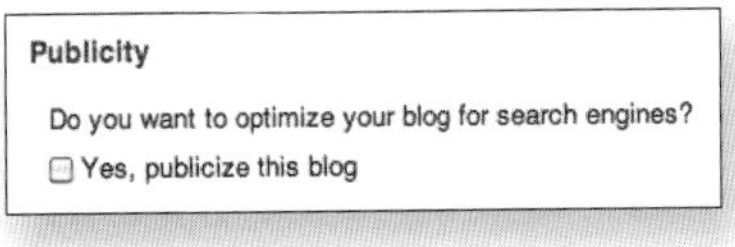

Publicity

Do you want to optimize your blog for search engines?

☐ Yes, publicize this blog

Figure 5.11 Publicity is a good thing for any blog.

Google Sitemap

When someone says "search engine," which one do you think of first? Google! Google is the de facto search standard, and you want to do everything in your power to have your blog rank high in Google searches. That's why you really should check the Yes, Generate Google Sitemap box (**Figure 5.12**). This setting creates a special file that Google will use to index your site fully. If you don't create one of this files, nothing bad will happen to your blog, but why not create one when it makes the top search engine on the planet happy? Trust me—you don't want to anger Google.

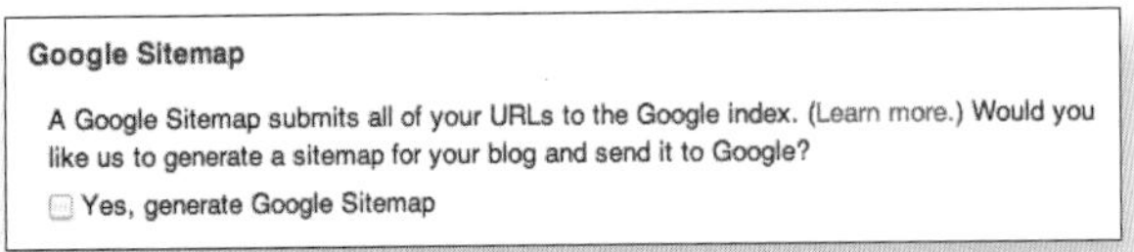

Google Sitemap

A Google Sitemap submits all of your URLs to the Google index. (Learn more.) Would you like us to generate a sitemap for your blog and send it to Google?

☐ Yes, generate Google Sitemap

Figure 5.12 A Google Sitemap makes it easier for Google to index your blog.

note This setting is grayed out until you enable the Yes, Publicize This Blog setting (see the preceding item), because if you don't want your blog showing up in search engines, you don't want to help Google index your blog. After you enable Publicity and save your changes, the Google Sitemap option becomes available.

Title Format

Every Web page has a title displayed at the very top of the browser window. Generally, folks overlook page titles as they browse the Web, but search engines see all, and they place some weight on your page titles. The drop-down menu in the Title Format section (**Figure 5.13**) offers a few options for titling the various pages of your blog (**Figure 5.14**).

note This format applies to both pages and posts, which I discuss in Chapter 7.

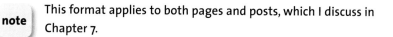

Title Format

What information should be included in the title tag of your posts?

Post Title – Blog Name

Post title followed by blog name is generally best for SEO. This setting applies to Pages as well.

Figure 5.13 You can choose how TypePad formats your blog's page titles here.

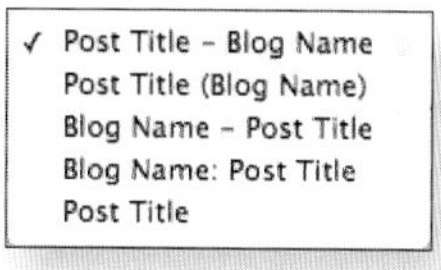

| ✓ Post Title – Blog Name |
| Post Title (Blog Name) |
| Blog Name – Post Title |
| Blog Name: Post Title |
| Post Title |

Figure 5.14 Pick the format that works best for you.

Each option includes the post title, and the first four include both the post title and the name of your blog. The default is Post Title - Blog Name. For my blog, Scott Explains, if I posted an entry with the title "TypePad blog settings explained," the default page title would be "TypePad blog settings explained —Scott Explains."

I recommend accepting the default setting, because search engines tend to put more emphasis on the beginning of a page's title, and you want all the keywords you've used in the entry's title to work for you.

Meta Keywords

Keywords (also called *tags* and *meta information*) describe something. Search engines use keywords to figure out what a Web site is all about. In the Meta Keywords section (**Figure 5.15**), enter the terms that best describe your blog, separating the terms with commas as shown in the figure.

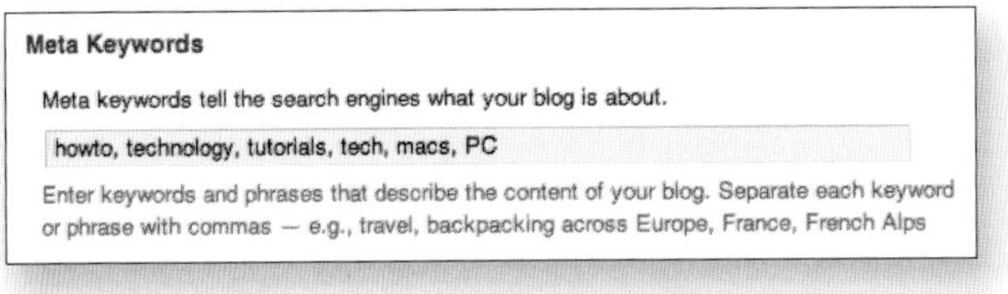

Meta Keywords

Meta keywords tell the search engines what your blog is about.

howto, technology, tutorials, tech, macs, PC

Enter keywords and phrases that describe the content of your blog. Separate each keyword or phrase with commas — e.g., travel, backpacking across Europe, France, French Alps

Figure 5.15 Keywords give you an opportunity to describe your blog. Your readers won't see these keywords, but search engines will.

Meta Description

Yes, another description for your blog! Only search engines use this one, though. Enter a descriptive few sentences in the Meta Description section (**Figure 5.16**), because search engines generally display this information in their results for your blog. This description will not show up in your blog itself, so feel free to be a little long-winded here.

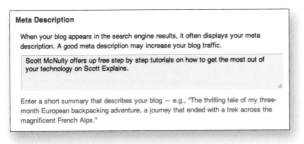

Meta Description

When your blog appears in the search engine results, it often displays your meta description. A good meta description may increase your blog traffic.

Scott McNulty offers up free step by step tutorials on how to get the most out of your technology on Scott Explains.

Enter a short summary that describes your blog — e.g., "The thrilling tale of my three-month European backpacking adventure, a journey that ended with a trek across the magnificent French Alps."

Figure 5.16 This description will be displayed in your search-engine results.

Sharing Settings

We were all taught that "sharing is caring," and TypePad certainly subscribes to that maxim. In fact, sharing is a key component of social media in general: You share your thoughts, you share links to cool stuff, and you share experiences. You can configure the following settings in the Sharing page.

When you're happy with your Sharing settings, be sure to click Save Changes.

Share Your Posts with Friends on Other Social Networks

The first section of the Sharing settings page (**Figure 5.17**) controls which external social networks (Facebook, Twitter, and the like) you can share your posts with automatically. Check one of the boxes to have TypePad share your new posts automatically, though you can override these settings on a per-post basis (see Chapter 4).

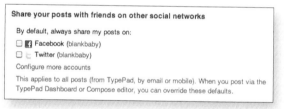

Figure 5.17 TypePad will happily post your entries to a variety of social networks.

The social networks that are listed in this section depend on what accounts you added to the Your Other Accounts section of your TypePad account (see Chapter 2). If the social network you want to be able to share posts with isn't listed in the Sharing page, click the Configure More Accounts link, which takes you to your TypePad Account Summary page so that you can add any number of social-networking accounts.

note Posting things to social networks automatically is always a tricky proposition. On one hand, it allows you to repurpose your content and share it with the largest audience possible; on the other hand, some people don't appreciate automated posts of any kind. The key to success is using a mixture of handcrafted and automated posts to social networks.

Share This Blog on Your TypePad Profile

Unless you aren't ready to share this blog with anyone (if you're still setting it up, for example), it's a good idea to select the check box in this section (**Figure 5.18**). This setting automatically updates your TypePad Profile every time you post something. Why would you want to do that? It also allows your blog posts to show up in your TypePad followers' Dashboards, and the more places your content shows up, the better your readership numbers.

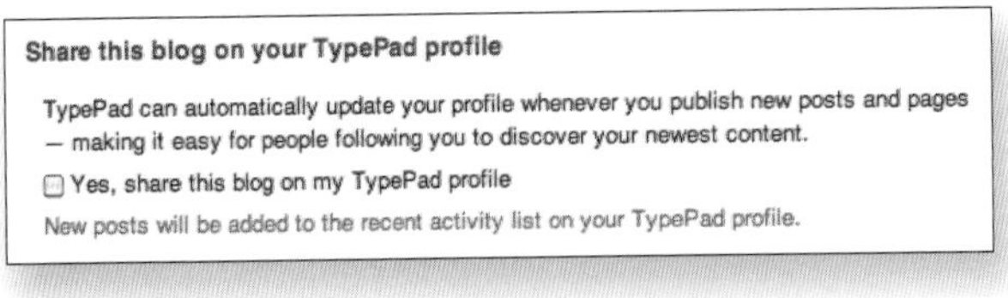

Share this blog on your TypePad profile

TypePad can automatically update your profile whenever you publish new posts and pages — making it easy for people following you to discover your newest content.

☐ Yes, share this blog on my TypePad profile

New posts will be added to the recent activity list on your TypePad profile.

Figure 5.18 Even if you don't want to share your blog on other social networks, you should share it in your TypePad Profile.

Let Your Readers Share Their Comments

This setting (**Figure 5.19**) affects the people who leave comments on your blog. By default, people can log into your blog through accounts they already have, such as TypePad, Twitter, and Facebook. This arrangement cuts down on the scourge of comment spam (which I talk about in "Comments Settings" later in this chapter) and allows people with TypePad accounts to share, via their TypePad Profiles, the fact that they've left a comment on your blog. If you want to change this setting, click the Manage Your Comments Settings link, which takes you to the Comments page, which I cover shortly.

Let your readers share their comments

When your readers sign in to leave a comment on your blog, their comments and a link to your blog will be displayed both on their profile and also on the dashboard of anyone who follows them.

◉ Congratulations, you already make the most out of your readers by allowing them to sign in when commenting.
Manage your comment settings

Figure 5.19 If you enable this option, your commenters' comments will show up in their followers' Dashboards.

Feeds Settings

Feeds are, in many respects, the lifeblood of a blog. Readers with a news-reader can subscribe to your blog's feed to find out when you've published something new (and, one assumes, exciting) for them to check out.

As always, don't forget the trusty Save Changes button. Click it after you're made any changes in your blog's Feeds settings.

Published Feeds

The Published Feeds section (**Figure 5.20**) allows you to decide what content in your blog gets its very own feed.

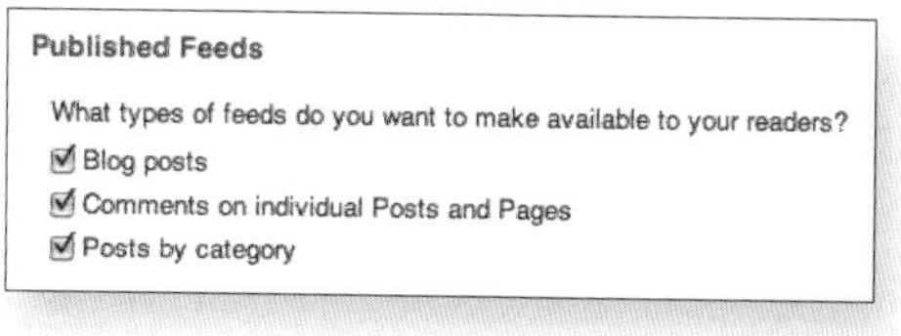

Published Feeds

What types of feeds do you want to make available to your readers?

☑ Blog posts
☑ Comments on individual Posts and Pages
☑ Posts by category

Figure 5.20 The more feeds, the better, if you ask me.

TypePad can provide the following three types of feeds for you (and you can choose to offer any of them, none of them, or mix and match):

- **Blog Posts.** All of your blog posts are included in this feed. This setting enables the bare-minimum feed that you should provide your readers.

- **Comments on Individual Posts and Pages.** People can leave comments on your blog posts and pages (if you allow them to), and some folks like to make sure that they can keep up with the conversation. Allowing people to subscribe to comment feeds per post ensures that they will never miss a comment.

- **Posts by Category.** Some of your readers may not be interested in everything you write but want to stay on top of whatever you have to say about a particular topic or in a particular category. Category feeds allow your readers to choose which topics they want to follow and ignore the ones they don't. These feeds will consist only of posts in the category that they've subscribed to.

tip How do you decide which feeds to offer? I suggest offering them all, because you want to make it as easy as possible for people to keep up to date with your blog.

Feed Content

You can offer two kinds of feeds with your TypePad blog: full and partial (**Figure 5.21**). What's the difference?

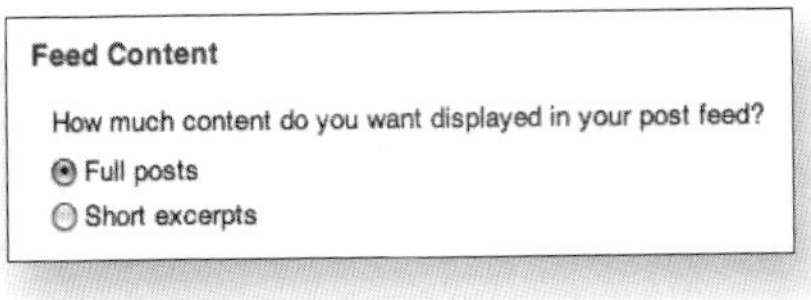

Figure 5.21 Your feed can have full posts or short excerpts. I recommend going with full posts.

The Full Posts setting creates a feed that includes the entire body of your posts. Everything is included—which, some people would argue, means that readers using newsreaders won't bother to come to your Web site (and, therefore, won't click any advertisements you may have).

The Short Excerpts option is known as a *partial feed* in blogger lingo. Instead of being able to read an entire post in their newsreaders, your blog's subscribers will be able to read a short excerpt containing a link back to your blog so that they can read the entire post on your Web site. This setting, therefore, forces people to come to your Web site to read your full content.

Whichever setting you decide to use is up to you, but because you've turned to me (in book form) for some blogging advice, let me lay some wisdom on you. Chances are that the only people using a newsreader to visit your blog are technology-savvy folks. Tech-savvy people tend to have their own blogs, Twitter accounts, and what have you. If you allow them to consume your blog in a way that they enjoy (with a full feed in a newsreader), they're more apt to share whatever you write with their circle. That situation means more potential eyeballs for your blog, which is never a bad thing.

Optional: Connect to FeedBurner

Google FeedBurner (www.feedburner.com) is a free service, offered by Google, that hosts your feeds instead of TypePad. Why would you want to use it? FeedBurner offers many features that TypePad doesn't, such as complete feed statistics, advertising, and promotion.

note I generally don't use FeedBurner because I don't want another layer between me and my feed. If my feed is acting up, I want the fewest variables possible so that I can troubleshoot easily.

That being said, FeedBurner offers a boatload of functionality that many bloggers find indispensable. I suggest that you check out all the features that FeedBurner has to offer and figure out whether the benefits outweigh the increased complexity.

To take advantage of this service, you need to have a Google account. If you don't have one, just click the Get One Now link (**Figure 5.22**) to set one up.

Figure 5.22 No Google account? No problem. Just click this link.

After you have your account sorted out, follow these steps to burn your feed:

1. Log in to FeedBurner via your Google account.

2. Enter your blog's URL in the Burn a Feed Right This Instant field, and click Next.

    FeedBurner scans the address you entered and returns a list of any feeds that it finds (**Figure 5.23**).

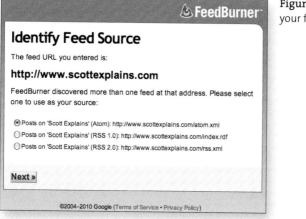

Figure 5.23 Pick one of your feeds to burn.

3. Select the feed you want to burn, and click Next.

    Sticking with the one that FeedBurner chooses by default is OK, as long as the feed is identified with the word *Posts*.

4. Set the name of your feed and your feed address.

    Make a note of the feed address you enter (mine is http://feeds. feedburner.com/ScottExplains, for example), because you'll need it in a second.

5. Click Next (or Cancel and Do Not Activate, if you've changed your mind).

    Clicking Next takes you to a list of options that you can activate for your new feed (**Figure 5.24**). I'm not going to cover them, because this book isn't about FeedBurner, but they're pretty straightforward.

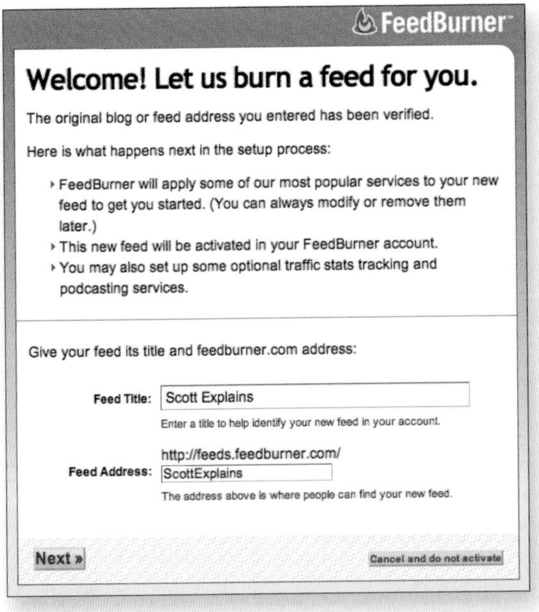

Figure 5.24 This page is the last step in the FeedBurner setup.

Now that you have a FeedBurner feed set up and know your FeedBurner URL (which you entered in step 4), you can tell TypePad to use that feed instead of its own.

6. In the Optional: Connect to FeedBurner section of the Feeds settings page, click the Connect to FeedBurner button (refer to Figure 5.22).

    The FeedBurner Feed URL dialog box opens.

7. Paste your FeedBurner URL into the text field (**Figure 5.25**), and click Save.

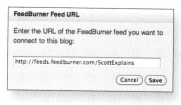

Figure 5.25 Enter the FeedBurner URL to complete the setup on the TypePad side.

Now the Optional: Connect to FeedBurner section informs you that the feed for this blog *is* connected to FeedBurner (**Figure 5.26**). If you decide to disconnect, just click the cleverly named Disconnect from FeedBurner button.

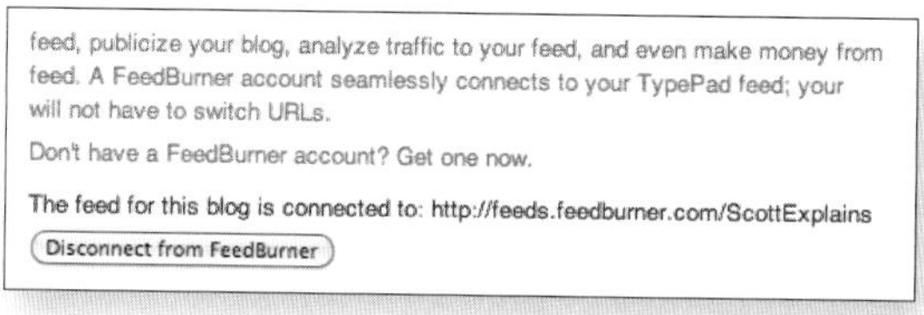

feed, publicize your blog, analyze traffic to your feed, and even make money from feed. A FeedBurner account seamlessly connects to your TypePad feed; your will not have to switch URLs.

Don't have a FeedBurner account? Get one now.

The feed for this blog is connected to: http://feeds.feedburner.com/ScottExplains

Disconnect from FeedBurner

Figure 5.26 If you get tired of FeedBurner, you can disconnect it from your blog and use the included TypePad feeds.

note You may be thinking, "Isn't it bad to change the URL of my feed like this, because people may be subscribing to the feed in their newsreaders? I don't want to lose readers! And am I locked into FeedBurner forever?" Excellent questions! Luckily, your feed's URL never actually changes, thanks to some magic on the TypePad side. You can change your feed as much as you like, and no one will become unsubscribed (but your subscribers may see your entire feed come up as unread in their newsreaders, which could be a little annoying).

Add-Ons Settings

We all know what *adds-ons* are: those little extras that aren't included in the price of the product you just bought. For a fee (or with a little work), however, you can have them.

Only two add-ons are available for TypePad at the moment: Google Analytics and Typekit fonts. I cover them both in the following sections. Remember to click Save Changes if you make any changes in the Add-Ons settings page.

Google Analytics

Google Analytics (www.google.com/analytics) is another free Google product that you can integrate with your blog for free. (As Crazy Eddy used to say, "My prices are insane!") This service tracks a bunch of statistics about your blog, such as how many visits it gets per day and where the clicks come from.

 note   **A full overview of Google Analytics is beyond the scope of this book, but I recommend that you set up an account. If you have a Google account, you can use it to log into Google Analytics and set it up for your blog.**

After you've set up your Google Analytics account, you need to create a new profile for your blog by following these steps:

1. Click the Add New Profile link in the Google Analytics dashboard (**Figure 5.27**).

   This link takes you to the Create New Website Profile page (**Figure 5.28**).

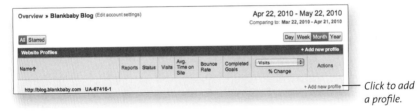

Click to add a profile.

Figure 5.27 To add a new profile to your Google Analytics account, click the link.

Figure 5.28 Creating a new Web-site profile in Google Analytics.

2. Select the Add a Profile for a New Domain radio button.

3. In the Add a Profile for a New Domain section, enter your blog's URL in the text field.

4. Set your time zone in the drop-down menus.

5. Click Finish.

   The Tracking Code page opens (**Figure 5.29**). The only bit of information you're interested in at the moment is Web Property ID, which is the string of letters and numbers beginning with *UA*.

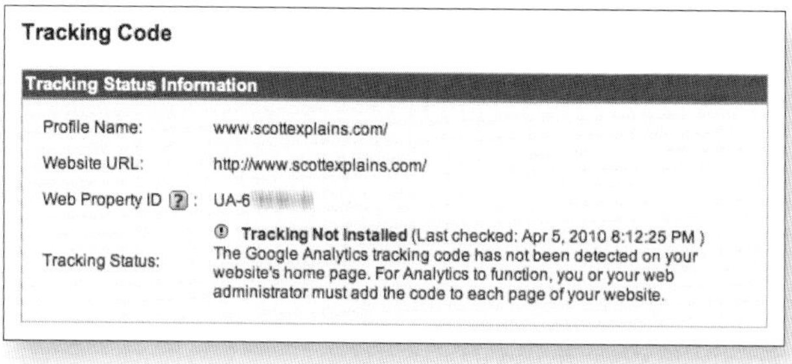

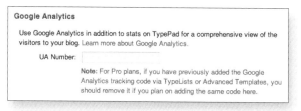

Figure 5.29 The code you need for TypePad is the Web Property ID.

6. Copy the Web Property ID to your computer's clipboard.

7. In the Add-Ons settings page of TypePad, paste the copied UA number into the UA Number field of the Google Analytics section (**Figure 5.30**).

Google Analytics

Use Google Analytics in addition to stats on TypePad for a comprehensive view of the visitors to your blog. Learn more about Google Analytics.

UA Number: [   ]

Note: For Pro plans, if you have previously added the Google Analytics tracking code via TypeLists or Advanced Templates, you should remove it if you plan on adding the same code here.

Figure 5.30 Paste the Web Property ID into the UA Number field.

8. Click Save Changes.

   Your TypePad blog is now using Google Analytics in addition to TypePad's built-in Web analytics (which I cover in Chapter 6).

Typekit Fonts

Designers have long bemoaned the state of typography on the Web. Traditionally, you've had to code your Web site to use fonts that you know will be available on the computers of most of the people who view your Web site. This fact has confined designers to a limited number of fonts, but Typekit hopes to change the situation.

Typekit uses some clever JavaScript that allows you to use fonts that render in your blog even if the person who's viewing it doesn't have those fonts installed. All you need to do is create an account and enter your Typekit Kit ID in the Typekit Fonts section of the Add-On settings page (**Figure 5.31**). Then follow the instructions at http://typekit.com to start using Typekit in your blog.

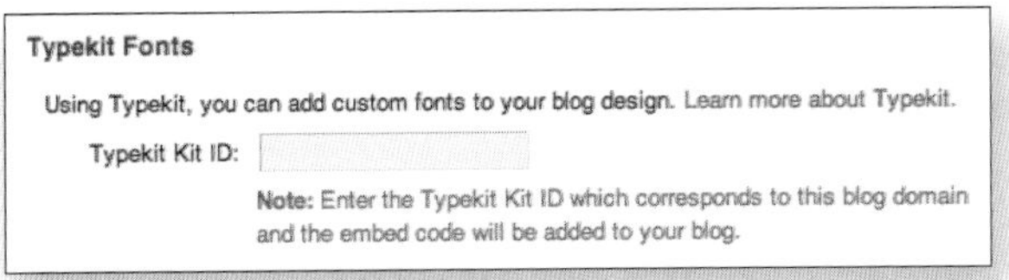

Typekit Fonts

Using Typekit, you can add custom fonts to your blog design. Learn more about Typekit.

Typekit Kit ID: _____

Note: Enter the Typekit Kit ID which corresponds to this blog domain and the embed code will be added to your blog.

Figure 5.31 Typekit is a third-party service that allows you to use more than just Web-safe fonts.

Posts Settings

If you were to ask me what the most important part of any blog is, I would readily answer, "The posts." When you get right down to it, stripping away all the technology and terminology, writing is what gets you noticed. Your posts are your currency in the crazy mixed-up world we call the blogosphere.

As befits the importance of posts, TypePad offers a bevy of settings that affect the way posts are displayed in your blog. Make sure that you click the Save Changes button if you change any of the following settings.

Default Publishing Status

To publish now or to draft: that is the question (**Figure 5.32**). When you're in the Compose section of your blog, this setting determines what happens when you click the Save button. The default, Publish Now, means that when you click Save, TypePad will publish your post for all to see. If you toggle this setting to Draft and click Save in the Compose page, your post won't be posted to your blog, but it will be saved so that you can go back and edit it.

Figure 5.32 The default publishing status for this blog.

Posts to Display

This setting (**Figure 5.33**) controls how many posts are displayed on the page people get when they type the URL, also known as your blog's *index page*. The index page for Scott Explains, for example, is at www.scottexplains.com.

Figure 5.33 You can set how many posts show up on each page of your blog's archives and index pages.

By default, your blog displays ten posts on your archive and index pages. You can change this setting simply by changing the number in the text field (to a maximum value of 50).

For your blog's index page, you can choose to either show a given number of posts or a given number of days' worth of posts. You can show a maximum 365 days' worth of posts, though that setting may be overkill. (The index page generally is the first page people see when they visit your blog, so you don't want it to take forever to load.)

Navigation Links

People can't read your archives if they can't page back through your blog to see what you've written. The settings in the Navigation Links section (**Figure 5.34**, on the next page) allow people to explore your content. You can enter whatever text you want in both text fields; just make sure that people can figure out what the text means.

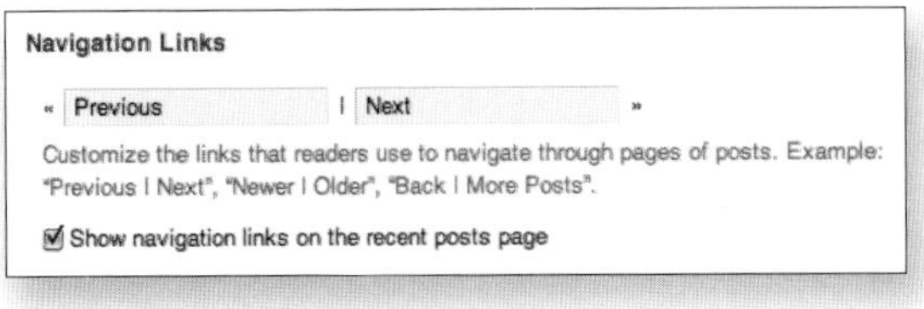

Figure 5.34 Navigation Links settings.

If you check the box titled Show Navigation Links on the Recent Posts Page, two links appear at the bottom of your blog pages, displaying the text that you set here (**Figure 5.35**). If you choose not to enable the navigation links, people will have to check out your blog's archives to delve into your previous writings.

Figure 5.35 Navigation links displayed on a blog page.

Post Date Format

Every one of your posts is time-stamped, and all the included TypePad themes display this stamp. The Post Date Format section (**Figure 5.36**) allows you to choose a date format for the time stamp.

Figure 5.36 A veritable cornucopia of date-format options.

No date format has any advantages over another, so pick the one you like best.

Post Time Format

Time stamps are composed of both the date and the time, so it's fitting that TypePad allows you to format them in multiple ways. (Two choices count as multiple choice, right?) **Figure 5.37** shows your options.

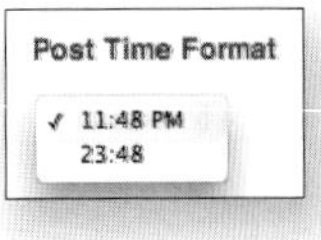

Figure 5.37 Both post-time formats are good.

Front Page

Front Page (**Figure 5.38**) is one of the most intriguing settings—one that can transform your blog in radical ways. The default setting, Display My Recent Posts on the Front Page, is how a blog is traditionally set up, and if you use TypePad for your blog, it's the way to go.

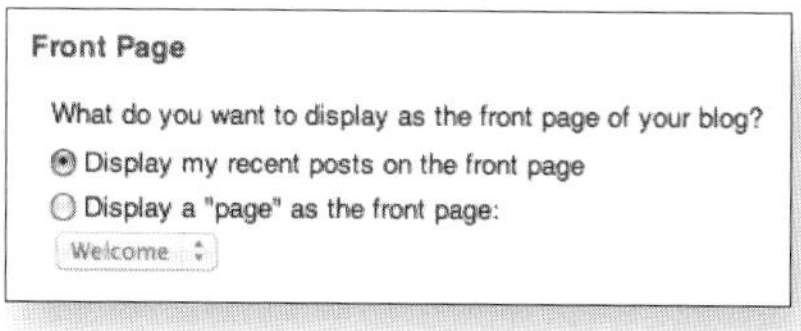

Front Page

What do you want to display as the front page of your blog?
⦿ Display my recent posts on the front page
◯ Display a "page" as the front page:
[Welcome ⬍]

Figure 5.38 You can choose to use blog posts as your front page or use a static page.

If you want to replace your business's Web site with TypePad, however, you may want to have a welcome or landing page serve as the index page of your site and display your blog posts on a secondary page. You can do this by selecting Display a "Page" As the Front Page. When you do, the drop-down menu becomes active (**Figure 5.39**), allowing you to set any of your existing pages as your blog's front page. (See Chapter 7 for more information about pages.)

Figure 5.39 If you decide to make your blog's front page a static page, you have to decide which page to display.

If you want to display a page as your front page, click the Save Changes button at the bottom of the page. The Front Page section changes as shown in **Figure 5.40**. Notice the link below the drop-down menu. TypePad automatically creates a new page that displays your recent posts for you. Pretty nifty, huh?

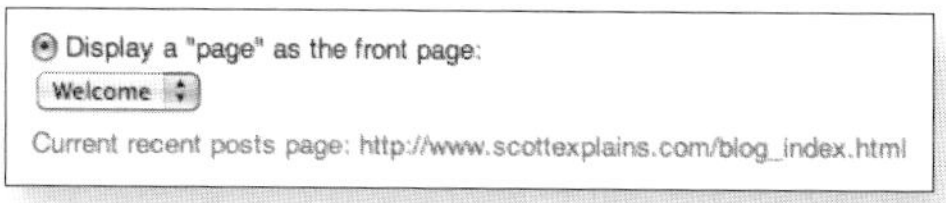

⦿ Display a "page" as the front page:
[Welcome ⬍]
Current recent posts page: http://www.scottexplains.com/blog_index.html

Figure 5.40 When your blog's front page is a static page, TypePad moves your blog to a new location and gives you a link to it.

Order of Posts

Blogs are known for displaying posts in reverse chronological order—that is, with the newest stuff at the top. If you'd rather use chronological order, though, just select Oldest First (Ascending) in the Order of Posts section (**Figure 5.41**). This settings applies to both your archive pages and your index page.

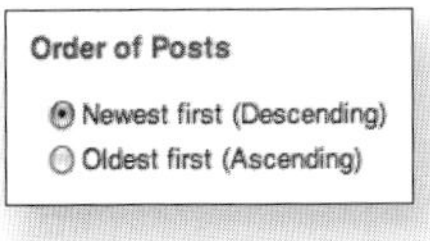

Order of Posts

⦿ Newest first (Descending)
◯ Oldest first (Ascending)

Figure 5.41 Traditionally, blogs display posts in reverse chronological order, but you don't have to be a slave to convention.

Limit Recent Posts

Generally, bloggers have their index pages display a certain number of posts (refer to "Posts to Display" earlier in this chapter), no matter what category those posts happen to be in. The Limit Recent Posts section (**Figure 5.42**) allows you to be a little more selective.

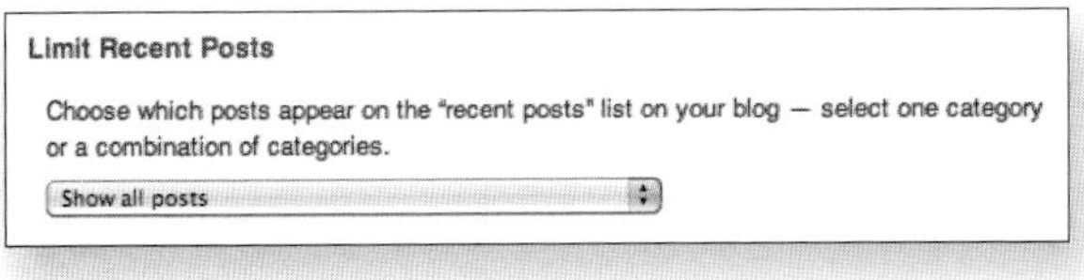

Limit Recent Posts

Choose which posts appear on the "recent posts" list on your blog — select one category or a combination of categories.

Show all posts

Figure 5.42 You can show only a limited subset of posts on your blog's index page.

You can think of this setting as being a filter for your index page (which probably is the front page of your blog). The drop-down menu allows you to display just one category of posts, all categories, or multiple categories (**Figure 5.43**).

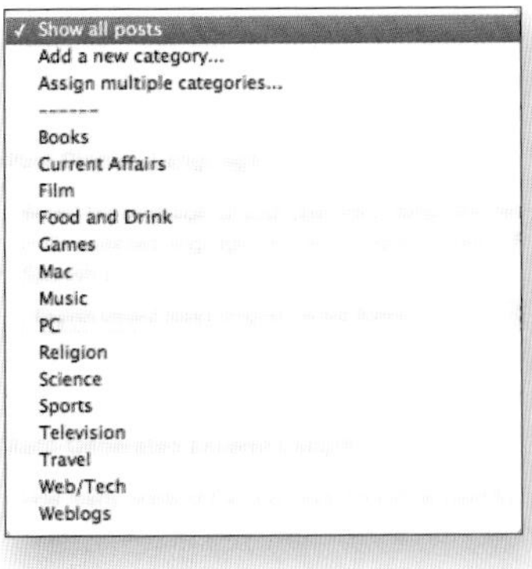

✓ Show all posts
Add a new category...
Assign multiple categories...

Books
Current Affairs
Film
Food and Drink
Games
Mac
Music
PC
Religion
Science
Sports
Television
Travel
Web/Tech
Weblogs

Figure 5.43 You can choose to show all posts, posts from one category, or posts from several categories.

Why would you want to show only certain posts on the front page? Perhaps you're running a flower shop, and you want to display only posts from your News and Specials categories on the front page. You also want to post pictures of your arrangements but don't want to clutter the recent posts with all those pictures.

For this example, you would choose Assign Multiple Categories from the drop-down menu in the Limit Recent Posts section. When you do, the Select Categories dialog box opens (**Figure 5.44**).

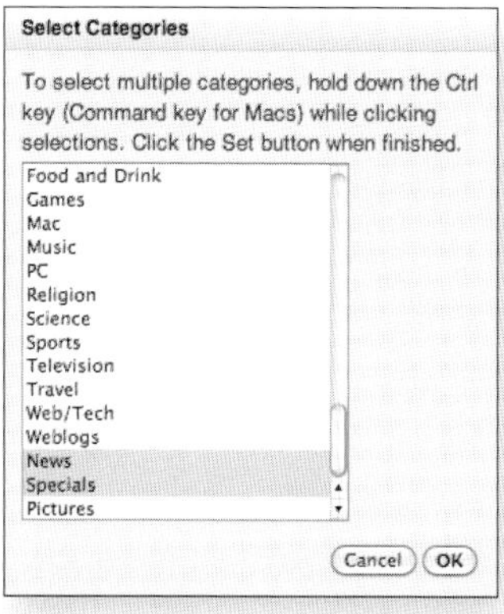

Figure 5.44 Select the category you want to display on your front page.

Depending on your operating system, the selection process is slightly different. On a Mac, hold down the Command key and click each category you want; on the PC, hold down the Ctrl key while you make your selections. When you're finished, click OK. Now the drop-down menu in the Limit Recent Posts section displays the categories that you've selected so you won't forget your settings (**Figure 5.45**).

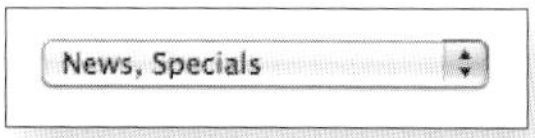

Figure 5.45 Posts in the categories News and Specials will be the only posts displayed on the front page.

If you think of a great new category that you'd like to add on the spot, choose Add a New Category from the drop-down menu; the Create Category dialog box opens (**Figure 5.46**). Type the name of the category in the text field, and click Create. Now you have a brand-new category.

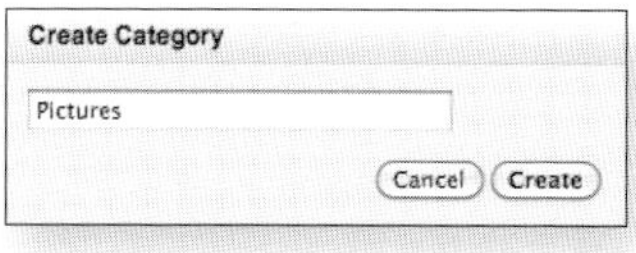

Figure 5.46 You can create a new category here.

Post Display Language

TypePad has been localized for several languages, meaning that common elements of your blog (such as headers, post links and dates) can be displayed in another language automatically. Select a language from the extensive drop-down menu in the Post Display Language section (**Figure 5.47**), and TypePad will take care of the rest.

Figure 5.47 TypePad can display headers, dates, and links in several languages.

This setting isn't a translation feature, so the posts themselves won't be translated into this language, but when you're composing a post, TypePad uses the spell checker for the language you set here.

Auto-Generated Excerpt Length

Back in the "Feeds Settings" section, I went on and on about full and partial feeds. The Auto-Generated Excerpt Length section (**Figure 5.48**) allows you to create excerpts for all your posts automatically. By default, automatically generated excerpts consist of the first 100 words. You can change this setting to any number you like, though the higher the number, the more reason you have simply to publish a full feed.

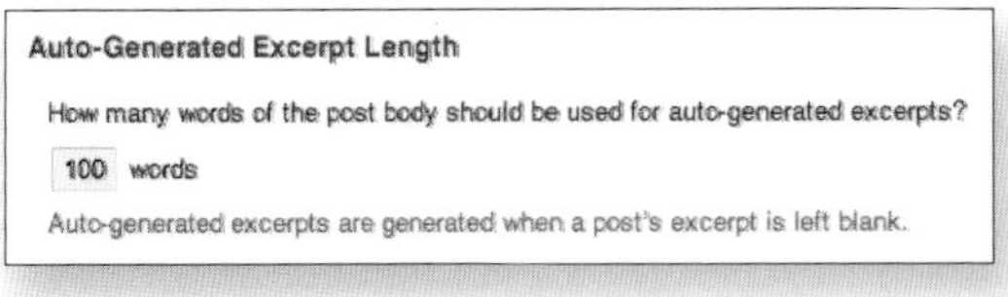

Figure 5.48 This setting tells TypePad how much of a post should appear in an autogenerated excerpt.

No matter what you set this number to be, you can override it for individual posts by creating a custom excerpt (see Chapter 5).

Categories Settings

Each of your blog posts can be slotted into one or more categories. Depending on how you have your blog set up, some posts in certain categories may not be included in your index page, and people can subscribe only to categories that they find interesting. Categories give you the opportunity to give your blog a little organization. Categories are optional, however. You can publish a blog post without any category, if you like.

TypePad supplies the default categories shown in **Figure 5.49**.

Categories		
Add a new category:		Add
Books	Edit	Delete
Current Affairs	Edit	Delete
Film	Edit	Delete
Food and Drink	Edit	Delete
Games	Edit	Delete
Music	Edit	Delete
Religion	Edit	Delete
Science	Edit	Delete
Sports	Edit	Delete
Television	Edit	Delete
Travel	Edit	Delete
Web/Tech	Edit	Delete
Weblogs	Edit	Delete

Figure 5.49 You can edit, delete, and add categories.

Adding a category

Chances are that TypePad's default categories don't cover every subject you're interested in blogging about. (Heck, they may not cover any of the topics you want to write about!) Luckily, adding a new category to a blog is very easy.

note Keep in mind that categories are set per blog, so if you add a category to one blog, it won't be added automatically to any other blog associated with your TypePad account.

In **Figure 5.50**, I'm adding a category called Software. All I have to do is type the name in the text field and click the Add button. A message tells me that the new category has been added to the list in the Categories page.

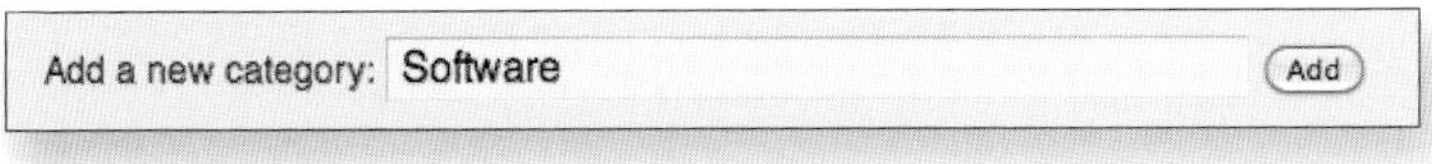

Add a new category: Software   (Add)

Figure 5.50 Adding a new category called Software.

Editing and deleting a category

Each category entry sports Edit and Delete buttons (refer to Figure 5.49). If you want to edit a category, click the Edit button; it and the Delete button become Save and Cancel (**Figure 5.51**). Change the category name in the text field, and click Save. TypePad updates your category list, and any post that had the previous category value applied to it will now use the new one.

Software   Save   Cancel   **Figure 5.51** Editing the category called Software allows you to rename that category.

As you may be able to tell from the Delete button, you can also delete categories that you won't be using. If you delete a category that has posts in it, the posts aren't deleted; they just have that category removed.

When you click Delete, a dialog box asks you whether you're certain, because there's no way to undo a category deletion. Click OK if you're sure that you want to delete the category in question, or click Cancel to return to the Categories page without deleting the selected category.

 note Remember to click the Save Changes button at the bottom of the Categories page to save your changes.

Comments Settings

Comments allow your readers to have a conversation with you on your blog. But you should take some precautions with them, due to the evils of *comment spam:* automated programs that scan the Internet for blogs on which they can leave spurious comments chockablock with links to Web sites in a vain attempt to game search engines. The Comments settings offer you rather fine-grained control of who can comment on your blog and how they go about it. Remember to click Save Changes if you change any settings on this page.

Comment Authentication

One way to fight comment spam is to require commenters to sign in with some sort of account (such as TypePad, Facebook, or Twitter) before they leave a comment. You enable this feature in the Comment Authentication section (**Figure 5.52**).

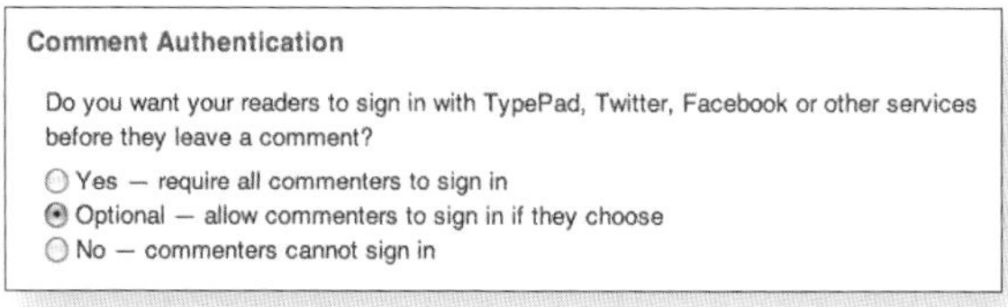

Comment Authentication

Do you want your readers to sign in with TypePad, Twitter, Facebook or other services before they leave a comment?

○ Yes — require all commenters to sign in
⦿ Optional — allow commenters to sign in if they choose
○ No — commenters cannot sign in

Figure 5.52 Comment authentication can help combat comment spam.

If you select the Yes radio button, no one without an account will be able to leave a comment. This setting surely protects your blog against comment spam, but it also means that people who don't have one of the acceptable accounts won't be able to leave you a comment.

Optional is the optimal comment-authentication setting, in my opinion. When you enable it, people who have one of the suitable account types can use it to log in and reap the benefits (such as being able to control the picture that accompanies their comments).

Select No to prevent anyone from logging in using any accounts. This setting is great if you just want to have plain old comments and aren't interested in integrating with other accounts.

Unauthenticated Commenters

I don't know about you, but to my eyes, the phrase *unauthenticated commenters* seems a little harsh. Don't worry—these commenters aren't doing anything wrong. They just aren't logging in with an account (see the preceding section). You can specify how to handle them in the Unauthenticated Commenters section of the Comments page (**Figure 5.53**).

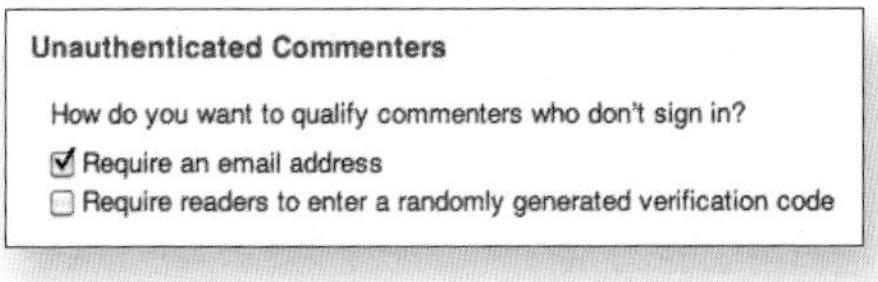

Unauthenticated Commenters

How do you want to qualify commenters who don't sign in?

☑ Require an email address
☐ Require readers to enter a randomly generated verification code

Figure 5.53 Handle unauthenticated commenters' behavior here.

Enabling the Require an Email Address option is a good idea for unauthenticated commenters, though keep in mind that someone with naughty intentions can easily pose as someone else, using that person's name and email address. We all know that not everyone is who they seem on the Internet.

The second option, which requires readers to enter a randomly generated verification code, may seem complicated, but chances are that you encountered one of these codes during your Web surfing today.

When you enable this option, a reader enters a comment, supplies an email address, and clicks Submit. TypePad checks your Comments settings and sees you have this setting enabled, so it previews that person's comment and displays a picture along with a random assortment of letters and numbers (**Figure 5.54**). The commenter must enter the sequence just as it appears in the picture and click Continue before his comment is approved for posting.

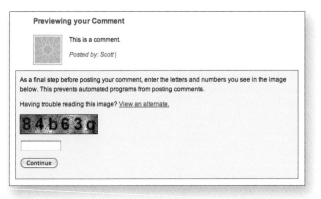

Previewing your Comment

This is a comment.
Posted by: Scott |

As a final step before posting your comment, enter the letters and numbers you see in the image below. This prevents automated programs from posting comments.

Having trouble reading this image? View an alternate.

84b63q

(Continue)

Figure 5.54 Requiring your commenters to use a randomly generated verification code looks like this.

Comment Moderation

Are you a control freak? There's nothing wrong with being one; you just have to be able to answer that question as it pertains to your blog. (I won't judge you.) Comment moderation is great for a control freak, because when this setting is enabled (**Figure 5.55**), no comments appear in your blog without your express permission.

Comment Moderation

Do you want to read comments before they appear on your blog?

☐ Yes, hold comments for my approval

Figure 5.55 Moderation allows you to approve or reject every comment.

When you're just starting your blog, chances are that you won't get many comments, so moderating comments won't take much time. If your blog becomes a vibrant community with lots of commenters, however (and generally, that's the goal), you'll have more moderating to do. People expect to see their comments appear in rather short order and tend to think that they're being censored if a comment doesn't appear within a day at most.

You have many reasons to moderate comments. I run a corporate blog for a major cable company during the day and moderate all comments on the blog. (One entry alone received more than 1,000 comments, all of which I read and approved myself.) The decision to moderate all comments was made to ensure that the comments were on topic, respectful, and free of naughty words. No computer program in existence can replace the judgment of a good old human being, so moderating comments it was.

If you fear that the comments section of your blog would be akin to something out of the Wild West, comment moderation is a sensible choice. I cover the actual process of moderating comments in Chapter 8.

Auto-Close Comments

Enabling the Auto-Close Comments setting (**Figure 5.56**) automatically closes comments on entries past a certain date. Simply select the check box and then choose a time period from the drop-down menu.

Auto-Close Comments

☐ Automatically close comments after [1 week ⬍]

Figure 5.56 This setting allows you to leave comments open for a certain period.

After a post has been on your blog longer than the set period, people won't be able to leave comments about it. The reasoning is that people are likely to leave comments on fresh content, whereas spammers don't care how old the posts are.

Comment Formatting

HTML is the tag-based language that's used to create Web pages. Because your blog posts are simply Web pages, the settings in the Comment Formatting section (**Figure 5.57**) allow commenters to use a subset of HTML to insert links and use some text controls.

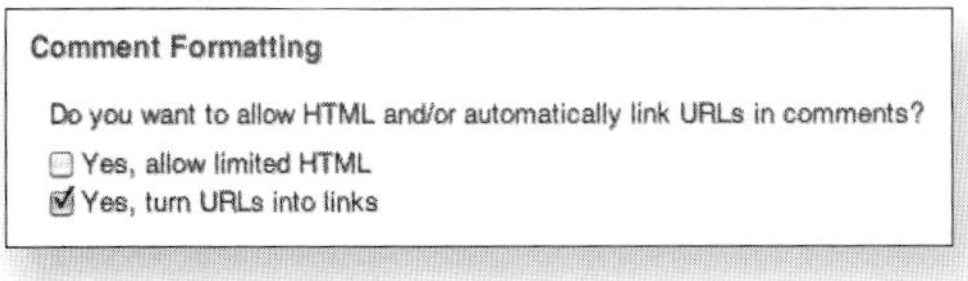

Comment Formatting

Do you want to allow HTML and/or automatically link URLs in comments?

☐ Yes, allow limited HTML
☑ Yes, turn URLs into links

Figure 5.57 Most people don't know HTML, but turning URLs into links automatically is a no-brainer.

If you allow limited HTML, people will be able to apply boldface and italic formatting and to create lists by using the appropriate HTML tags (<b>, <i>, and <li>, respectively). If your audience isn't too tech-savvy, you can get away with not enabling this option.

The second setting automatically changes URLs in comments to clickable links, making it easier for the people reading comments to visit any links that a commenter may have shared.

Comment Display Order

Comments are displayed on each post page, right below the meat of your post. By default, TypePad lists the oldest comments first and then displays the newer ones in chronological order, with the latest comment all the way at the bottom of the comment list. If you'd rather display the newest comments first, just toggle the Comment Display Order setting to Newest First (Descending) (**Figure 5.58**).

Comment Display Order

What order do you want your comments to be displayed?

◉ Oldest first (Ascending)
○ Newest first (Descending)

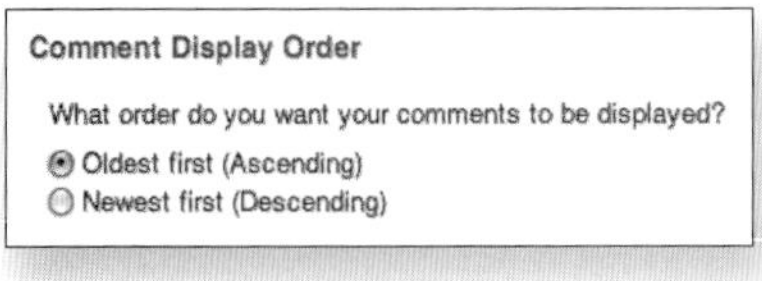

Figure 5.58 Generally, comments are displayed oldest first so that the conversation flows in the right way for reading.

Comments to Display

TypePad automatically paginates comments for you, which is great because it keeps page-load times down. (Nothing is worse then having to wait 5 seconds for a post to load. I'm a busy man!) Also, pagination makes it easier to read a large volume of comments.

As you can with posts, you can set how many comments to display per page (**Figure 5.59**). The default value is 25, but you can max out at 100 or have only 1 comment per page, if you want.

Figure 5.59 You decide how many comments should appear on each page.

Comment Userpics

The check box in the Comment Userpics section (**Figure 5.60**) simply enables or disables the display of user pictures next to comments. The picture that gets displayed depends on whether the commenter has logged in from a particular account. If so, the picture associated with that account will be displayed. If no picture is associated with the account, or if the commenter isn't logged in, TypePad creates a random picture (**Figure 5.61**).

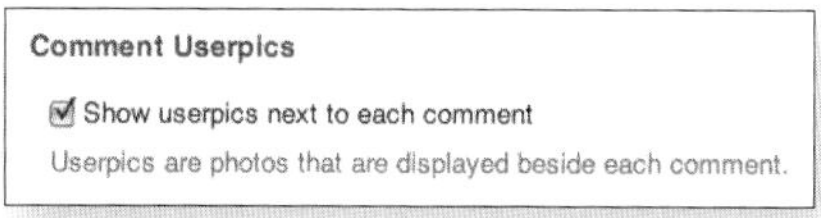

Figure 5.60 You can display user pictures next to people's comments.

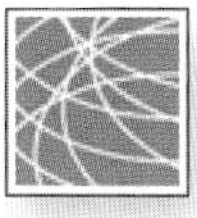

Figure 5.61 An autogenerated user picture.

Comment Sharing

I've said over and over again that blogging is all about sharing, so why not extend that philosophy to comments? If you enable the Comment Sharing setting (**Figure 5.62**), commenters who logged in to leave a comment can post a link to that comment automatically. This feature allows your commenters to share their pithy comments with friends and also exposes a new circle of people to your blog.

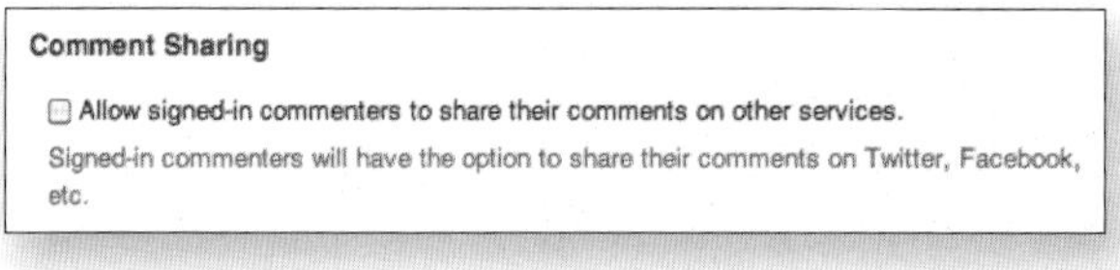

Comment Sharing

☐ Allow signed-in commenters to share their comments on other services.

Signed-in commenters will have the option to share their comments on Twitter, Facebook, etc.

Figure 5.62 Commenters can share links to their comments if you allow them to.

Navigation Links

If you read the "Comments to Display" section earlier in this chapter, you already know that TypePad paginates comments for you automatically. The Navigation Links setting (**Figure 5.63**) allows you to set the text for the links that people use to navigate your pages.

Navigation Links

« | Previous | | Next | »

You can customize the links that readers use to navigate through pages of comments. Examples: "Previous | Next", "Older | Newer", "Back | More Comments".

Figure 5.63 Text for the navigation links at the bottom of your comment pages.

Email Notification

Want to get an email every time someone leaves a comment or trackback on your blog? The Email Notification section is where you enable that feature (**Figure 5.64**).

Email Notification

☑ Notify the author of the post when new comments are submitted
☑ Notify the author of the post when new TrackBacks are submitted

Figure 5.64 Email notifications can be set on a per-blog basis.

By Default, Accept Comments

You can turn comments on and off for each post individually, but the By Default, Accept Comments setting (**Figure 5.65**) allows you to tell your blog that you want to accept comments on posts and pages (or both) by default. The settings in Figure 5.65 allow comments by default on new posts, but not on new pages.

Figure 5.65 These settings can be overridden on a per-post (and per-page) basis.

By Default, Accept Trackbacks

The By Default, Accept Trackbacks setting (**Figure 5.66**) is the same as the preceding setting except that it applies to trackbacks. I suggest leaving both of these boxes unchecked, because trackbacks are almost entirely overridden by spam. Not accepting them gets rid of one small management task and lets you concentrate on blogging.

Figure 5.66 Trackbacks can also be set for specific posts and pages.

TypePad Connect Comments (Beta)

The last setting in the Comments page is more like a switch than a setting. TypePad Connect Comments (Beta), a new commenting system that TypePad is working on, offers a few new features. You can toggle it on or off without fear that any of your existing comments will disappear.

Authors Settings

TypePad supports multiple authors per individual blog. The settings on the Authors page (**Figure 5.67**) allow you to invite people to become authors of your blog and to manage the authors you already have.

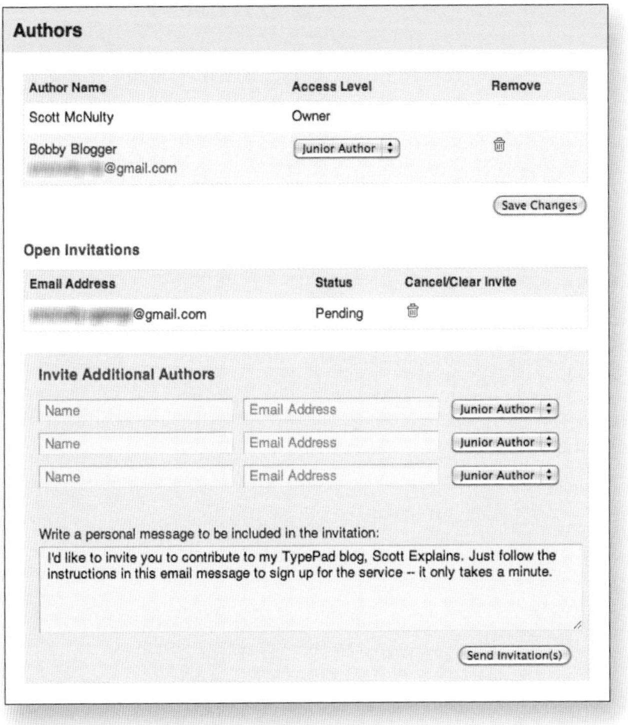

Figure 5.67 The Authors settings.

Current authors

The first section of the Authors page lists all the authors currently associated with this blog (**Figure 5.68**). If you're just getting started with this blog, only one author may be listed: you.

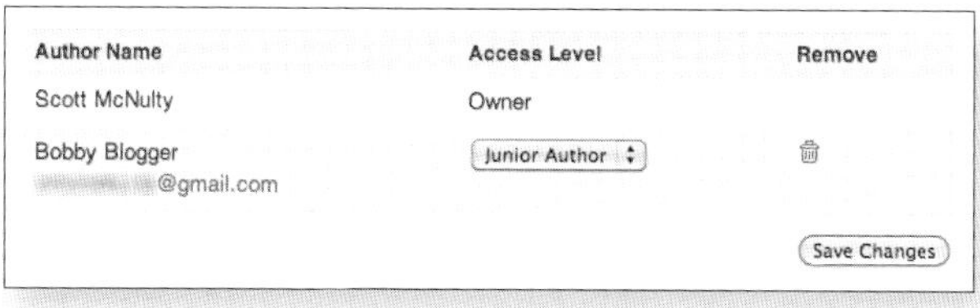

Author Name	Access Level	Remove
Scott McNulty	Owner	
Bobby Blogger ▓▓▓▓▓@gmail.com	[Junior Author ⬍]	🗑
		[Save Changes]

Figure 5.68 Current authors of your blog.

The Access Level column shows what privileges each author has. TypePad provides only three levels of access. From least to most powerful, those levels are

- **Junior Author.** Junior authors are the low men on the totem pole. They can create new posts but can't publish them; all their posts must be approved by the administrator of the blog (you). Also, these authors can't edit or delete posts by anyone, including themselves. Further, they can't upload any files to your blog, so their posts won't have pictures in them. They can publish comments on their own posts, however.

- **Guest Author.** Guest authors have a little more power. They can write posts and save them as drafts, just like the junior authors, but they can publish their own posts to the blog without any approval. They can also delete their own posts but can't edit or delete posts by anyone else.

- **Owner.** Every blog has only one owner, and that person generally is you. Accordingly, you can do whatever you want: edit, delete, and publish all content; approve comments on all posts; upload files; and access all statistics and settings for the blog.

If you decide that you don't want to have an author contribute to the blog anymore, just click the little red trash-can icon in that author's Remove column, and click OK in the confirmation dialog box. That author is deleted, though any posts he or she created still appear in your blog.

Open Invitations

You have to invite authors to participate in your blog (see the next section), and while they ponder your invitation, you see an Open Invitations section in your Authors page (**Figure 5.69**). The Status column for each invited author will display either *Pending* or *Declined*.

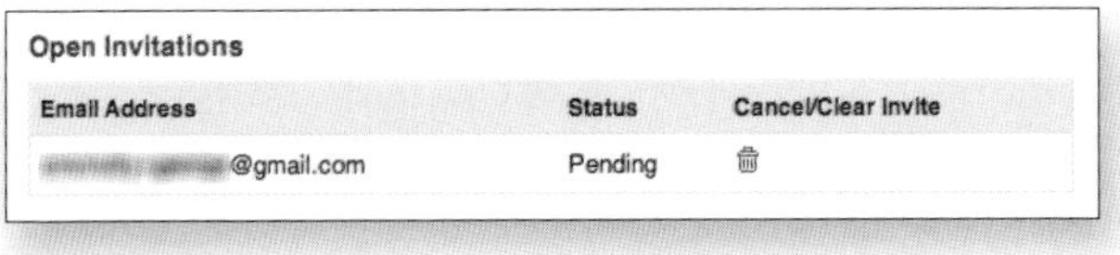

Figure 5.69 Invitations that are pending appear here.

You can cancel a pending invite, or clear a declined one, by clicking the red trash icon in the Cancel/Clear Invite column and clicking OK in the confirmation dialog box.

Invite Additional Authors

The Invite Additional Authors section (**Figure 5.70**) is where you actually invite people to join your blog. Enter each person's name and email address, and set the access level you want to grant that person. You can invite up to three people at the same time.

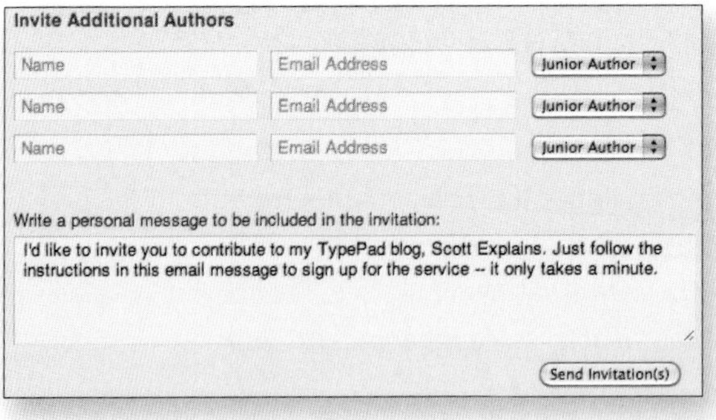

Figure 5.70 Use this form to invite authors.

Invitations are send out via email, so the final part of this section allows you to write a personal message to include with the invitation. The default text includes the name of the blog and a little explanation of what the heck the email is all about. Feel free to write whatever you like, however.

When you're all set with your invitations, click the Send Invitation(s) button. **Figure 5.71** shows what the invitees get in their mailboxes.

Figure 5.71 A received invitation. The recipient can accept or decline by clicking the appropriate button.

Post by Email Settings

One of my favorite features of TypePad is Posts by Email (**Figure 5.72**, on the next page). As the name suggests, this feature allows you to send an email to a secret email address and have whatever you sent posted to your blog. (I cover posting by email in detail in Appendix B.)

Post by Email

Posting Email Address

Use this custom email address to send posts and photos to this blog:

Secret Address: df377e0c767ac601 @typepad.com

Don't have time to copy this? Send yourself an email containing the secret address and easily add it to your address books.

smcnulty@gmail.com   (Send Email)

Reset Address

(Reset)

Just click the reset button to generate a new secret address at any time.

Notifications

☐ Notify me via email when my email post has been successfully submitted

(Save Changes)

Figure 5.72 One of the coolest features of TypePad: Post by Email.

Don't forget to save your changes when you're done with this page.

Posting Email Address

The most important thing in this section is your blog's secret address. There's no way to force someone to log in when he's posting via email, so you can't tell whether the person who's sending email to your blog is actually allowed to post. To get around this situation, TypePad creates a secret— and very difficult to guess—email address that only you know. As you can see in Figure 5.72, no one will be guessing that email address.

> **tip**
>
> Because the secret address is rather long, you can email it to yourself and then add it to your address book, using the name of your blog as the name of the contact for quick posting. Enter the email address you want to send the secret address to and then click Send Email.

When you send a post to your blog via email, the Subject line of the email becomes the post's title.

You don't have to limit yourself to posting pictures via this meth
send a text email, and it will be posted as well.

note For more information about posting via email, see Appendix B.

Reset Address

You may have a reason to generate a new secret address for your blog.
Perhaps you printed your old secret address in a book about TypePad, and
you want to make sure that none of your lovely and very smart readers
start posting things to your blog via email. Click the Reset button to
generate a new secret email address. The old address will no longer work.
(Nice try, though.)

Notifications

Select the check box in this section if you want to get an email confirmation
when a post has been sent via your secret email address.

Import/Export Settings

No blogging engine is an island, and the good folks at TypePad know that
yes, Virginia, there are other blogging platforms. If you're making the switch
from WordPress, Movable Type, or another blogging platform that can
export in either WordPress or MTIF format, you can import your content into
TypePad. You can also export all your posts in case you want to back up your
blog or decide that your time with TypePad is over.

To illustrate how these settings work, I'll start by showing you how to
import content from another blogging system.

Importing content

The Import section (**Figure 5.73**, on the next page) offers two kinds of
imports, even though three options are listed. The first and third options are
file-based—that is, you need to have an export file handy to import from.
The middle option—importing from WordPress.com—is slightly different.
In the following sections, I cover both file-based and WordPress options.

Import

Import content from another blog:

○ TypePad, Movable Type, or other MTIF file
○ WordPress.com
○ WordPress WXR file

(Import)

Figure 5.73 You can import content from other
blogging platforms.

File-based import

Select the first or third radio button in the Import section (refer to
Figure 5.73), and you'll get the option to find the file containing your
exported blog content on your computer or point TypePad to the file's
URL (**Figure 5.74**).

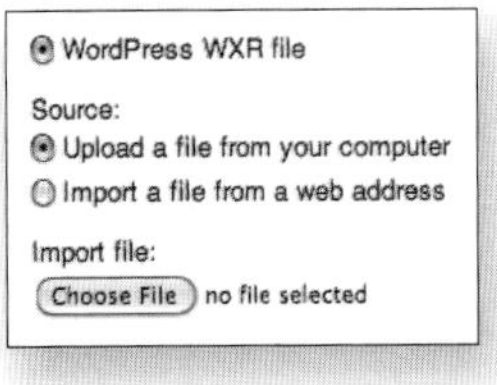

● WordPress WXR file

Source:
● Upload a file from your computer
○ Import a file from a web address

Import file:
(Choose File) no file selected

Figure 5.74 Importing content from
WordPress into TypePad.

Click the Choose File button, and use your operating system's file browser to
find the file you want to import. After you've located it, click the Import
button. TypePad will happily start chugging along, importing the blog
content (**Figure 5.75**). This process may take a while, so grab yourself a nice
cold beverage while you wait or click the links to fiddle with your blog's
design or create a new post.

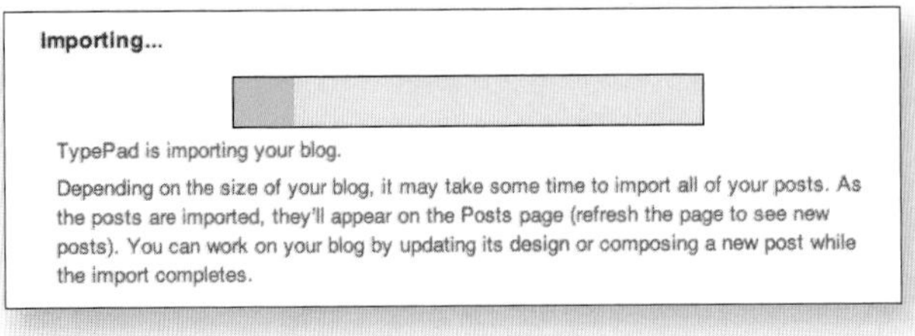

Importing...

TypePad is importing your blog.

Depending on the size of your blog, it may take some time to import all of your posts. As
the posts are imported, they'll appear on the Posts page (refresh the page to see new
posts). You can work on your blog by updating its design or composing a new post while
the import completes.

Figure 5.75 The import process can take a while, depending
on the size of the import file.

When TypePad finishes importing the posts, an alert lets you know that all your content has been imported (**Figure 5.76**).

> **Done!**
>
> **TypePad is finished importing.** Your imported posts will now appear on the Posts page as well as your blog.
>
> View your blog

Figure 5.76 Success! Your content has been imported.

 note   All the posts imported via this method will appear to have been written by you, no matter who the original author was.

WordPress import

You can also import content from WordPress.com, which is a hosted version of WordPress. This import process is slightly different from the one I just described for the self-hosted version.

Select the middle radio button in the Import section (refer to Figure 5.73), and you'll be prompted to enter your WordPress.com blog URL, user name, and password (**Figure 5.77**). When you've entered that information, click Import. You'll see the same progress and completion alerts that you'd see for the preceding import method.

> Blog URL:
>
> `http://blankbaby.wordpress.com`
>
> The web address of your WordPress blog.
>
> Username:
>
> `blankbaby`
>
> Your WordPress username. (Only used to import your blog, never saved.)
>
> Password:
>
> `••••••••`
>
> Your WordPress password. (Only used to import your blog, never saved.)

Figure 5.77 You can import WordPress.com content by entering your WordPress credentials.

Exporting content

There may come a time, in the distant future, when you decide to move your blog from TypePad. I won't ask you why, but I will show you how to create a file with all the text you've posted to this blog,

note   The TypePad export function exports only the text of posts and comments. Any images or other media that you've posted to your blog aren't included in this file.

Exporting your posts and comments is simple. Click the Export button in the Export section (**Figure 5.78**), and you'll see the Exporting progress bar (**Figure 5.79**). Depending on the amount of content in your blog, the export process can take a good while (much like the import process). Might I suggest grabbing another frosty beverage, perhaps?

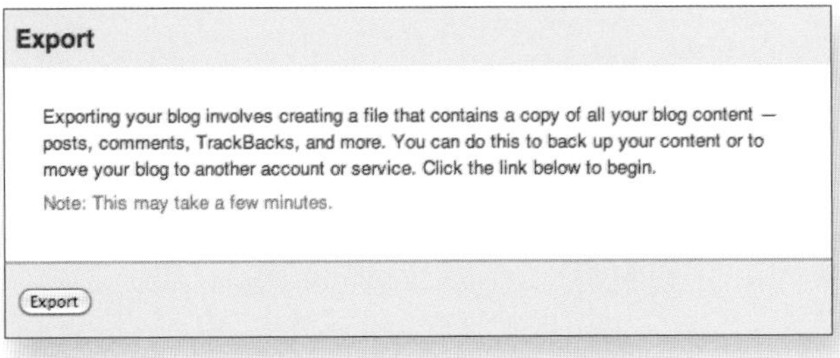

Export

Exporting your blog involves creating a file that contains a copy of all your blog content — posts, comments, TrackBacks, and more. You can do this to back up your content or to move your blog to another account or service. Click the link below to begin.

Note: This may take a few minutes.

(Export)

Figure 5.78 Exporting your content from TypePad is as easy as clicking the Export button.

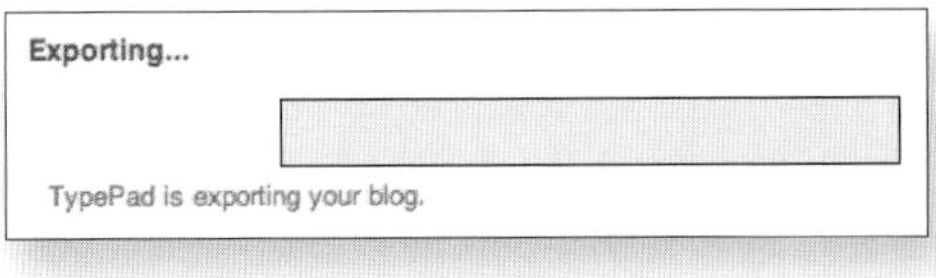

Exporting...

TypePad is exporting your blog.

Figure 5.79 The Exporting progress bar.

When TypePad is done exporting your blog, you'll see a confirmation screen with a Download link (**Figure 5.80**). The Download link points to the actual export file that TypePad created, so click it to save it to your computer. That's it. Your blog has been exported. All your posts and comments are still available in your TypePad blog, however; this export is just a backup copy.

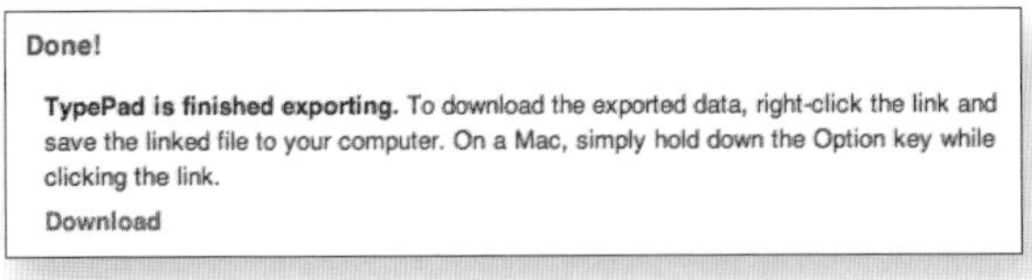

Done!

TypePad is finished exporting. To download the exported data, right-click the link and save the linked file to your computer. On a Mac, simply hold down the Option key while clicking the link.

Download

Figure 5.80 Click the Download link to finalize the export.

6

Viewing Your Blog's Statistics

Everyone wants to be popular, right? I'm sure you also want people to like your blog. (Otherwise, why are you reading this book?) In this chapter, I look at a couple of ways you can see how many people are reading your blog and what's bringing them in.

Getting to the Blog's Dashboard

The first thing you have to do is navigate to the blog you want to see statistics for. If you're in the TypePad Dashboard, you can click the blog's name in the Manage My Blogs module or choose it from the Blogs drop-down menu in TypePad's global navigation bar (**Figure 6.1**, on the next page).

Either action takes you to that blog's own dashboard, or administrative interface (**Figure 6.2**).

Figure 6.1 The Blogs drop-down menu is the gateway to your blog.

Figure 6.2 Each blog has its own dashboard.

 note This small-d dashboard shouldn't be confused with the TypePad Dashboard, which I cover in Chapter 4.

The series of tabs at the top of the page functions as your blog's administrative navigation bar (**Figure 6.3**). To the left of those tabs is the name of the blog, which is also a link that takes you back to the Overview page (see the next section), no matter where you are in the blog's administrative interface.

Figure 6.3 A blog dashboard's tabs give you quick access to various aspects of the blog's administrative interface.

Working with the Overview Page

Whenever you enter a blog's dashboard, the Overview page (**Figure 6.4**) is open by default. This page gives you a quick look at some of your blog's traffic statistics, along with some tips from the folks behind TypePad.

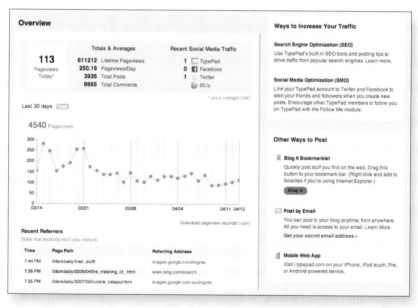

Figure 6.4 The Overview page gives you lots of information at a glance.

Checking traffic

The first section of the Overview page is the handy-dandy traffic summary
(**Figure 6.5**).

	Totals & Averages		Recent Social Media Traffic
113	**611212** Lifetime Pageviews	1	TypePad
Pageviews Today*	**250.19** Pageviews/Day	0	Facebook
	3936 Total Posts	1	Twitter
	8665 Total Comments		Bit.ly
			* since midnight GMT

Figure 6.5 The traffic summary.

The summary breaks down this way:

- **Page views.** That white square on the left side of the traffic summary
  displays how many page views your blog has received today. (TypePad
  defines *today* as "since midnight GMT," so you may have to adjust that
  definition for your time zone.)

- **Totals and averages.** Next to the page-views square is a list of
  fun totals and averages: lifetime page views, average page views
  per day, total posts, and total comments.

- **Social-media traffic.** The final section of the traffic summary, titled
  Recent Social Media Traffic, lists four social-media entities: TypePad,
  Facebook, Twitter, and Bit.ly. This section displays the number of folks
  who came to this blog via your TypePad Profile or the listed social
  networks. (The blog also shows up in your followers' TypePad
  Dashboard if you decided to share the blog in your TypePad Profile;
  see Chapter 3.)

  TypePad keeps track of people who recently found your blog via Twitter
  and Bit.ly links, as I discuss in the nearby sidebar "Tracking Twitter Traffic."

Tracking Twitter Traffic

The Recent Social Media Traffic section of the traffic summary provides links to real-time tracking data from Bit.ly, which is a URL-shortening service popularly used with Twitter. (You can find other URL-shortening services out there, but Bit.ly is the one that TypePad uses.) Click the Bit.ly link in the traffic summary (refer to Figure 6.5), and you'll see all the traffic that your blog is getting from Bit.ly links in real time (**Figure 6.6**).

Figure 6.6 Real-time Bit.ly traffic statistics.

The final column, Bit.ly Info, includes the Bit.ly links associated with the blog posts in question. A plus sign at the end of a link points to a page on Bit.ly's servers that gathers detailed statistics (**Figure 6.7**, on the next page). You can also access this page by typing the link in a Web browser and adding a plus sign to the end.

continues on next page

Tracking Twitter Traffic *continued*

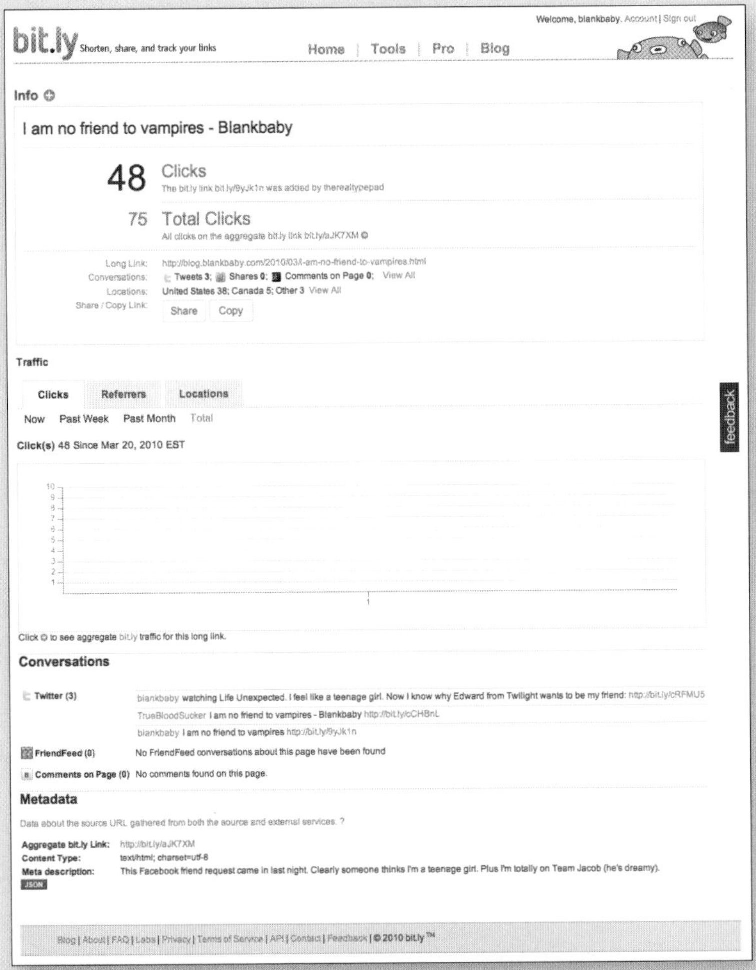

Figure 6.7 Detailed traffic stats for a Bit.ly URL.

To return to your blog's Overview page from the real-time Bit.ly traffic page, click the Overview tab or the Return to Overview link at the top of the page.

Viewing the traffic graph

Who doesn't love a good graph? The traffic graph on the Overview page gives you a great look at how your blog's traffic is doing (**Figure 6.8**). By default, the graph charts page views over the past 30 days.

Click to change the time period.

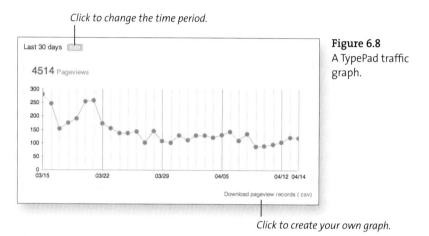

Figure 6.8
A TypePad traffic graph.

Click to create your own graph.

The large number at the top of the graph tells you the total number of page views during the specified period. If you place your mouse pointer over one of the green dots, which represent individual days, a little pop-up window shows you exactly how many page views your blog got on that day (**Figure 6.9**).

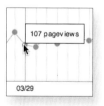

Figure 6.9 Hovering over a day's plot point reveals the number of page views recorded that day.

Traffic Isn't Everything

Traffic is only one of many metrics of success (can you tell I've been working in Corporate America for a while?) that you should take into account. Here are some others:

- **Audience.** Success is also about the audience that's reading your blog. If you have a flower shop, you want people who are interested in flowers reading your blog and sharing it with their friends. You can tell when your blog is being mentioned by looking at your referrers (see the next page).

- **Engagement.** Are people commenting on your posts? Do they post links to your blog on Twitter and Facebook? Are you getting emails from readers thanking you for posts? All these things are a sign that your blog has high reader engagement. Engaged readers are loyal readers—and a good indication that you're doing something right with your blog.

- **Sales.** If you notice an uptick in sales after you launch a blog, chances are that your blog is a success. This factor counts only if you can attribute the increase in sales to your blog, however. To find out, perhaps you can run some blog-based promotions, using a special code tied to your blog to track sales.

- **Influence.** By some accounts, influence (or mindshare) is the most important aspect of a blog, yet it's the most difficult to measure in a meaningful way. That being said, you'll know when you see it. You'll start being asked to speak on panels about your topic, for example, or people will ask you for your thoughts on whatever your blog subject is about, and your blog will start showing up on people's blogrolls. Slowly, your blog will become a trusted source. I run a blog for a big company as my day job and saw this influence firsthand when reporters starting quoting the blog's posts—a very cool situation for someone trying to get a message out.

Editing the graph

What if you want to look at statistics for a longer or shorter period? Click the Edit button at the top of the graph, and a drop-down menu lists several choices (**Figure 6.10**). Just choose the time period you're interested in seeing, and the chart will repopulate with that traffic information.

Figure 6.10 The TypePad traffic graph can display statistics for several periods.

Creating your own graph

Now, I know that some of you Microsoft Excel junkies out there are thinking, "If only I had access to the raw data, I could whip up some super-cool charts that would put this chart to shame." I admire your confidence, and you'll admire the fact that the TypePad team thought of this option. In the bottom-right corner of the traffic graph (refer to Figure 6.8) is a link titled Download Pageview Records (.csv). Clicking that link gets you a .csv (comma-separated values) file containing the data on which the chart is based. You can put this .csv file in Excel or any other number-crunching application and have your way with it.

note   Keep in mind that the .csv file contains information only from the selected time period.

Seeing recent referrers

The final section of your blog's Overview page is my favorite: Recent Referrers (**Figure 6.11**). It's my favorite because it shows where blog visitors are coming from. A *referrer* is a site on which someone clicked a link to visit your site. This section is a great way to see what sites are linking to your blog. (Perhaps you should be linking back to those sites.)

Recent Referrers
Sites that recently sent you visitors.

Time	Page Path	Referring Address
7:21 AM	/	twitter.com/marusula
6:40 AM	/about.html	www.scottexplains.com
6:39 AM	/	www.blankbaby.typepad.com
3:18 AM	/about.html	www.scottexplains.com/archives.html
3:18 AM	/archives.html	www.scottexplains.com/ipad
3:17 AM	/ipad/	www.scottexplains.com/how-to

Figure 6.11 Recent Referrers shows sites that have been linking to your blog.

This section shows three types of information:

- **Time.** The first column lists the time when your blog was visited.

- **Page Path.** The second column tells you what page on your blog was visited.

- **Referring Address.** The last column provides a link to the source of each visit (the referrer).

 note **Sometimes, an entry's Referring Address column is blank or contains only a slash. This doesn't mean that ghosts are visiting your blog (though that would be awesome); it just means that the visitor went directly to your blog by typing the URL in a Web browser or using a bookmark.**

You'll probably see your own URL listed as a referrer, which is a good thing. It means that visitors are clicking around into your archives and checking out other things that you've posted. A blog with this sort of traffic is said to be *sticky*—that is, folks get stuck reading it because of all the compelling content. The longer you can get someone to spend reading your blog, the more likely she is to subscribe to your blog or to buy your products or services.

Another common source of traffic is search engines. Google in particular will probably send a good amount of traffic to your blog. Clicking a referring link from Google takes you to the query that resulted in a person's visit to your site. You can take note of the search keywords that are listed most often and build more traffic by blogging about the same topics that people are searching for (though you should always write for your audience, not for a search engine).

The Recent Referrers section is paginated, with 50 referrers appearing on each page. At the bottom are navigation links that allow you to see some historical data about your blog's referrers.

tip **Keep in mind that as its name suggests, the section lists only about 24 hours' worth of referral data for your blog. If you want more detailed analytics—and you do; trust me—you should install Google Analytics (see Chapter 5) or another third-party analytics package.**

The Linking Economy

This sidebar is a great place to talk about the linking economy, which has helped grow the blogosphere tremendously. Blogs are all about pointing to other places on the Internet that might be of interest to your readers. The concept is very simple: If you like someone's work, link to it from your site. Linking helps spread the word about that person's site, and thanks to the magic of referrers, it brings your Web site to the attention of the linkee. (You're the linker.)

At first, it may seem odd to send readers of your blog off to some other site, but never forget what happened in *Miracle on 34th Street*. Kris Kringle, working as a Santa at Macy's, was asked whether the store carried a particular toy. Kris consulted his book and told the woman that Macy's didn't have that item, but its archrival had it in stock (and at a good price). The manager of Macy's overheard and was outraged that Kris hadn't suggested buying something that Macy's had in stock. But the woman was so impressed that she vowed to shop only at Macy's from then on.

The moral of the story? Building long-term loyalty is more important than short-term gain. To put it another way, people like it when you point them to cool stuff.

7

Posts and Pages

Posts and pages make up the bulk of your blogging experience and represent almost the entirety of what brings people to your blog. I've spent a good deal of this book talking about what some people might consider to be the bones of a blog. If everything I've talked about up to this point represents the skeleton of a blog, posts and pages are the flesh and muscle.

Posts are what you traditionally think of when you think of blogs. They're chronological, displayed on the front page of your blog, and usually have comments enabled.

Pages, on the other hand, are used for static content that can stand on its own. Two common pages used in blogs are About Me, which tells your readers a little about yourself and your blog, and Contact Me, which allows blog visitors to send you a note. Pages can have comments enabled, though they're traditionally disabled.

Because posts and pages are so important to your blog, you have several ways to jump into writing them from within TypePad. This chapter covers writing a blog post in the TypePad Web interface.

Composing a Post

You've probably noticed the big yellow Compose button in your blog's navigation bar. Clicking it opens a drop-down menu listing two choices: New Post and New Page (**Figure 7.1**).

Figure 7.1 The Compose menu is always just a click away.

For purposes of this chapter, choose New Post to open the New Post page (**Figure 7.2**), which is where the proverbial blogging magic happens. In the following sections, I explain each part of it.

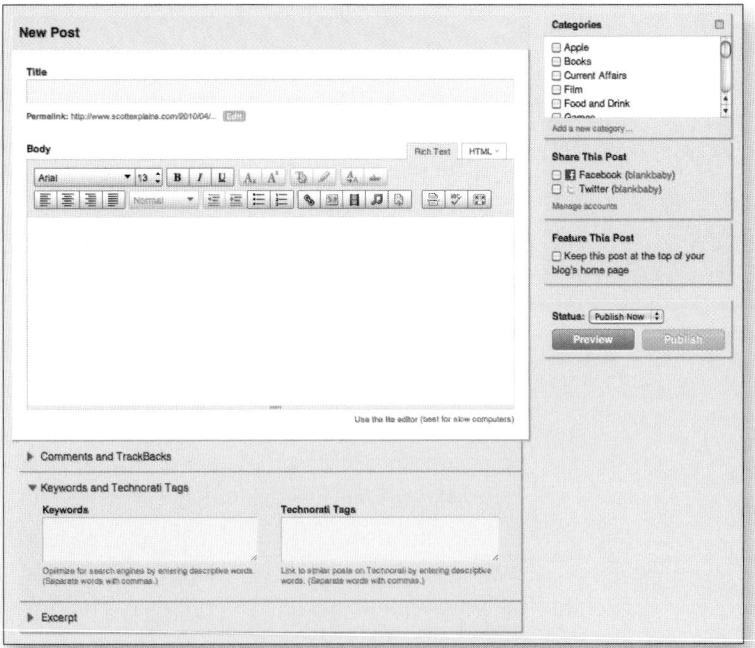

Figure 7.2 The New Post page is where you create blog posts.

Title

A good title is among the first things you should think about when you compose a post. Search engines put a lot of weight on a post's title, which is also the title of the Web page on which the post is displayed.

In **Figure 7.3**, I'm writing a post about how to change your email signature on an iPad. Clearly, a few words have to be in the title so that both my readers and search engines know what the post is about. *iPad, email,* and *signature* are key search terms, so I made sure to use them.

Title

Changing your iPad's email signature

Permalink: http://www.scottexplains.com/2010/04/changing-your-ipads-email-signature.html [Edit]

Figure 7.3 Keywords in a post title.

> **tip** TypePad allows you to enter up to 255 characters for a title. Search engines emphasize the first 62 characters, so make sure to include important terms at the beginning.

Permalink

TypePad automatically creates a permalink for your post based on the title you entered, using hyphens instead of spaces to separate words. As you type a title in the Title field, you'll notice that the permalink starts to populate below that field (refer to Figure 6.3). If you happen to change the title wording before you publish the post, the permalink automatically changes to reflect the new title.

This behavior may lead you to believe that the permalink and post title are intertwined and that nothing shall ever come between them. Although this notion is a romantic one (well, as romantic as anything related to a Web form can be), it's inaccurate. The blue Edit button to the right of the permalink allows you to edit the permalink independently of the title. When you click this button, a text field appears, and the button's *Edit* label changes to *Done* (**Figure 7.4**, on the next page). You can type any URL-safe characters in this field—that is, letters, numbers, and some symbols but no spaces, using hyphens to separate words.

Figure 7.4 You can edit a permalink manually here.

When you're happy with your new permalink text, click the Done button. When that post is published, it will use your new custom permalink.

note It isn't a good idea to change a permalink after you've published a post on your blog, but the permalink Edit button is available for all your posts and pages, published or not. When you attempt to edit the permalink of a published post, a warning pops up (**Figure 7.5**). You can ignore the warning and edit the permalink, of course.

Figure 7.5 TypePad warns you about breaking links to the post in question.

Body

The Body section is the real meat of any blog post. As you can see in **Figure 7.6,** a lot is going on here.

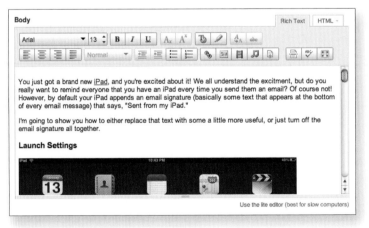

Figure 7.6 The body of a post in progress.

Rich Text and HTML tabs

First, take a look at the Rich Text and HTML tabs in the top-right corner of the posting form (**Figure 7.7**). Rich text renders the post just as it will look in a browser. The Rich Tab text is selected by default because that format is easy for new bloggers to use. If you're more comfortable hand-coding HTML, click the HTML tab to open a different kind of post window.

Figure 7.7 You can compose a post in rich text or HTML.

Rich Text and HTML toolbar

Whether you choose the Rich Text or HTML tab (see the preceding section), the toolbar—the row of buttons above the post entry field—is the same.

tip   Hover your mouse over a toolbar button to see a tool tip containing the keyboard shortcut for that command.

The first two controls in the post toolbar control the font and font size. If you don't make choices here, the post will use the default font you defined for your blog.

To boldface some text, select it and click the B button. The other two buttons work in a similar way, though with different results. The I button applies italics to selected text, and the U button underlines it.

These two buttons apply subscript and superscript formatting, respectively.

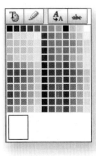

Generally, your blog's styling code dictates what color the text will be, but these buttons give you some control of font color in your post. If you want to highlight some text in a certain color or change the color of some text, just select it and click the appropriate button. A color palette pops up. Click a color, and the selected text will be displayed or highlighted in that color (**Figure 7.8**). (If you don't choose a color from the palette, TypePad uses your blog's default text color.)

Figure 7.8 You can use the highlight tool to highlight any words you choose in one of the available colors.

Both of these buttons are about correcting errors, though in slightly different ways. The first button removes any formatting that has been applied to the selected text. The second button, which applies strikethrough formatting, is a great way to acknowledge a mistake without actually removing the erroneous information.

The next set of buttons lets you align the text of your post in any of four common ways: left, center, right, and justified. TypePad defaults to left-aligned text.

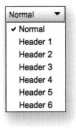

The Format menu gives you access to several text-formatting options. Select the text you want to format, and choose an option from the drop-down menu. Normal, of course, is what the vast majority of the text in your posts will be. You can also apply one of six headers to selected text if you want to break up a long post. Header 1 produces the largest header; use the smaller ones for subheadings.

The Indent and Outdent buttons let you indent and outdent paragraphs. Position your cursor where you want to indent or outdent text, and click the appropriate button.

The next two buttons let you create lists (which I enjoy using, if you can't tell from reading this book!). The first button creates a bulleted list. Select some text or an image to be your first list item, and TypePad inserts a bullet before it. Press Return or Enter to add another item to the list; when you're done with the list, press the same key twice to end it and go back to writing normally. The second button works the same way but creates a list whose items are numbered.

The button with the three links of chain on it turns any selected text into a hyperlink. When you select a bit of text and click this button, the Insert/Edit Link dialog box opens, displaying the selected text in the Link Text field (**Figure 7.9**). Unless you decide to change it, this text will be displayed in your post as a link.

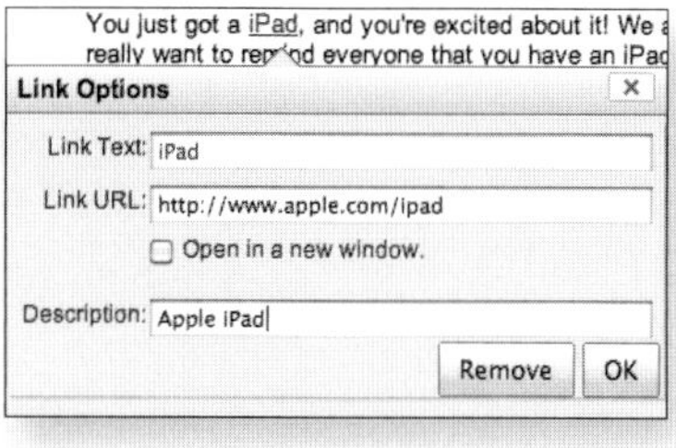

Figure 7.9 The link options allow you to control the behavior of links in your post.

The Link URL field is where you set the destination for the link. By default, the linked page opens in the same browser window that the user has open, but if you want it to open in a new window, select the check box titled Open in a New Window. The Description field is optional, but if you enter something here, it shows up when someone hovers over the link or accesses your site in a text-only browser. Click the OK button when you're happy with the link information you've filled in, and TypePad transforms the text you've selected into a link.

note If you want to change any of the values of an existing link, click the Hyperlink toolbar button again and make the changes in the Insert/Edit Link dialog box.

tip Turning a link back into plain old text is easy too. Just select the link that you want to de-linkify, click the Hyperlink button to open the Insert/Edit Link dialog box, and click the Remove button.

This button allows you to insert images into your blog post. I cover all the image options in "Putting Images in Your Posts and Pages" later in this chapter.

 Click the button with the filmstrip on it to open the Insert Video dialog box, which lets you embed a video from several video-sharing sites, including YouTube and Vimeo, in your post (**Figure 7.10**). You can select the top radio button and paste the video's URL in the URL field, or you can select the bottom radio button and paste the video's embed code in the Embed text box. (You'll find this code on the video-sharing site you're using. You have to use the code exactly as is; TypePad doesn't let you set any options.) When you're done, click Insert Video, and the video will be displayed in the Body field of the New Post page (refer to Figure 7.6).

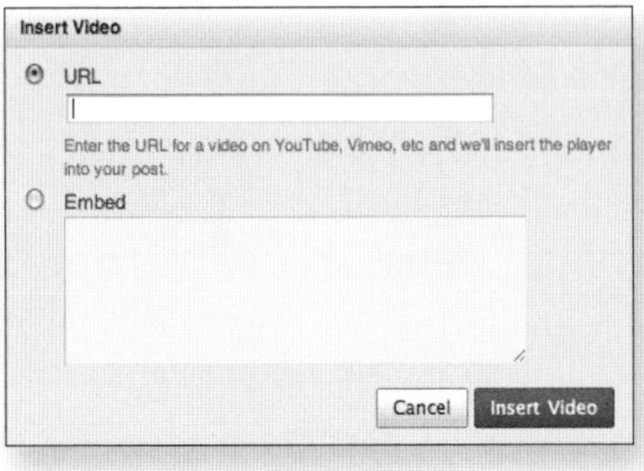

Insert Video

○ URL

```
[                    ]
```

Enter the URL for a video on YouTube, Vimeo, etc and we'll insert the player into your post.

○ Embed

```
[                    ]
```

Cancel   Insert Video

Figure 7.10 Who doesn't like videos? Just paste in a URL or embed code from your favorite video-sharing site, and you're all set.

If you want to delete the video later, select it and press the Delete key on your keyboard.

note **To see your video previewed live, you must have Adobe Flash Player installed.**

This button allows you to upload audio files directly to your post, in case you want to post an audio podcast. Click it, and the Upload an Audio File dialog box opens, offering very few options (**Figure 7.11**). In fact, the only thing you can do is launch your operating system's file browser so you can select the audio file that you want to upload. When you've done that, click the Upload File button to get that audio file up to TypePad and into your post. The upload time will vary depending on the file size and the speed of your Internet connection.

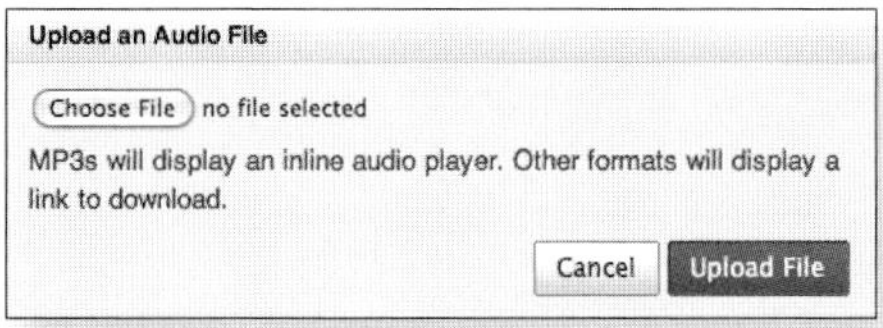

Upload an Audio File

Choose File   no file selected

MP3s will display an inline audio player. Other formats will display a link to download.

Cancel   Upload File

Figure 7.11 You can include audio in your post. Just find the file and click Upload File.

If you upload an MP3 file, TypePad not only inserts the file into your post, but also places a player in the post itself so that people can enjoy your audio right there (**Figure 7.12**). This player works only for MP3 files.

Figure 7.12 Visitors can play an uploaded MP3 file directly in a post, thanks to TypePad's audio player.

The Insert File button allows you to upload pretty much any kind of file to your post, including video files that you want to host in TypePad as opposed to linking to them on a sharing site. Click this button to open the Upload a File dialog box (**Figure 7.13**), click the Choose File button, select the file on your computer that you want to use, and click Upload File. TypePad places a link to that file in the post. You can change the link text by double-clicking the link in the New Post page.

Upload a File

Choose File   no file selected

To insert a file into your post, click the button above and select a file on your computer to upload.

Cancel   Upload File

Figure 7.13 You can upload any file to a blog post, including PDFs and Microsoft Office documents, via the Upload a File dialog box.

 Clicking this button splits your post in two and displays a dotted line across the Body field. Anything that falls before the dotted line will be displayed on the front page of your post. At the end of that section, TypePad will display a link that says Continue Reading (*title of your post*). Clicking that link takes readers to a page that contains the full text of the post.

Spell checking in TypePad works much the way you expect it to. Click the Spell Check button to start the check. Any word that TypePad's dictionary doesn't recognize is highlighted in yellow; click a highlighted word to see spelling suggestions (**Figure 7.14**, on the next page). Select or skip the suggestions, and TypePad continues checking until it reaches the end of the text or you click the X to cancel the spell check.

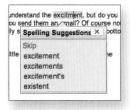

Figure 7.14 The spell-check feature scans your blog post and highlights any misspelled words.

The Full Screen button expands the posting field to take up your entire browser window. Click it again to toggle back to normal view.

HTML tab

If you prefer to hand-code your posts in HTML, just click the HTML tab at the top of the Body section to switch to a coding-friendly display (**Figure 7.15**). This display allows you to edit your post's HTML instead of depending on the HTML that TypePad generates for you when you use Rich Text mode.

Figure 7.15 Click the HTML tab to compose your post by entering HTML code manually.

If you click the small triangle on the right side of the HTML tab, a three-option menu drops down (**Figure 7.16**).

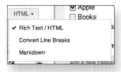

Figure 7.16 HTML mode offers a few options that Rich Text mode doesn't.

Each of these options tells TypePad to interpret the text you enter in slightly different ways:

- **Rich Text/HTML.** This setting (the default) allows you to enter straight HTML. TypePad won't do anything to what you enter; it just posts that code as is.

- **Convert Line Breaks.** If you opt for HTML mode, you need to make sure to use paragraph tags (<p>) so that your text will display properly. If you choose Convert Line Breaks, TypePad automatically adds the tags for you based on the line breaks in your text.

- **Markdown.** Markdown is an alternative to HTML that uses much more natural text markup. When you choose this option, you type your text in Markdown (http://daringfireball.net/projects/markdown), and TypePad converts that text to HTML and displays it properly. Markdown does require a little bit of a learning curve, but when you have it down, it's quite natural.

Finally, if you notice that the post editor isn't responding quickly on your computer (which might happen if you have an older computer), you can use a less-resource-intensive editor that offers almost all the same functionality. When you click the Use the Light Editor link in the bottom-right corner of the compose page, an alert dialog box tells you to save your post and reload the page to switch editors (**Figure 7.17**). When you're using the light editor, the link changes to read Use the Full Editor; click it to switch back to the full editor.

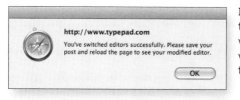

Figure 7.17 TypePad reminds you that when you switch to the light version of the post editor, or vice versa, you need to reload the page to see the changes.

HTML toolbar

The toolbar remains the same no matter which mode you're using, but in HTML mode, some of the functions are disabled. The controls that you can't use are as follows:

- Font and Font Size controls

- Subscript and Superscript buttons

- Font-color and highlighting controls

- The Style controls

- The spelling checker

Comments and Trackbacks

Your blog has a default setting for both trackbacks and comments (see Chapter 8). You can override these defaults on a per-post basis, however, by changing the settings in the Comments and Trackbacks section of the New Post page (**Figure 7.18**).

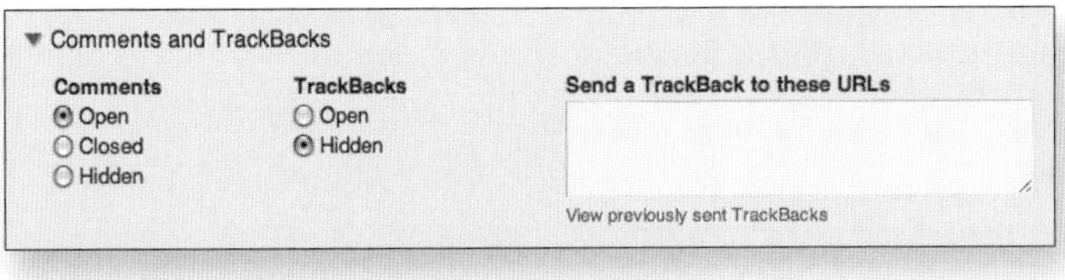

Figure 7.18 Comments and Trackbacks options.

You can set three options for comments on a per-post basis:

- **Open.** People can post comments, though they may need to sign in with a certain account, depending on how you have your comments set up at blog level.

- **Closed.** No one can leave a comment on the post. If you decide to close comments after folks have left comments on a post, those older comments will still be displayed, but new ones won't be accepted.

- **Hidden.** Comments that were previously left for this post will no longer be displayed, and new comments won't be accepted.

You also have a couple of trackback options:

- **Open.** This setting accepts trackbacks.

- **Hidden.** As with hidden comments, when you hide trackbacks, no new trackbacks will be accepted, and older ones are hidden from sight.

While I'm on the subject of trackbacks, take a look at that text box titled Send a Trackback to These URLs. To send a trackback, you'll need the special trackback URL (which usually is displayed on the post that you want to track back to). When you have it, paste it in this box. You can enter more than one trackback URL, if you want.

Keywords and Technorati Tags

The settings in the Keywords and Technorati Tags section (**Figure 7.19**) are optional, but they allow you to describe your post further and perhaps scare up a little more traffic—and who doesn't want to get a couple more readers?

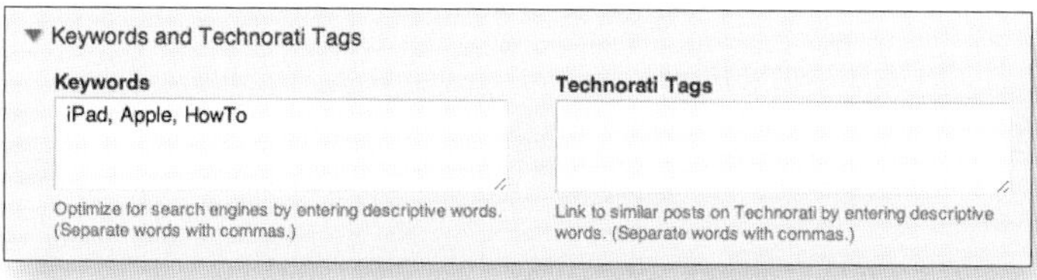

Figure 7.19 Use these settings to describe your post in extra detail.

Enter keywords, separated by commas, in the Keywords box. Keywords are useful because they allow you to associate words related to the post but not used in the post (such as *HowTo* in Figure 7.19), so that the post shows up in searches even for keywords that aren't in the text.

Technorati tags are slightly different from keywords. Named after the blog directory Technorati (www.technorati.com), these tags are displayed in your post as links back to Technorati searches. A post tagged with the word *Mac*, for example, would link to http://technorati.com/tag/mac, which compiles all the posts across Technorati that are also tagged with *Mac*.

Excerpt

TypePad can be set to automatically generate an excerpt, or brief preview, of your blog post (see Chapter 5). Enter new text in the Excerpt text box (**Figure 7.20**) to replace TypePad's automatically generated excerpt with your handcrafted one.

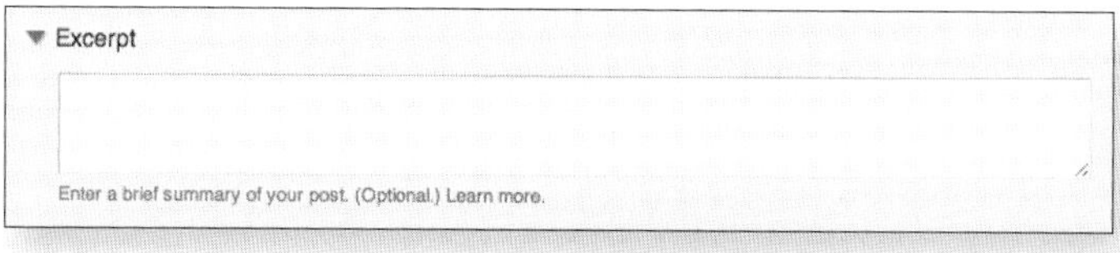

Figure 7.20 You can enter a custom excerpt for this post.

Categories

You can assign one or more categories to your post by making a selection in the Categories list (**Figure 7.21**). Just select the check box next to each category you want this post to appear in, and that's it! You can select as many categories you like.

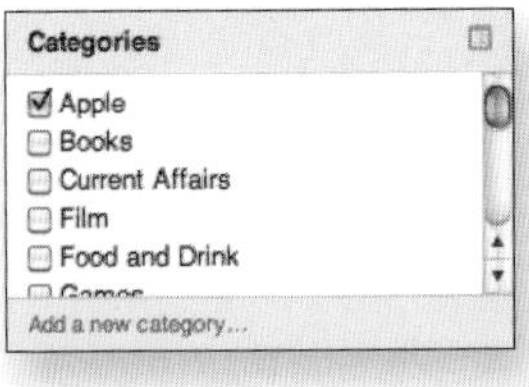

Figure 7.21 The Categories section lists all the categories available for your post.

If you can't find an appropriate category for the post, you can create a new one by clicking the Add a New Category link at the bottom of the list. When you do, the Create Category dialog box opens (**Figure 7.22**). Type the name of the new category in the text field, and click the Create button. The new category appears at the bottom of the list and is selected automatically (**Figure 7.23**).

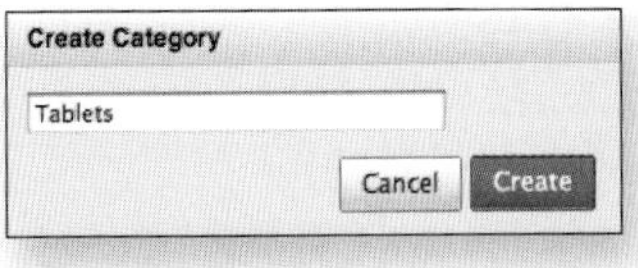

Figure 7.22 Come up with a name for the new category, and click Create.

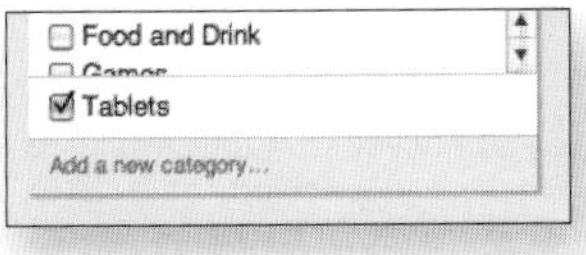

Figure 7.23 TypePad automatically applies the new category to the post you're writing.

You can expand the Categories list by clicking the expansion icon (**Figure 7.24**). When you're done, click the icon again to return the list to its original height.

If you decide to remove a category from a post, clear the appropriate check box and then either save or republish the post.

Expansion icon

Figure 7.24 Expand the list to see more of your categories.

Share This Post

I've said many times that social media is all about sharing items of interest with your social circle. That's an oversimplification, of course, but I think that it covers about 98 percent of the reasons why people use social media. As I discuss in Chapter 5, TypePad wants to help make your blog the hub of your social-media sharing, and that's where the Share This Post section comes in (**Figure 7.25**).

Figure 7.25 All the other accounts that support posting from TypePad are listed here.

This section lists all the social-network accounts that you've configured for sharing on your blog (see Chapter 2). If you want to share a particular post on one of your social networks, just select that network's check box in the Share This Post section. (You can pick more than one network, if you want.) When you publish the post, TypePad will automatically share the title of your post along with a shortened URL that links back to your blog (**Figure 7.26**, on the next page).

Changing your iPad's email
signature http://bit.ly/aV9naS
less than 10 seconds ago via TypePad

Figure 7.26 A tweet sent from TypePad.

tip Don't forget that you can set TypePad to share your posts auto-matically with all, or some, of your social-media accounts. See Chapter 5 for details.

Feature This Post

note Only users with TypePad Pro–level plans can feature posts.

Your blog's post index is arranged chronologically, in either ascending or descending order. Most of the time, this arrangement is great. But what if you want to highlight a certain post or perhaps display a welcome post at the top of your blog? Do you have to change the publication date (a trick that I show you in "Setting publishing status" later in this chapter) every day to keep that post at the top of the list? No—just feature the post via the Feature This Post section (**Figure 7.27**).

Feature This Post
☐ Keep this post at the top of your
blog's home page

Figure 7.27 Check this box to feature a post.

Selecting the check box titled Keep This Post at the Top of Your Blog's Home Page allows this post to break free from the chains of time; it will be the first post displayed in your blog no matter when it was published or what your blog's display order is.

note You can have only one featured post at a time. If you already have a featured post and later enable this option for another post, the new featured post supersedes the old one.

Status

OK, you've picked a great title, written a fantastic post, tagged it, categorized it, enabled sharing for it, and decided to feature it in your blog. There's only one more step: publishing the darned thing.

Setting publishing status

First, check out that drop-down menu in the Status section (**Figure 7.28**).

Status: [Publish Now ‡]
[Preview]   [Publish]

Figure 7.28 These settings control when the post appears on your site.

When you click this menu, you see three options:

- **Publish Now.** This status means that the post is ready to go live on your blog, and you can publish it by clicking the green Publish button.

- **Draft.** Sometimes, you want to work on a post that isn't quite ready for prime time. To keep the New Post window open while you work on it, you can save the post as a draft. Just choose this option from the Status drop-down menu and click the green Save button.

- **Publish On.** TypePad allows you to schedule posts to appear in your blog on a future date. Why would you want to do this? Suppose that you've scheduled a special sale at your store and want a post to appear on the first day of the event, but you'll be traveling that day. Write the post and then choose Publish On from the Status drop-down menu. The Published Date and Time dialog box opens, allowing you to pick the exact date and time when the post should appear. When you have a date and time all set, click the OK button. The date you selected appears in the Status section (**Figure 7.29**). Click the green Schedule button to schedule the post.

Status: [Publish On... ‡]
April 29, 2010 5:19:00 PM EDT
[Preview]   [Schedule]

Figure 7.29 A post scheduled to be published on a specific date.

If you want to adjust the date and time of posting later, click the date listed in the Status section to reopen the Published Date and Time dialog box and make your changes.

> **tip** You aren't limited to scheduling posts in the future; you can back-date posts too. I don't suggest doing this, however, unless you have a very good reason. People might think that something is fishy when "old" posts suddenly appear in your blog.

Previewing the post

Before you publish your post, wouldn't it be a good idea to see how it will look in your blog? Click the Preview button in the Status section (refer to Figure 7.28), and another browser window opens, displaying the post you're working on as it will look in your blog. Don't worry—this display is just a mockup. The post isn't available for public consumption just yet.

If everything looks to be in order, click the green Publish button (or the green Save button, if you want to save the post as a draft). TypePad takes the appropriate action and displays a yellow alert at the top of the Edit Post page (**Figure 7.30**), which I cover in "Editing a post or page" later in this chapter. If you published the post, this alert contains a link to it.

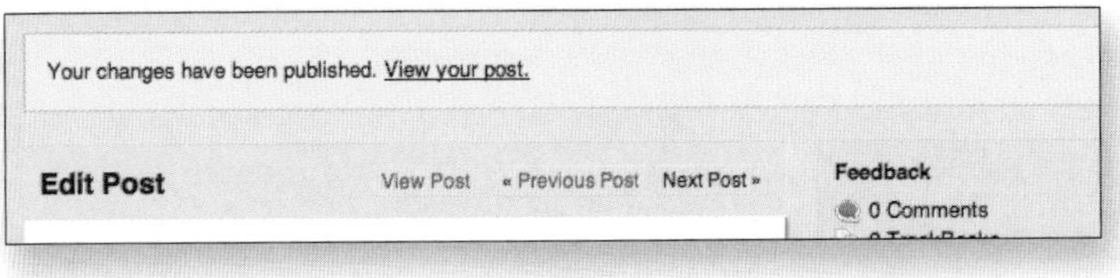

Your changes have been published. View your post.

Edit Post   View Post   « Previous Post   Next Post »   **Feedback**
                                                                        0 Comments

Figure 7.30 Whenever you save or publish a post, TypePad displays a yellow alert to tell you that the action was successful.

Putting Images in Your Posts and Pages

As they say, a picture is worth a thousand words, so you're going to want to gussy up your posts and pages with an image or two. The Image toolbar button (refer to "Rich Text and HTML toolbar" earlier in this chapter) allows you to insert an image into your post and control some related settings.

Inserting an image with default settings

To insert an image into a post or page, follow these steps:

1. Click the Image toolbar button.

The Insert Image dialog box opens (**Figure 7.31**).

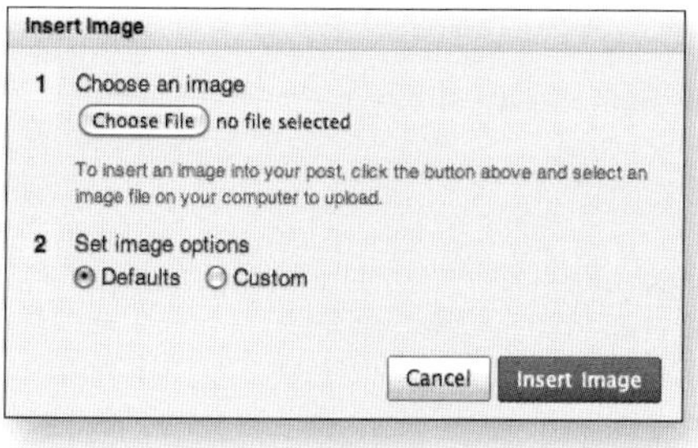

Figure 7.31 The Insert Image dialog box lets you set a bunch of image options.

2. Click the Choose File button, and use the file browser to find and select the image on your computer.

3. Set your image options by selecting the appropriate radio button.

As shown in Figure 7.31, Defaults is selected automatically.

4. If you accept the default image options, click the Insert Image button.

TypePad inserts the image into your post or page.

Inserting an image with custom settings

But where do the default image settings come from? Why, right from the Insert Image dialog box itself. To set your own, follow these steps:

1. Complete steps 1 and 2 of "Inserting an image with default settings."

2. Select the Custom radio button in the Insert Image dialog box to display the Custom options (**Figure 7.32**, on the next page).

These options give you a lot of control over the way images appear in your blog. You can set them just the way you like them and then make that setup the new default.

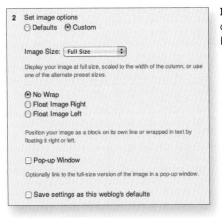

Figure 7.32 You can save these image options as a default so that you don't have to keep setting them manually.

3. Make a choice from the Image Size drop-down menu (**Figure 7.33**).

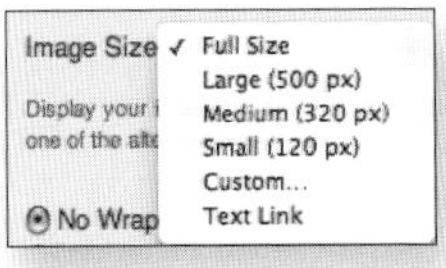

Figure 7.33 Image Size options.

Your options are

- **Full Size.** The default option is Full Size, which inserts the image either full size or scaled to fit your post's width. (If you're uploading an image that's 1000 pixels wide, but your blog is 500 pixels wide, TypePad will display the image 500 pixels wide. If the image is 400 pixels wide, TypePad will display it in its full glory.)

- **Large, Medium,** and **Small.** These options are self-explanatory.

- **Custom.** When you choose the Custom option, you can enter whatever pixel width you want.

- **Text Link.** This option doesn't actually insert the image into your post. Rather, it inserts a text link that points to the image, which will be uploaded and stored in your blog, not displayed in the post itself.

4. Choose a wrapping option.

If you choose No Wrap, the image will stand on its own, with no text wrapping around it. Generally, this option is best for images that take up the entire width of the post column. You'll probably be more likely to use either Float Image Right or Float Image Left to have text flow to the right or left of the image.

5. Check or clear the Pop-Up Window check box.

   When you enable this option, TypePad inserts a small version of the image into your post and makes it a link to the full-size version. Then, when someone clicks the image in your blog, a pop-up window opens, displaying the full-size image.

6. When you've set all the image options just the way you like them, you can make this set of settings the default by checking the box titled Save Settings As This Weblog's Defaults.

7. Click the Insert Image button to insert the uploaded image and save the new defaults (if you've changed them).

Changing an image's settings

After you successfully inserted a picture into your post, the Image toolbar button serves a dual purpose. Sure, you can use it to add more pictures—there's no limit to the number of pictures you can have in one post—but you can also use it to modify images that are already in the post.

To do so, double-click a picture that you want to edit, and click the Image toolbar button. The Image Options dialog box opens (**Figure 7.34**).

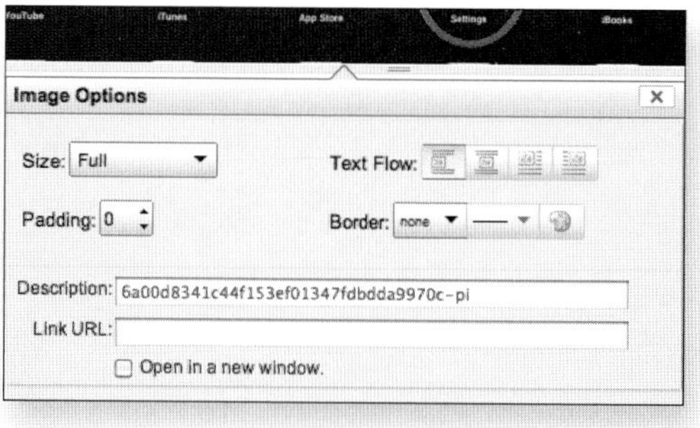

Figure 7.34 After you've inserted an image into your post, you can bring up some more image options by double-clicking the image.

A couple of options in Figure 7.34 could use some explanation:

- **Padding.** This option adds a little white space around your image. Click the up and down arrows to add or subtract padding. If you're using Rich Text mode (refer to "Rich Text and HTML tabs" earlier in this chapter), you'll see the padding changes live in the Edit Post page.

- **Border.** The first drop-down menu in this section sets the thickness of the border from 0 to 5 pixels. The second menu (**Figure 7.35**) lets you draw a solid, dashed, or dotted line around the image to create a nice effect (*nice* being a highly subjective adjective, of course). The final menu lets you set the color of the border by making a choice from a color palette.

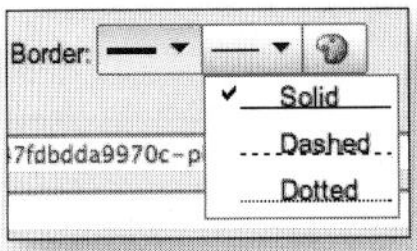

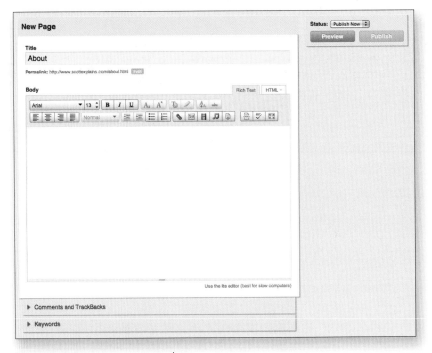

Figure 7.35 Borders come in three flavors: solid, dashed, and dotted.

Creating a Page

The process of creating a new page is strangely similar to that of creating a new post. Click the yellow Compose button in your blog's navigation bar and choose New Page from the drop-down menu, and you're in the New Page page (**Figure 7.36**), which bears a striking resemblance to the New Post page. (Notice a trend?)

Figure 7.36 Compose your pages here.

Composing a new page is almost exactly like creating a new post. In fact, there are so many similarities that it makes sense just to point out the few differences:

- **Comments and trackbacks.** You can enable comments and trackbacks on a per-page basis, much as you can for posts, but you don't have a way to enter trackback links to other blogs.

- **Keywords and Technorati tags.** You can assign keywords to a page, but you can't assign Technorati tags.

- **Categories.** Pages can't be placed in categories, so you don't have a way to pick a category.

- **Sharing.** If you want to tweet a link to one of your pages, you'll have to do it manually, because TypePad doesn't support automatic sharing of pages.

- **Featuring.** You can't feature a page.

- **Excerpts.** Pages don't have excerpts, because they don't show up in your blog's feeds.

- **Publishing status.** You can assign only two publishing statuses to a page: Publish Now (or Published, if the page has already been published) and Draft.

- **Permalinks.** A page's permalink is simply your blog's URL followed by the page's title, with hyphens used in place of spaces. (If I were to create a page called All about Scott for Scott Explains, for example, the URL would be www.scottexplains.com/all-about-scott.html.) Just as you can with posts, you can edit a permalink both before and after you publish a page.

Managing Posts and Pages

Now that you know how to write posts and create pages, I'm sure that you'll start blogging like mad in no time. Sooner or later, though, you'll want to manage a post or page in some way—delete a post, add a category, or correct a misspelling. (It happens to the best of us.)

To access your management tools, click the Posts tab on your blog's navigation bar (**Figure 7.37**). When you do, the Posts page opens (**Figure 7.38**).

| Compose ▼ | Overview | Posts | Comments | Design | Settings |

Figure 7.37 Click the Posts tab to manage both posts and pages.

| Posts | | Posts | All posts | or | | Search | ⊕ New Post |

Posts All posts ▼ or _____ (Search)   ⊕ New Post

Pages

☐ **What the heck is e-Ink anyway?**
Apr 28, 2010 by Scott McNulty

☐ **Marking videos as TV shows in iTunes**
10 hours ago by Scott McNulty

☐ **Improving your WordPress blog's permalinks**
View | 3 days ago by Scott McNulty
Categories: How To, WordPress

☐ **Changing your iPad's email signature**
View | 7 days ago by Scott McNulty
Categories: Apple, How To, iPad

☐ **Welcome to Scott Explains**
View | 7 days ago by Scott McNulty ⭐ Featured
Categories: Site News

☐ PUBLISH DRAFT DELETE   More actions... ▼ (Go)

Figure 7.38 The Posts page. Select a post or page to edit it.

As you can see in Figure 7.38, all your posts are nicely displayed in a list that
shows 20 posts at a time. (If you have more than 20 posts in your blog—and
eventually, you will—TypePad paginates the list and displays navigation
links at the bottom of the page.)

On the left side of the page is a blue navigation menu with two options:
Posts and Pages. Because the tab you click to get here is called the Posts tab,
TypePad shows you your lists of posts by default. If you're looking to
manage your blog's pages instead, click Pages in this menu.

 note   You can even compose a post from this page by clicking the New
Post link in the top-right corner.

Filtering posts

At the top of the post list, you'll see a couple of controls that make finding
the item you're looking for a little easier:

- **Posts drop-down menu.** The default setting is All Posts. Click the drop-down menu to see more options (**Figure 7.39**). You can filter the list of posts based on their publication status (Draft Posts, Published Posts, and Future Posts) or based on categories. Your list of categories won't match the list in Figure 7.39 unless you think exactly like I do, which probably wouldn't be good for you (and isn't all that great for me!).

Figure 7.39 All the filters that you can apply to the post list.

- **Search controls.** If filtering isn't your thing, or if you remember a word or phrase that you used in the title of the post you're looking for, you can use the search controls to find it. Just type a word or phrase in the text field, and click the Search button. TypePad will search your posts' titles and categories and return any matches.

Viewing the post list

The post list shows a lot of information about your blog's posts in an easy-to-read format. The title of each post is listed first. Clicking the title allows you to edit that post (see "Editing a post or page" later in this chapter). Below the title are the date and time when the post was—or will be—published and the author's name (or authors' names, if there are more than one).

To the right of that information are three icons. The first two icons represent whether the post accepts comments and trackbacks, in that order. As you might guess, a green check mark on the icon means that comments or trackbacks are being accepted. (In Figure 7.38 earlier in this chapter, you can see that comments are open for all the posts.) A red "prohibited" symbol on the icon (a circle with a line through it) means that the post doesn't accept either comments or trackbacks.

note A black dash through the icon signifies that comments or trackbacks are hidden for a post or page.

The final icon is the status icon, which can have one of three values (**Figure 7.40**):

- The yellow pencil icon means that the post is a draft.

- The green check means that the post is published.

- The blue clock icon denotes a post that's scheduled to be published in the future.

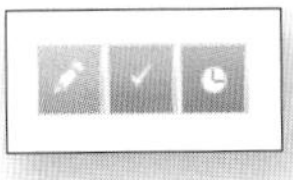

Figure 7.40 These icons represent the three possible post statuses: draft, published, and scheduled.

Clicking a post's status icon opens a menu that allows you to change that post's status (**Figure 7.41**).

Figure 7.41 You can take any of three publishing actions on posts.

One final note about the post list: If you've featured a post in your blog (refer to "Feature This Post" earlier in this chapter), that post gets a jaunty star icon denoting its special status. You can feature only one post at a time.

Performing bulk operations on posts or pages

Each post has a check box next to it, so you can select several posts (or all of them, by checking the box at the bottom of the post list) and perform bulk operations on them. Make your selections; then click the Publish, Draft, or Delete button at the bottom of the post list to apply that action to all the selected posts. Ah, the power.

Bulk operations aren't limited to those three actions, however. You can also make a choice from the More Actions drop-down menu at the bottom of the post list (**Figure 7.42**) to affect all the selected posts at the same time.

Figure 7.42 The More Actions menu lets you apply an action to several posts at the same time.

note Page management is virtually identical to post management. Click Pages in the blue navigation menu on the Posts page, and you'll see a table listing all your blog's pages along with their titles, authors, and publication dates. The only difference is that the More Actions drop-down menu omits any actions related to categories, because pages don't have categories.

Editing a post or page

To edit an existing post, click the Posts tab in your blog's navigation bar to open the Posts page, and click the title of the post in the post list. TypePad takes you to the Edit Post page (**Figure 7.43**). If you want to edit a page instead, choose Pages from the navigation menu in the Posts page (refer to Figure 7.38), and click the title of the page you want to edit. The options for posts and pages are the same.

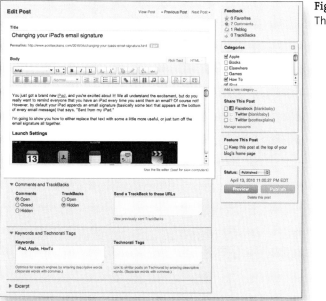

Figure 7.43
The Edit Post page.

Right off the bat, you'll see three new links at the top of the page. View Post links to the post on your blog (and serves as a handy link to the post's permalink); the Previous Post and Next Post links allow you to jump directly to the Edit Post page for older or newer posts.

The Status section also has a couple of new options (**Figure 7.44**). First, you can adjust the post's publication time by clicking the date above the Preview and Publish buttons. Also, below those buttons is a small link titled Delete This Post. Clicking this link deletes the post or page that you're editing. A confirmation dialog box appears, asking you whether you're sure that you know what you're doing, because you can't undelete a post or page. Click the appropriate button to confirm or cancel the deletion.

Figure 7.44 Delete This Post is a tiny link so that you won't click it inadvertently.

You'll also find a new Feedback section on the right side of the Edit Post page (**Figure 7.45**), listing the number of people who have left comments or trackbacks, favorited, and reblogged this post. By looking at this list, you can tell whether folks are enjoying your post.

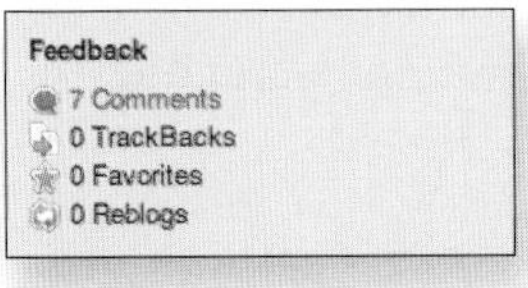

Figure 7.45 This section gives you a quick look at the feedback the post has received.

In the case of both comments and trackbacks, when the number displayed is greater than zero, the number becomes a link that you can click to manage those comments and trackbacks. I show you how to do that—and much more—in Chapter 8.

 note For a few alternative ways to create posts in TypePad, turn to Appendix B.

8

Managing Feedback

Blogging is all about having a conversation, but that doesn't mean that your blog has to be a free-for-all. TypePad has tools that allow you to manage comments and trackbacks, as well as create a blacklist of words and addresses that aren't allowed in your blog.

Working with Comments

Comments are both boons and busts for blogs. On the boon side, many people met their significant others in the comments section of a blog (including my blog, though I met my own wife at a blogger meetup). On the bust side are the scourges of the blogosphere—comment spam and jerks—which can ruin a perfectly good comments section.

Luckily, you can manage your blog's comments. To do so, make sure that you're viewing the dashboard of the blog you want to manage comments for. (I cover individual blog dashboards in Chapter 6.) Then click the Comments tab in the navigation bar at the top of the dashboard. TypePad opens the Comments page (**Figure 8.1**), which lists all the comments on your blog, with the most recent at the top.

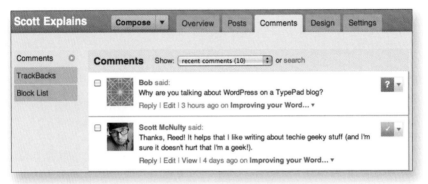

Figure 8.1 When you click the Comments tab, TypePad displays a page that looks something like this one.

Filtering comments

You can filter what comments are displayed by making a different choice from the Show drop-down menu (**Figure 8.2**).

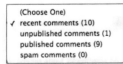

Figure 8.2 The available filters to help you keep your comments under control.

Your choices are

- **Recent Comments.** This option, which is the default setting, lists all comments left on your blog, no matter what their status.

- **Unpublished Comments.** This option shows only comments that haven't been approved yet. (If you don't have comment moderation enabled, there won't be any comments in this category.)

- **Published Comments.** This option lists only published comments.

- **Spam Comments.** If you want to check out your spam comments, choose this option.

The number in parentheses after each menu option represents the number of comments of that type.

Searching comments

In addition to filtering by comment type, you can search your comments. Click the Search link next to the Show drop-down menu, and a search field appears. From the Show menu, choose the criterion you want to search on: Author, Email, or IP Address (**Figure 8.3**). Then enter your search term and click the Search button. TypePad displays all the comments that match what you searched for (**Figure 8.4**).

Figure 8.3 You can search your comments by author, email address, or IP address.

Figure 8.4 The results of a comment search by author.

In the search results, you see a picture for each commenter who has a TypePad Profile picture. If you hover your mouse over one of these pictures, you see more information about that comment (**Figure 8.5**), including the commenter's email address and links to all comments left by that user and sent from the same IP address.

Figure 8.5 Details about the author of a comment.

Along with the picture, TypePad shows you the full text of each comment, with a few links below it:

- **Reply.** Click the Reply link to go the comment form of the blog post in question so that you can respond to the comment.

- **Edit.** The Edit link allows you to edit the comment—a topic that I cover later in this chapter.

- **View.** The View link takes you to the comment live on your blog, just the way visitors to your blog see it. (If the comment isn't approved and published, however, this link won't work. See "Viewing and changing comment status" later in this chapter for details on approval.)

The final tidbit of information displayed for each comment entry is a link based on the title of the post the commenter commented on. When you click this link, it doesn't take you to the post, but to the menu shown in **Figure 8.6**.

Improving your Word....
Posted: 4 days ago
Edit this post
View all comments on this post
Close comments on this post
View published post

Figure 8.6 The action menu for a comment.

This menu lists several actions you can take on the post in question:

- **Edit This Post** takes you to the post composition screen.

- **View All Comments on This Post** applies a filter to the comments list.

- **Close Comments on This Post/Open Comments on This Post** is a toggle command that closes or opens comments.

- **View Published Post** is a link to the post on your blog.

Viewing and changing comment status

At the right end of each comment listing is an icon that indicates the comment's status:

Approved. This comment is live and viewable in your blog.

Not published. You can approve this comment so that it appears in your blog, or you can mark it as spam or delete it.

 Spam. TypePad thinks, for whatever reason, that this comment is spam. You can publish it manually or delete it. After two weeks, TypePad automatically deletes any comment that's marked as spam.

To change a comment's status, click its status icon to open the status menu (**Figure 8.7**), which allows you to publish, unpublish, delete, or mark the comment as spam.

 **Figure 8.7** You can take four actions on each comment.

Be sure to mark as spam only those comments that look like actual spam—that is, a bunch of random words or short phrases with a link to a random Web site. Why? TypePad keeps track of all the comments you mark as spam so that it can do a better job of catching spam in the future. Marking legitimate comments as spam will lead to false positives. Just delete or unpublish comments that you don't want showing up in your blog.

Performing bulk operations on comments

At the bottom of the Comments page, you'll find buttons that perform the available bulk operations (**Figure 8.8**). Each comment has a check box next to it, and the check box at the bottom of the page selects all the comments on the page. If you want to include comments in a bulk operation, perhaps to delete a bunch of spam comments, just select the check boxes of the comments you want to act on and then click the appropriate bulk-action button.

 **Figure 8.8** Click these buttons to publish, unpublish, delete, and spam-mark multiple comments at the same time.

Editing comments

Clicking the Edit link displayed for each comment entry takes you to the Edit Comment page (**Figure 8.9**). You can change just about everything about a comment here, including the text of the comment, its author, the author's email address, and the URL used to leave the comment. Generally, you won't be changing any of these settings, but it's good to have that option.

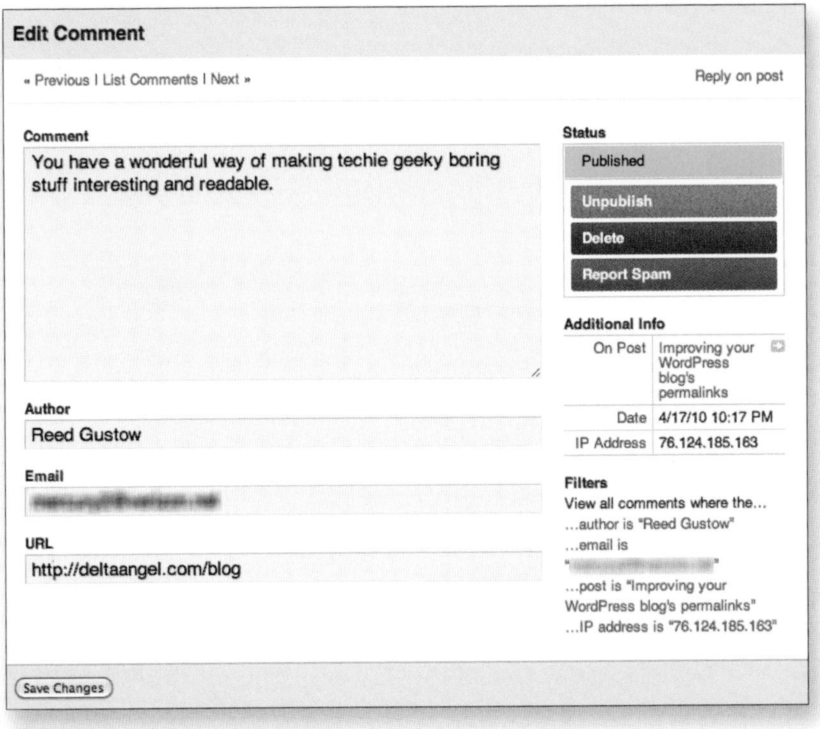

Edit Comment

« Previous I List Comments I Next »   Reply on post

Comment
You have a wonderful way of making techie geeky boring
stuff interesting and readable.

Status

| Published |
| Unpublish |
| Delete |
| Report Spam |

Additional Info

On Post | Improving your WordPress blog's permalinks

Author
Reed Gustow

Date | 4/17/10 10:17 PM
IP Address | 76.124.185.163

Email

Filters
View all comments where the...
...author is "Reed Gustow"
...email is

URL
http://deltaangel.com/blog

..."post is "Improving your
WordPress blog's permalinks"
...IP address is "76.124.185.163"

(Save Changes)

Figure 8.9 You can change anything about a comment in this page.

At the top of the page are a few links. Previous and Next let you cycle through your blog's comments, in case you're mass-editing comments (see the preceding section). The List Comments link takes you back to the comments list, and Reply on Post works just like the Reply link in individual comments. (Reply on Post is active only for published comments, because you can't reply to comments that aren't public.)

The right side of the page lists the comment's current status. Clicking any of the buttons below the comment status performs the labeled action. If you're viewing a comment that isn't published, the Unpublish button will be a Publish button.

The Additional Info section lists...well, some additional information about the comment: a link to the post in question, the date and time of the comment, and the commenter's IP address.

The final section lists a few filters that you can apply right from the Edit Comment page. Clicking any of those filters displays a list of comments that meet the parameters of that filter: all comments by the same author, all comments associated with the comment author's email address, all comments left for the same post, and all comments sent from the same IP address.

When you're happy with your changes in this page, click the Save Changes button.

Edit Comments Carefully

I've found that editing comments can be a slippery slope. When I leave a comment on someone's blog, I expect it to be published untouched or not published at all.

You risk losing your audience's trust if someone finds that the text of his comment has been altered—especially if you change the meaning of a comment through a well-intentioned edit. I've been tempted to edit comments to correct a spelling error or a slight grammatical mistake, but if I start editing comments, where do I draw the line? That's why I have a strict no-editing policy when it comes to comments.

That's not to say that commenters should be allowed to say whatever they want. Your blog is your blog, so you should feel free to delete abusive, profane, or off-topic comments as you like.

Monitoring Trackbacks

The second item in the blue navigation menu on the Comments page (refer to Figure 8.1) is Trackbacks (which TypePad displays as *TrackBacks*). Choose that option to open the Trackbacks page (**Figure 8.10**), where you handle all your trackback-management needs if you have trackbacks enabled for your blog.

Figure 8.10 TypePad's Trackbacks page.

note Trackbacks need to be managed more closely than comments do because spammers use them more often.

Filtering and searching for trackbacks

You can filter and search for trackbacks, just as you can for comments. The Show drop-down menu at the top of the page lets you display recent, unpublished, published, or spam trackbacks (**Figure 8.11**). Notice how many spam trackbacks show up in Figure 8.11. This is why I suggest that you disable trackbacks.

Figure 8.11 Trackback filter options.

The Search link, to the right of the Show menu, allows you to search your trackbacks based on several criteria: the blog that sent the trackback, the title of the trackback (which is the title of the blog post from which the trackback originated), and the sender's IP address (**Figure 8.12**).

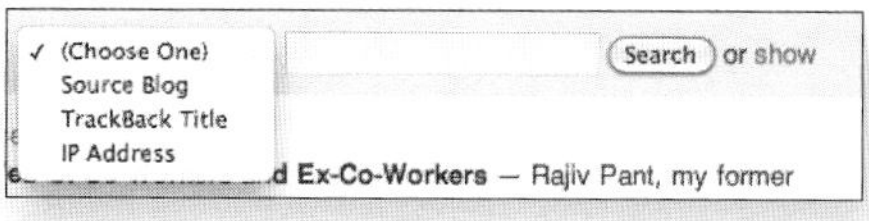

Figure 8.12 Searching trackbacks via source blog, trackback title, and IP address.

In the list of search results, TypePad displays trackbacks in reverse chronological order, with the most recent ones listed at the top. For each trackback, you see the name of the blog that sent it, the title of the trackbacked post, a short excerpt from that post, and the date when the trackback was sent.

Managing trackbacks

In the list of search results, the name of the trackbacking blog and the title of your post look like links, but they aren't. If you click either of those "links," you'll get a menu that provides a few options.

Clicking the blog's name, for example, produces the menu shown in **Figure 8.13**.

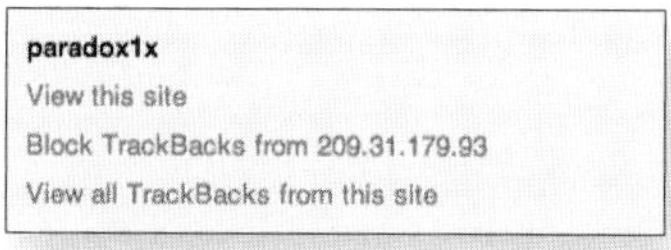

Figure 8.13 Details about the blog that sent the trackback.

This menu offers these options:

- **View This Site** links back to the site that sent the trackback.

- **Block Trackbacks from xxx.xx.xxx.xx** blocks all trackbacks from this particular IP address. This feature is useful for preventing spammers from sending spurious trackbacks to your blog.

- **View All Trackbacks from This Site** applies a filter to your trackbacks, limiting the display to trackbacks from the selected site.

If, instead of clicking the blog's name, you click the title of the post that received the trackback, the menu shown in **Figure 8.14** appears.

Figure 8.14 Actions you can take on the post that received the trackback.

First, you see the date on which the entry was posted. Then you can choose to do any of three things:

- Edit the post.

- View all the trackbacks on the post.

- Close trackbacks on the post.

Each trackback also has a publishing status, which you can change by clicking its status icon. These icons are identical to the status icons for comments (refer to "Viewing and changing comment status" earlier in this chapter). You can also apply bulk changes to your trackbacks by selecting the check boxes of the ones you want to change and then clicking one of the four bulk-operation buttons (Publish, Unpublish, Delete, and Mark As Spam; refer to Figure 8.8).

Blocking Unwelcome Comments

TypePad does a great job of catching most spammers, but some will still slip through. The Block List feature allows you to ban certain people from leaving comments or trackbacks on your blog and to create a list of words and phrases that aren't allowed in comments. Choose the Block List command—the final item in the blue navigation menu on the Comments page—to open the Block List page (**Figure 8.15**).

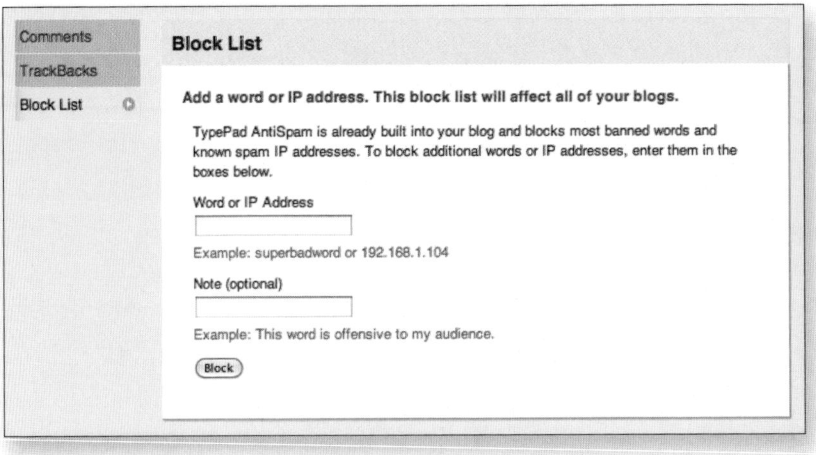

| Comments |
| TrackBacks |
| Block List |

Block List

Add a word or IP address. This block list will affect all of your blogs.

TypePad AntiSpam is already built into your blog and blocks most banned words and known spam IP addresses. To block additional words or IP addresses, enter them in the boxes below.

Word or IP Address

Example: superbadword or 192.168.1.104

Note (optional)

Example: This word is offensive to my audience.

(Block)

Figure 8.15 The Block List page allows you to ban specific people and words from the comments section of your blog.

Blocking a word or address

Here's how it works:

1. In the Word or IP Address field, enter a word or address to block.

    You can even enter an email address or Web-site URL.

2. In the Note field, describe why you're adding this word or address to your block list.

3. Click the Block button.

That's it. TypePad will block whatever you wanted to be blocked. Thereafter, whenever anyone sends a comment to your blog, TypePad checks your block list and marks the comment as spam if it contains anything that's also in your block list. Spam comments aren't published to your blog, but you can look at them in the Comments page (refer to "Filtering comments" earlier in this chapter).

Unblocking a word or address

Directly below the entry form in the Block List page (refer to Figure 8.15) is the Blocked Words and IP Addresses section (**Figure 8.16**).

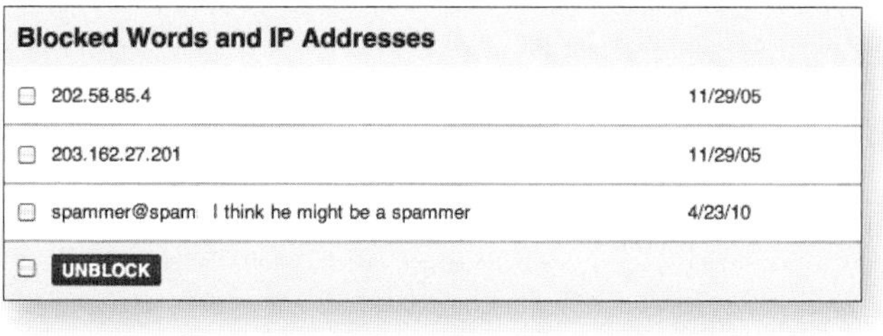

Blocked Words and IP Addresses

☐ 202.58.85.4		11/29/05
☐ 203.162.27.201		11/29/05
☐ spammer@spam I think he might be a spammer		4/23/10
☐ **UNBLOCK**		

Figure 8.16 The Blocked Words and IP Addresses section displays the items in your block list.

Below this list, you'll notice a red Unblock button. If you decide that you want to unblock something that you've blocked, select the check box next to that item (or items) and then click the Unblock button. Commenters can once again post comments using that phrase or originating from that IP address.

9

Designing Your Blog with Themes

The most important factor in your blog's success is compelling content. Despite common wisdom, however, many people *do* judge a book by its cover—and that's where your blog's design comes in. In TypePad, blog design is controlled by *themes*, which dictate color scheme, how the content is laid out, and what information is displayed about you and your posts.

This chapter covers all three of the theme options available for TypePad blogs: stock themes, Theme Builder, and Advanced Templates. This chapter also shows you how to manage your themes after you've gathered a few of your own.

Working in the Design Page

The Design tab in your blog's navigation bar (**Figure 9.1**) is your gateway to making your design stand out.

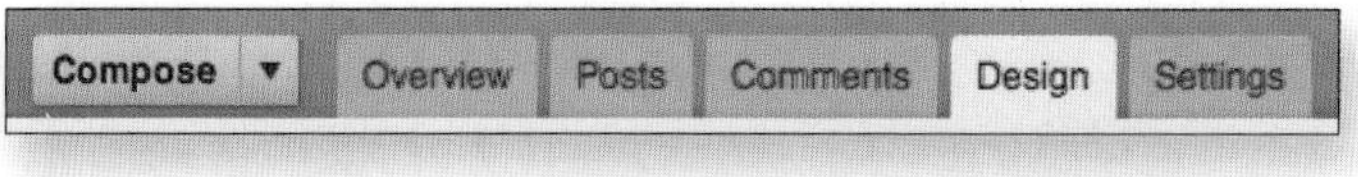

Figure 9.1 Click this tab to control the look and feel of your blog.

When you click the Design tab, TypePad takes you to the Design page for your blog (**Figure 9.2**). This page shows you what design is currently applied to your blog, lists options that you can set for the current design, gives you the choice to create your own design, and displays the designs that are applied to other blogs in your TypePad account and the custom designs you've created.

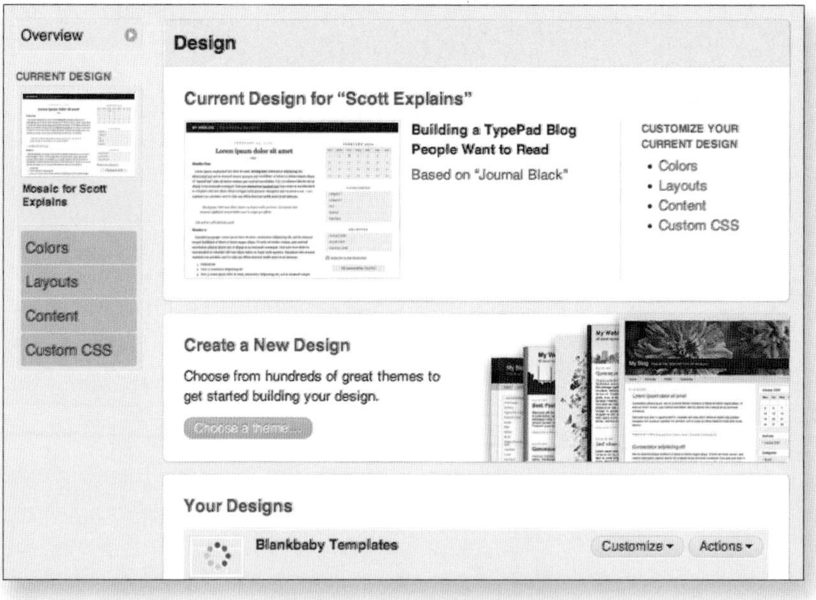

Figure 9.2 The Design page provides a few useful features.

Browsing the stock themes

The first thing you'll want to do is browse the available stock themes. In the Create a New Design section, click the Choose a Theme button to open a page titled Choose a Theme for Your New Design (**Figure 9.3**). For the sake of brevity, I call this page the *theme browser*.

Figure 9.3 The theme browser shows all the themes that TypePad has to offer.

The navigation menu on the left side of the theme browser has two sections: Themes and Categories (**Figure 9.4**).

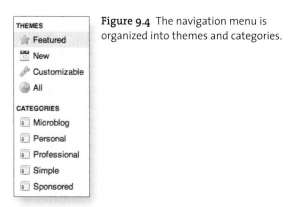

Figure 9.4 The navigation menu is organized into themes and categories.

Browsing by theme

The Themes section of the navigation menu breaks the available themes into four groups:

- **Featured.** This group includes themes that TypePad is featuring, for whatever reason. Featured themes may be popular, may include cool exclusive features, or may just strike the fancy of the kind folks at TypePad.

- **New.** This group is pretty obvious, containing the newest themes.

- **Customizable.** When you click this group name, you get two choices: Theme Builder and Advanced Templates (**Figure 9.5**). Each option allows you to create custom themes. I cover both Theme Builder and Advanced Templates later in this chapter.

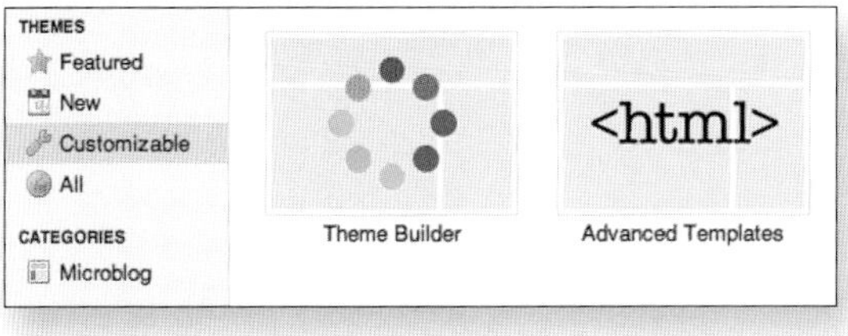

Figure 9.5 Theme Builder and Advanced Templates give you more control of your theme.

- **All.** If you want to scroll through all the available themes, this group is the one for you.

Browsing by category

Below the Themes section is the Categories section, which lists the following groups:

- **Microblog.** *Microblogs* are blogs geared toward sharing ephemera— links, images, and things of that nature. They generally have a two-column layout, with the first column showcasing content and the second column listing contact info and social-media accounts.

- **Personal.** These themes are a little more whimsical in nature, though depending on your business or professional persona, you may find a theme in this group that suits your blog nicely.

- **Professional.** TypePad considers these themes to look professional enough for business use. (They don't feature unicorns or kittycats.)

- **Simple.** Simple is the way I tend to go, because there's no need to let the design distract from the content. If you're a visual designer or an artist looking to set up a portfolio site, however, you may want something a little flashier.

- **Sponsored.** From time to time, TypePad works with companies or media properties to create a special sponsored theme. At this writing (spring 2010), the only sponsored theme available is Avatar.

Viewing theme thumbnails

The center section of the theme browser (refer to Figure 9.3) displays thumbnail images of all the themes included in whichever category is selected in the navigation menu. **Figure 9.6**, for example, shows themes in the Featured group, which I cover in "Browsing by theme" earlier in this chapter. Each theme's thumbnail image gives you an idea of what your blog might look like with this theme applied.

Figure 9.6 Thumbnail views of nine themes.

 The thumbnails aren't based on your blog's content; they're simply examples.

Previewing a theme

When you find a theme that you like in the theme browser, click its thumbnail. TypePad displays more information about that theme on the right side of the page (**Figure 9.7**). The thumbnail is enlarged a little so that you can get a better look at the theme. Below that image, you see the name and creator of the theme, followed by Choose and Preview buttons.

Figure 9.7 Detail view of the Chroma theme.

Go ahead and click the Preview button. TypePad previews the selected theme by displaying what your most recent blog post would look like with this theme applied (**Figure 9.8**). If you haven't posted yet, the preview won't include any post text, so you won't get a true feel of what the theme will look like populated with content. A banner at the top of the theme browser lets you preview all the other themes in the same category.

Figure 9.8 Previewing a theme.

At the bottom of the detail view (refer to Figure 9.7) is some important information about the selected theme: its features. You can apply a theme's features from within TypePad without fiddling with code of any kind, as I discuss in "Working with modules" later in this chapter.

Choosing a theme

When you've found a theme that you like, just click the green Choose button (refer to Figure 9.8). I'm going to use the Mosaic theme for Scott Explains because I like the way it looks and because it allows me to upload a custom banner. (I'm all about the branding.) If you're still undecided, click Go Back and browse the other available themes to your heart's content.

 tip   Be sure to choose a theme that reflects what you're trying to do with your blog. If you want to project a fun, relaxed image, you should pick one of the lighter themes. If you plan to blog about serious issues or business, a muted theme would be appropriate.

After you click Choose, TypePad opens an Overview page displaying the new theme (**Figure 9.9**). Don't worry—the new theme won't be applied to your blog until you select the Apply This Design to *yourblog* check box and click the Save Changes button.

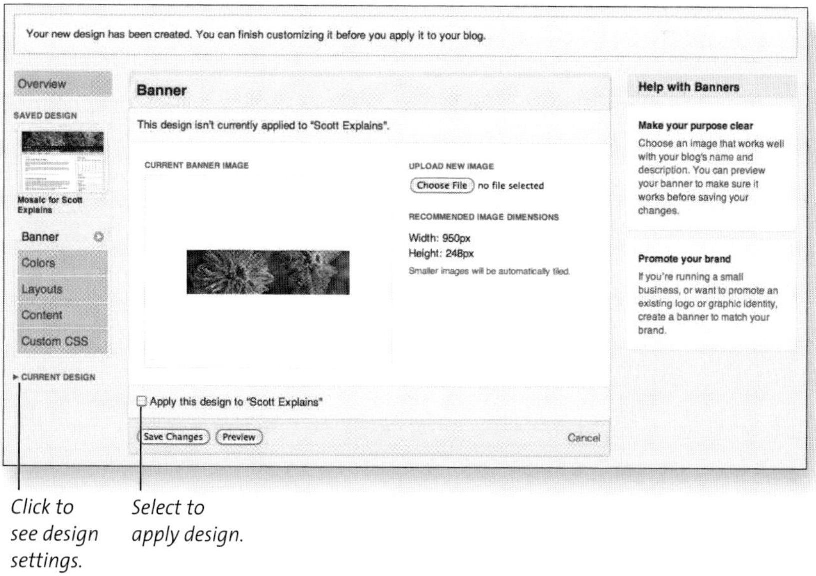

Click to see design settings.   Select to apply design.

Figure 9.9 The theme isn't applied until you check this box and click Save Changes.

tip You can see the design settings at any time by clicking the Current Design link at the bottom of the navigation menu.

If you just want to see how the settings will look without applying them to your live blog, click the Preview button to see a preview. Click the Cancel link to cancel out of the theme you've selected, if you want; then you can go ahead and select another one.

After you've chosen and applied a theme, you can customize it, as I explain in the following sections.

Viewing Theme Options

Each built-in TypePad theme has several features that you can change to customize the theme for your own use. Keep in mind, however, that not every theme has the same options. Mosaic, for example, allows you to set a custom header from within TypePad, but some other themes don't. When a theme doesn't offer a particular customization, such as a custom banner, that feature doesn't show up in the blue navigation menu on the left side of the Overview page (**Figure 9.10**).

Figure 9.10 A theme's navigation menu.

In the following sections, I delve into the options that are available for the Mosaic theme because they're available for the majority of TypePad's built-in themes.

Banner

A banner is a great way to brand your blog, so if you have a logo or some other image that you want to associate with your content, think about using a custom banner. (If you don't apply a custom banner, TypePad will use a default image.)

Mosaic allows you to set a custom banner for your blog, so you have a Banner option in the navigation menu. Choose it to open the Banner page (**Figure 9.11**). (Keep in mind that different themes have different options that you can set, so if you aren't using Mosaic, you may not have a Banner option available to you.)

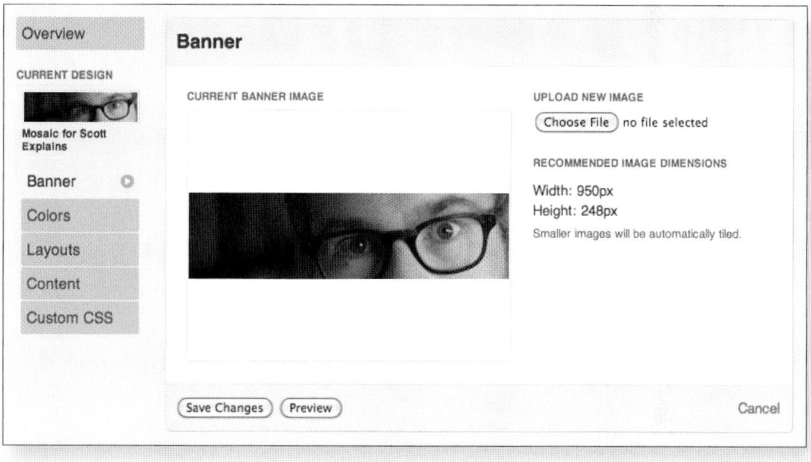

Overview	**Banner**	

CURRENT DESIGN

Mosaic for Scott Explains

| Banner ○ |
| Colors |
| Layouts |
| Content |
| Custom CSS |

CURRENT BANNER IMAGE

UPLOAD NEW IMAGE

(Choose File) no file selected

RECOMMENDED IMAGE DIMENSIONS

Width: 950px
Height: 248px

Smaller images will be automatically tiled.

(Save Changes) (Preview)   Cancel

Figure 9.11 The Mosaic theme allows you to set a custom banner image.

If your theme allows for a custom banner, the dimensions that you should use will be displayed in the Banner page. (For the Mosaic theme, the banner image should be 950 pixels wide and 248 pixels tall, as you see in Figure 9.11.) Images smaller than the recommended dimensions will be tiled to fill the space of the banner.

 note Be sure to keep your banner on the small side, because this image will be loaded on all your blog's pages.

Colors

When optional colors are available for a theme, the Colors option is available in the Overview page's navigation menu. When you choose it, the Colors page opens (**Figure 9.12**). As you see in Figure 9.12, Mosaic features a light and dark version; I'm partial to the light version.

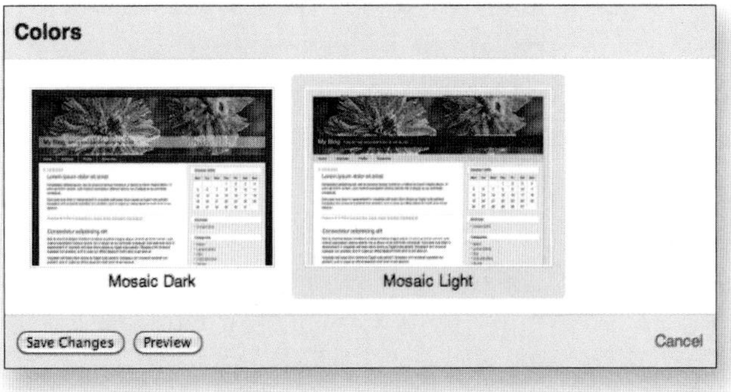

Figure 9.12 Color options for the Mosaic theme.

Layouts

Most themes provide several layout options. If your selected theme does, choose Layouts in the navigation menu to open the Layouts page (**Figure 9.13**). This page is where you decide how you want your blog's content to be laid out. Do you want one big column or three columns, for example? You get the idea.

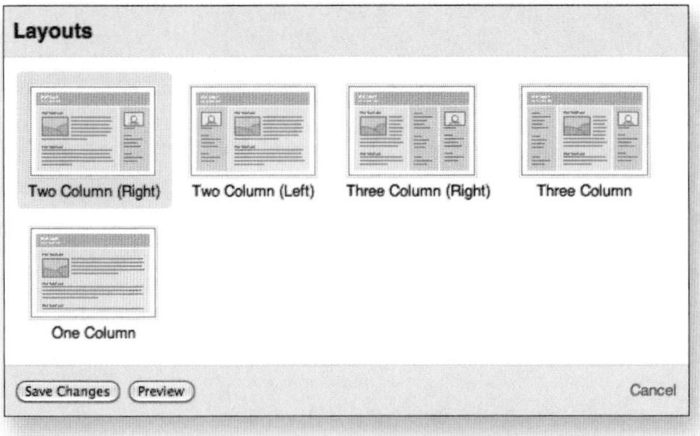

Figure 9.13 Many themes offer different layouts.

If you aren't sure how many columns would be best, don't be afraid to experiment. That's what the Preview button is for. Select a layout and click Preview to see what the blog will look like. Don't like the layout? Click the Cancel link and pick another layout option.

Content

Choose Content from the navigation menu to access the Content page, which gives you control of the content that fills the beautiful blog container you've chosen (its theme).

You can customize your blog's content in several ways, so this part of the design interface deserves its own section. I cover this page in more detail in "Displaying Content with a Default TypePad Theme" later in this chapter.

Custom CSS

This option enables you to use custom CSS (Cascading Style Sheets) for your blog design and is available only if you have a TypePad Pro Unlimited account or higher.

> **note** CSS is beyond the scope of this book, but you can find out more in *CSS3: Visual QuickStart Guide*, 5th Edition, by Jason Cranford Teague (Peachpit Press).

When you're happy with all your theme settings, click Save Changes. TypePad applies the theme, along with your settings, to your blog. Then it takes you back to the Overview page, where a yellow alert informs you that the theme has been applied and provides a link to your blog (**Figure 9.14**).

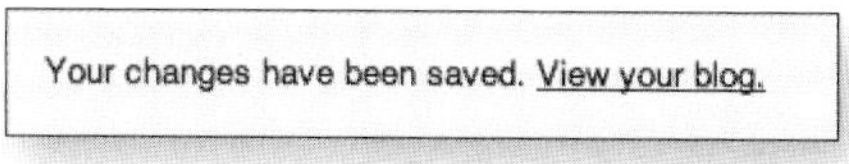

Your changes have been saved. View your blog.

Figure 9.14 Your design changes have been saved. Hurrah!

Displaying Content with a Default TypePad Theme

Up until this point, you've been able to change a few aspects of your chosen stock theme. Perhaps you've set a custom banner or changed the color scheme. But what about the real meat of any blog: the content?

As you might guess, the Content page of the theme editor (**Figure 9.15**) has a host of options that allow you to control how and where content appears in your blog's theme.

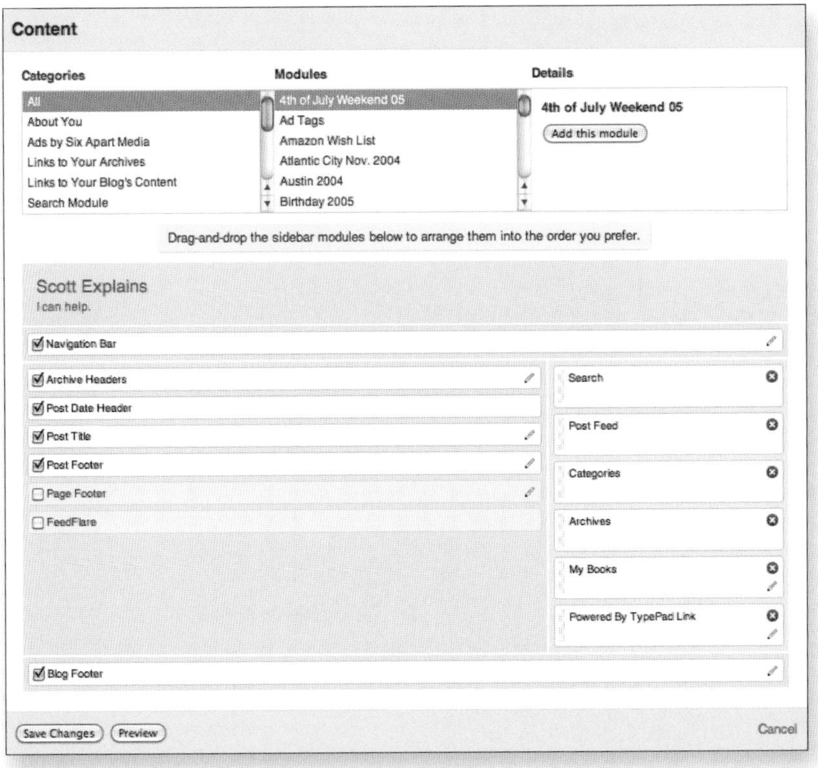

Figure 9.15 The Content page is where you decide what content to display where.

Working with modules

The first thing you see in this page is the module browser (**Figure 9.16**).

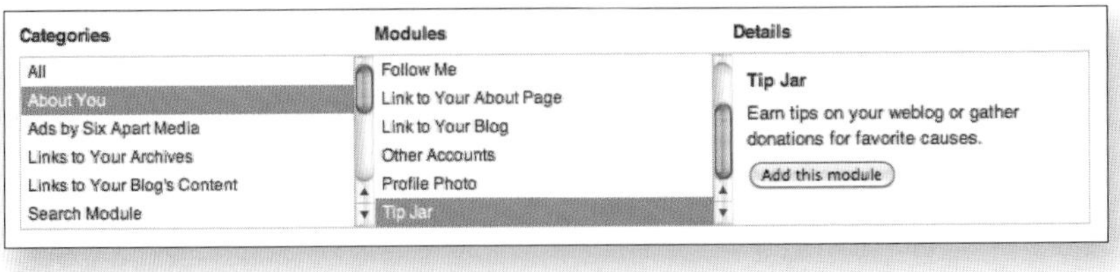

Figure 9.16 Modules allow you to add even more content to your blog.

Modules let you add all types of content—everything from search boxes to links—to your blog's *sidebars* (defined in "Adding a module" later in this chapter) without having to code a single thing. What if you're using a one-column layout? The module is displayed at the bottom of your blog.

Browsing the modules

TypePad offers too many modules for me to delve into each of them in this book, but as you can see in Figure 9.16, your choices are categorized, which makes it easy to find a module that can do what you need it to do. Want to add a link to your Amazon.com Wish List, for example? Chances are that this module will be listed in the About You category (and it is!).

Whenever you select a module in the browser, the Details column tells you a little bit about what the selected module does. Figure 9.16, for example, shows you a little information about the Tip Jar module, which allows your readers to send you money via PayPal if they want to show their appreciation for all your hard work. (If you're running a business blog, of course, this module probably isn't for you.)

> **tip** In the Categories list, you'll find a category of modules called widgets, which allow you to embed third-party functionality in your blog. Check out www.sixapart.com/typepad/widgets to find widgets for your blog. These widgets work just like the modules built into TypePad.

Adding a module

Click the Add This Module button in the module browser, and either of two things will happen:

- The module will be added to the section that represents your blog's layout.

  or

- Module options will appear (**Figure 9.17**, on the next page) so that you can set them before you add the module to your blog. Don't worry— you can change these options after you add the module, too. Read on to find out how!

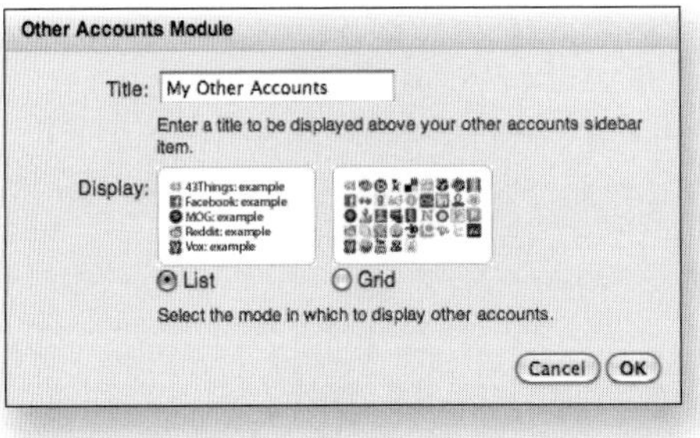

Other Accounts Module

Title: My Other Accounts

Enter a title to be displayed above your other accounts sidebar item.

Display:
43Things: example
Facebook: example
MOG: example
Reddit: example
Vox: example

○ List   ○ Grid

Select the mode in which to display other accounts.

Cancel   OK

Figure 9.17 The Other Accounts Module dialog box has some settings that you can specify. Each module offers different settings.

The various modules at your disposal can be added to your theme in several places, depending on how many columns you have in your layout. The only time you can add modules to a blog's main content column, however, is when it's the only column in your blog. Otherwise, modules always go in secondary (or tertiary) columns called *sidebars*.

Editing a module

Some modules have configuration options. To reveal those options, just click the Edit button, which looks like a pencil (**Figure 9.18**). You can also change the order of modules by dragging the module you want to move. Release the mouse button when you have the module in the position where you want it. If you have more than two columns in your blog's layout, you can even drag modules from one column to another.

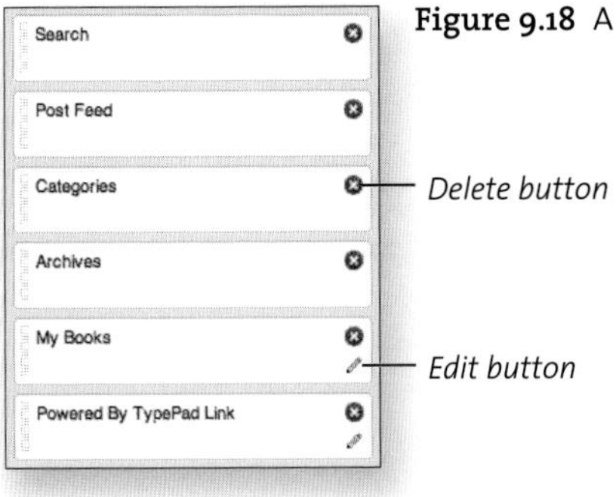

Search   ⊗

Post Feed   ⊗

Categories   ⊗——— *Delete button*

Archives   ⊗

My Books   ⊗
                              ✎——— *Edit button*

Powered By TypePad Link   ⊗
                              ✎

Figure 9.18 A bunch of modules, all in a row.

tip   To delete a module that you've added yourself, click the red X button next to that module.

Tweaking the layout

Right below the module browser, you'll see a display that mimics your blog's layout (refer to Figure 9.15). You can use this area to rearrange your modules, change their settings, and determine how your blog posts are displayed. Simply select the check box for each element you want to use, and if you see an Edit button (pencil icon) for a selected element, click that button to tinker with its settings. When you finish, click the Save Changes button in the Content page to save your changes.

I cover the layout elements individually in the following sections.

Navigation bar

The *navigation bar* is the bar of links that's usually displayed above or below your blog's banner. Clicking the Navigation Bar item's Edit button in the Content page brings up the Navigation Bar Configuration dialog box (**Figure 9.19**). You have two radio-button options here: Simple and Advanced.

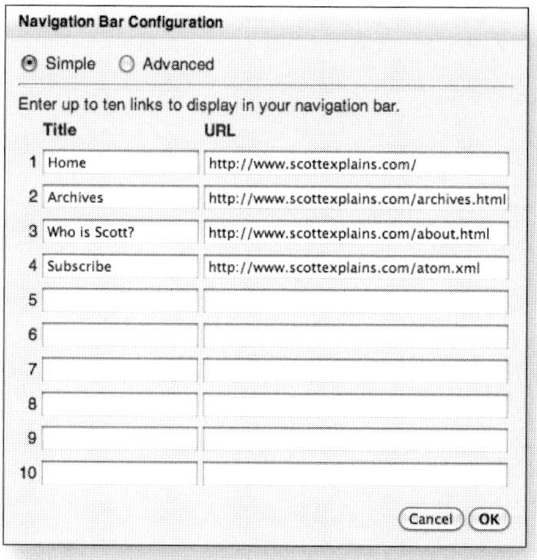

Figure 9.19 You can add links to your blog's navigation bar here.

If you don't know HTML, I suggest choosing Simple; then all you have to do is enter up to ten titles and URLs in the text fields. Each of these entries becomes a link in your navigation bar.

Figure 9.19 shows a few links that I want to have in my navigation bar. First, I want a Home link so that no matter where people land in my blog, they can always get to the main page. (Smart, right?) Second, I have a link to my archives so that folks can delve into all that great content I've built up. The third link goes to the About Me page for my blog. I'm calling it Who Is Scott? because the Scott Explains blog is personality-driven, and people may want to know a thing or two about me. (All you need to know about me is this: I'm awesome, and I don't like string beans.) The final link points to my blog's Atom feed, because I want readers to be subscribers.

When everything is set up, click OK to save your changes and create your navigation bar (**Figure 9.20**).

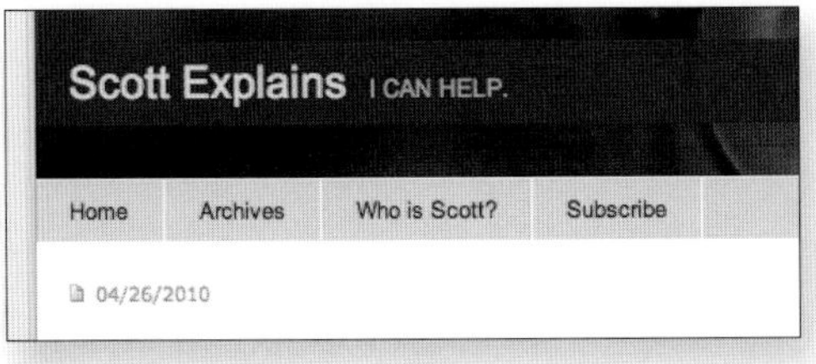

Figure 9.20 An example of a navigation bar, with the settings applied from Figure 9.19.

If you're comfortable with HTML, choose the Advanced option and enter whatever HTML you want to use. Remember that this code will be executed on every page of your blog.

Archive headers

The next things you can configure are your blog's archive headers. All your past posts make up your blog's archives, and the Archive Headers settings determine the appearance of the individual category- and date-based archive pages. That is, your main archive page links to subpages that display all the posts in a certain category or posted on a certain month.

To change the default settings, click the Archive Headers item's Edit button to open the Archive Headers Configuration dialog box (**Figure 9.21**). Make the appropriate choices (which are straightforward) from the Date-Based Archives and Category Archives drop-down menus, and then click OK.

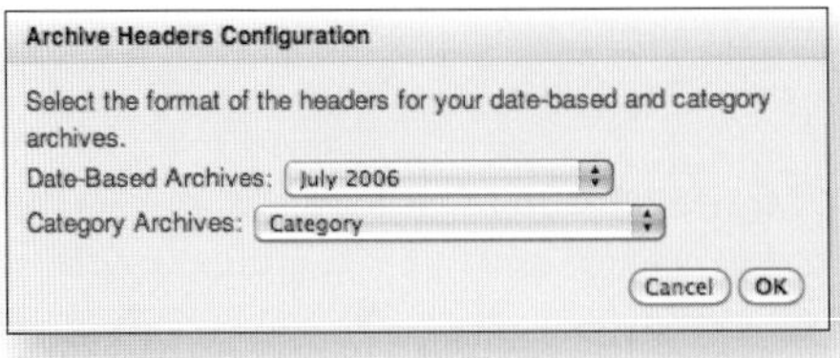

Figure 9.21 Control freaks are welcome in TypePad. Here, you can specify the date format of your archive headers.

Post date header

TypePad can display a header on your blog's index page automatically, showing the date when an entry was posted. (If you post more than one entry on the same day, all those entries are grouped below the same date header.) The Post Date Header setting determines whether this header is displayed: yes if the item is checked, no if it's unchecked. This item has no other options.

Post title

The Post Title Configuration dialog box (to open it, select Post Title and click its Edit button) allows you to display an author picture next to an entry's title—obviously, a pic of the person who wrote the entry. If you're the only blogger posting on your blog, this setting might be a little bit of overkill unless you're unusually attractive, as I am.

Post footer

Each post has a footer, and that's exactly what the Post Footer Configuration dialog box (**Figure 9.22**) allows you to configure. (You know the drill now: To get there, select the Post Footer item's check box and then click its Edit button.)

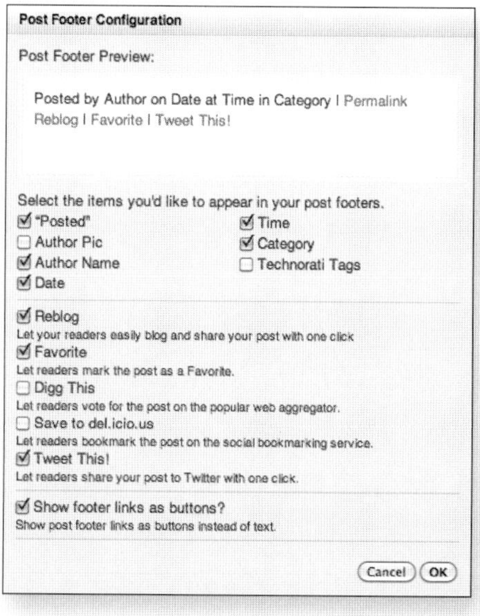

Figure 9.22 The settings in this dialog box control what appears at the bottom of every one of your posts.

In the first check-box section of the dialog box, check the options that you want to appear at the bottom of every one of your posts; TypePad previews them for you in the Post Footer Preview window at the top of the dialog box. I like to include Author Name, Date, and Time at the very least. Selecting Category adds a link to the category archive, allowing readers to dive deeper into a category if they want to.

The options in the second check-box section are all about letting people share your posts in a variety of ways. Reblog and Favorite are both TypePad–specific ways to share; Digg This, Save to del.icio.us (which is now known simply as Delicious), and Tweet This! allow people to share your post on those three social networks by clicking a button.

The final check box lets you display the links as fancy buttons or plain-Jane text links.

When you've configured everything to your liking, click OK. TypePad sets up your footer just the way you want it. **Figure 9.23** shows you what a footer looks like with the options set in Figure 9.22.

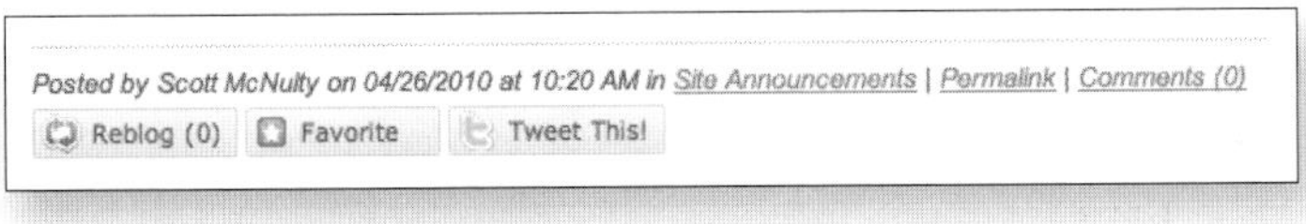

Posted by Scott McNulty on 04/26/2010 at 10:20 AM in Site Announcements | Permalink | Comments (0)
Reblog (0)   Favorite   Tweet This!

Figure 9.23 A post footer configured according to the settings in Figure 9.22.

Page footer

Pages can also have footers, though they're disabled by default. The only options available for the Page Footer item (select its check box and click its Edit button) are the social-media links (**Figure 9.24**). Select the ones you want and then click OK.

Figure 9.24 The Page Footer Configuration options for sharing.

FeedFlare

The FeedFlare item enables some FeedBurner options in your blog's feed. Check out Chapter 5 or www.feedburner.com for more details.

Blog footer

The blog footer is the final piece of your layout that you can configure. Think of a blog footer as being a navigation bar displayed at the bottom of your blog's pages.

Select the Blog Footer item's check box and click its Edit button to open the Footer Configuration dialog box (**Figure 9.25**). You'll see why I make that comparison: It looks exactly like the Navigation Bar Configuration dialog box (refer to Figure 9.19).

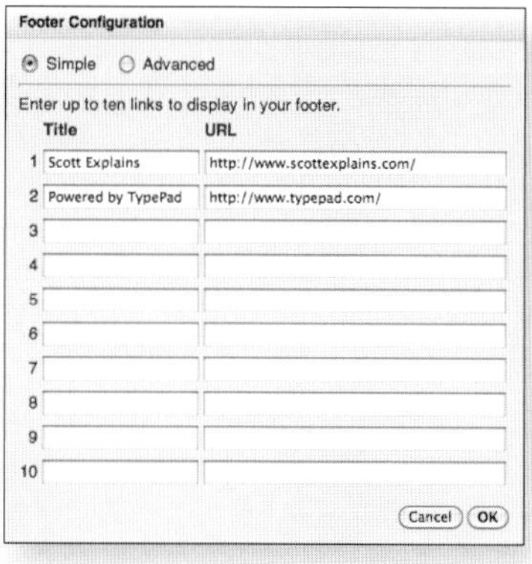

Figure 9.25 The blog-footer options should look familiar to you.

In Simple mode, you can add up to ten titles and URLs (though you can add a title without a link if you want to add copyright information). If you prefer, select Advanced mode instead and enter any HTML code you'd like to use.

Creating Your Own Theme with Theme Builder

If you want to have even more control of your blog's theme, Theme Builder is for you. To open it, choose Customizable from the theme browser's navigation menu (**Figure 9.26**, on the next page).

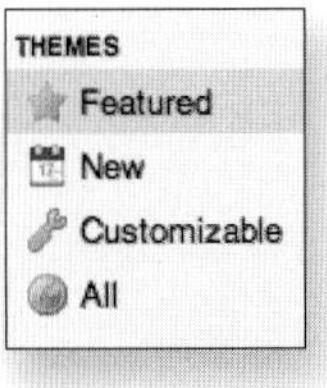

Figure 9.26 Choose Customizable from this menu to use Theme Builder.

Theme Builder (**Figure 9.27**) is just a long list of options, grouped in sections, that allows you to tweak each item displayed in your blog. Click the header of each section to reveal that section's options.

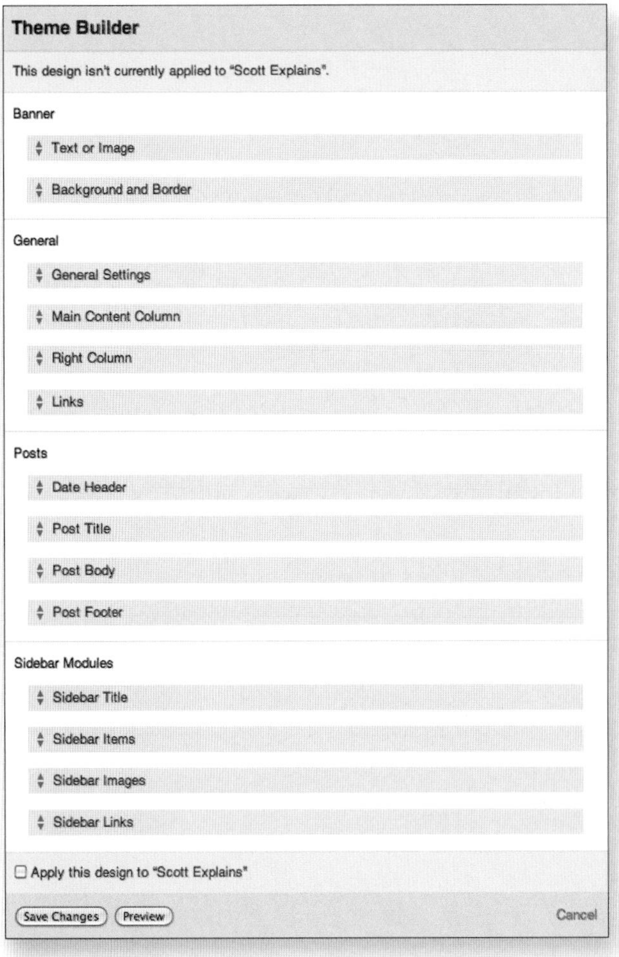

Figure 9.27 Theme Builder gives you many choices for your new theme.

I've found that the best way to create a theme with Theme Builder is to come up with a loose idea of the theme I want and then use Theme Builder to get as close as I can to that design. For Scott Explains, I'd like to have a custom banner and a two-column layout. The first column will contain the blog post, and the other will contain all the sidebar modules. I'd also like to use a large serif font and to use the color orange as much as possible.

In the following sections, I review Theme Builder's options, keeping in mind the preceding custom theme.

Banner

The banner is the first thing people see when they come to your blog, so you want it to stand out. You have a couple of options in Theme Builder (**Figure 9.28**).

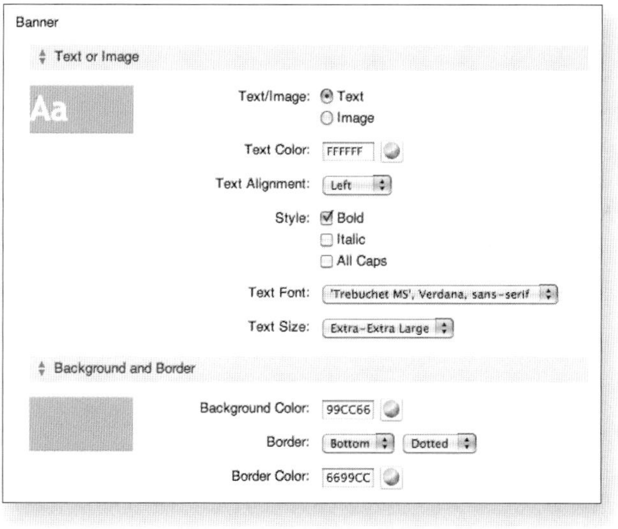

Figure 9.28 Available Banner settings in Theme Builder.

Text or Image

The first thing you have to decide is whether you want to go with a text banner or use an image (**Figure 9.29**, on the next page).

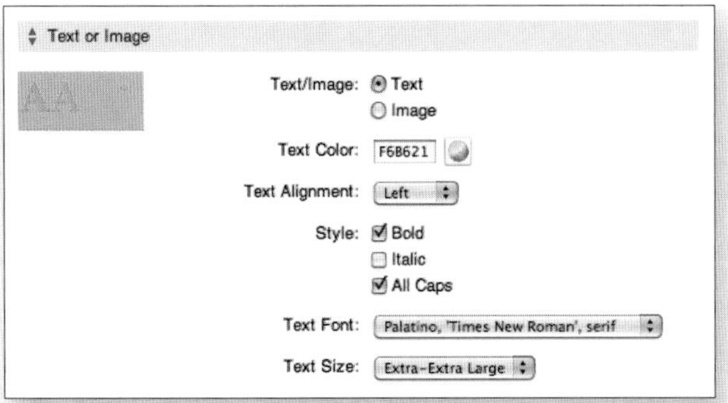

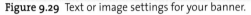

Figure 9.29 Text or image settings for your banner.

I suggest selecting Text, because this setting gives you a little more flexibility than the Image option. Using CSS, which is a method of applying styles to Web pages, you can create a custom banner behind the text. This method gives you the best of both worlds: text that is both clickable for your visitors and indexable by search engines, and a fancy custom image.

The text options include color (clicking the color wheel brings up a color selector), alignment (left is the common practice), and style (bolding is always a good idea, and I'm going to make my title all caps just for fun).

The final text settings are font and size. The Text Font drop-down menu lists several Web-safe fonts (meaning that most computers can display them), and the Text Size drop-down menu's options range from extra-small to extra-extra large. I'm going with Palatino, Times New Roman, and Serif at the extra-extra large size.

If you decide that you want to stick with an image for the banner, just select the Image radio button and upload your banner image.

note **If you select Image to use a custom image, keep in mind that your blog name and description (which you entered in the blog settings; see Chapter 5) won't be displayed. You have to make sure to have both of those pieces of information in the custom banner.**

Your choices are previewed right there in the Text or Image section. Clever!

Background and Border

You've told TypePad what you want to appear in the banner (either text or an image) and how you want it to appear. Now you need to set the background color and specify whether you want a border around part or all of the banner.

You have a few options for the border, which can run around the entire banner; run only on the right, left, bottom, or top side; or not appear at all. By default, TypePad gives you a solid border (you can also have a dashed or dotted border) at the bottom of your banner.

I'll set my banner background to be gray and have a solid orange border at the bottom.

General

The General section is where you set the options for the main layout of your blog. It's divided into four groups:

- **General Settings.** You have three options to set here: Background Color (for the entire page, not just the banner), Border (around the whole blog page), and Border Color (**Figure 9.30**).

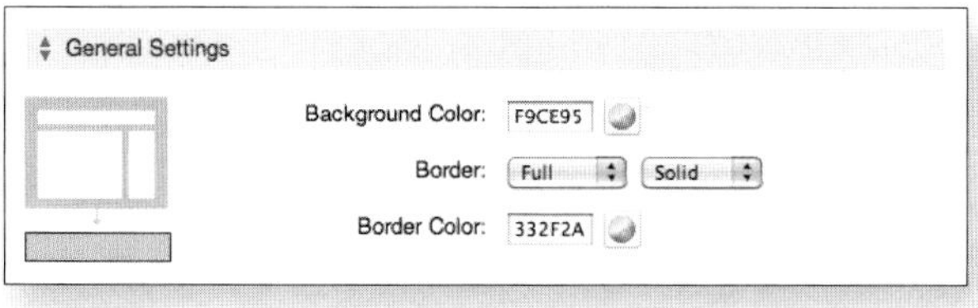

Figure 9.30 These settings apply to the whole blog.

The little box below the icon of a blog to the left of these options previews your color choices. (No, this theme isn't going to be pretty, but I'm sure that you're better at picking colors than I am!)

- **Main Content Column.** This column displays your posts (or the contents of your pages), so what you set here is pretty important (**Figure 9.31**, on the next page).

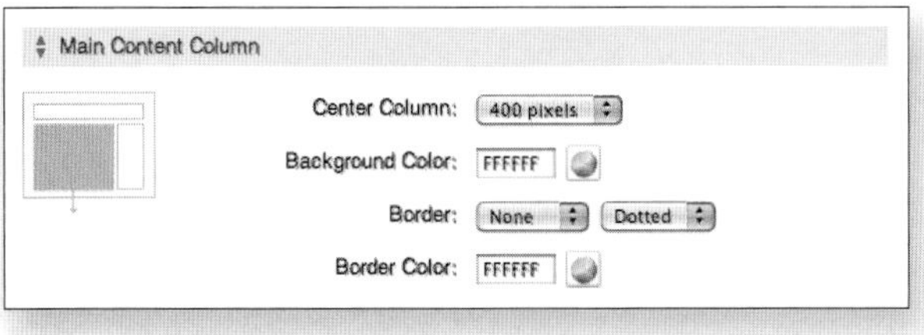

Figure 9.31 The Main Content Column options.

The most important setting here is Center Column. The drop-down menu provides a few options for setting the width of the main column: 300, 400, or 500 pixels, or fluid. The first three options are known as *fixed widths*, meaning that no matter the size of a visitor's browser window, the column will always be *x* pixels wide. *Fluid* just means that the column will resize itself according to the visitor's browser window.

I generally go with 500 pixels because my images usually are 500 pixels wide. (I think images that take up the entire width of a column are quite striking.)

- **Right Column.** The Right Column section (**Figure 9.32**) has the same basic options as the Main Content Column section but traditionally is the home of your sidebar modules. The width options are a little narrower, however, at 150, 200, or 300 pixels (which you add to the width of the main column to get the full width of your blog).

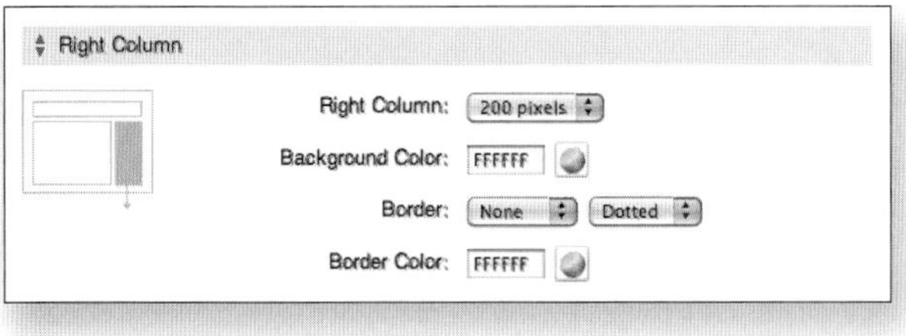

Figure 9.32 These settings affect your blog's right column, which houses your sidebar full of modules.

- **Links.** We're all familiar with links, but did you know that a link can find itself in any of four states? All these options are available to you in the Links section (**Figure 9.33**).

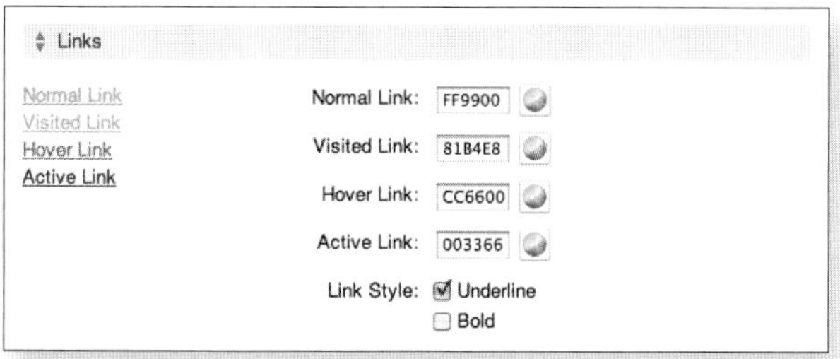

Figure 9.33 The Links settings.

The four states are

- **Normal.** A *normal* link is a link that hasn't been clicked yet. It's the default state of links in your blog.

- **Visited.** *Visited* links point to a site or post that the visitor has already been to (which is why they're usually displayed in a lighter color than normal links).

- **Hover.** Hovering over a link puts it in the *hover* state and often changes the color of the link (depending on the settings).

- **Active.** The *active* state is over before the visitor might register it. It's that moment after the user clicks the link but before the new page loads.

You can also set the color and style for each type of link. Customizing your links can be fun, but it's easy to go overboard by using wacky color combinations.

Posts

What's a blog without posts? Quiet, I suppose, but also a little boring. The Posts section controls how four aspects of your posts appear in this theme:

- **Date Header.** Posts are chronological, so your blog groups posts by date. Each day that includes a post (or posts) is signified by a date header in your blog. The Date Header section (**Figure 9.34**, on the next page) is where you control how that date header looks. You see all the by-now-familiar controls that have to do with text, allowing you to set the font, size, color, alignment, style, border, and border color.

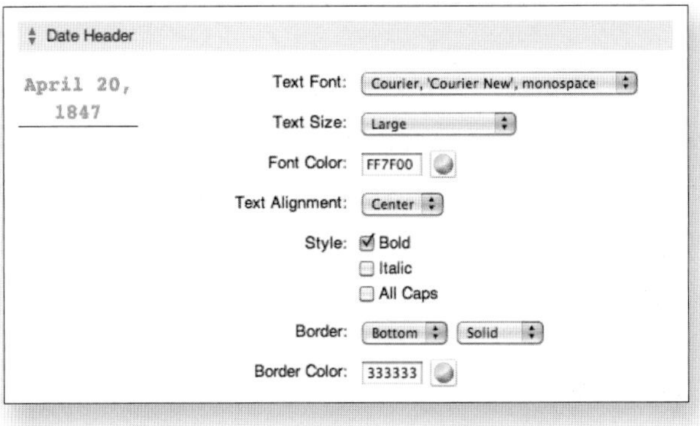

Date Header

April 20,
1847

Text Font:	Courier, 'Courier New', monospace
Text Size:	Large
Font Color:	FF7F00
Text Alignment:	Center
Style:	☑ Bold ☐ Italic ☐ All Caps
Border:	Bottom · Solid
Border Color:	333333

Figure 9.34 Date Header options let the date stand out,
or fade into the background, as much as you want.

- **Post Title.** You can style your post's titles to your heart's content. The
Post Title options are exactly the same as the Date Header options,
because they also involve text.

- **Post Body.** The meat of your post shows up in the post body, and all the
same text options are available in the Post Body section, with one addition: Line Spacing (**Figure 9.35**). If you want to keep your lines of text
close together, go for the Tight option; if you want to give them a little
breathing room, opt for Loose. Normal works fine in most cases if you
don't have a strong yearning either way.

Figure 9.35 The Line Spacing setting controls how much
white space is displayed between lines of text on your blog.

- **Post Footer.** The Page Footer section has all the text options that I've
already covered, as well as the border options. You'll probably want to
display a border on the top of the footer to act as a buffer between the
footer and the post.

Sidebar Modules

Finally, the sidebar needs some styling of its own. Most of the options in the Sidebar Modules section are identical to those in the other sections, because your sidebars generally are made up of text and links. Your options are

- **Sidebar Title.** Each sidebar module includes a title, which can be styled with the usual text controls.

- **Sidebar Items**. Items listed in the sidebar are sort of like blog posts, so it makes sense that you have the same options here as in the Post Body section (covered in the preceding section).

- **Sidebar Images.** Images can appear in a sidebar, so why not make them pop a little with a border? As you can see in **Figure 9.36**, the options dictating how the border appears are the same as those in the Border section, except that this border will appear around any images in your blog's sidebar. You also have a few new options here. You can set the border weight, or thickness, to normal, hairline (thin), or wide; you can also set the border's color and the alignment of images in it (right, left, or center).

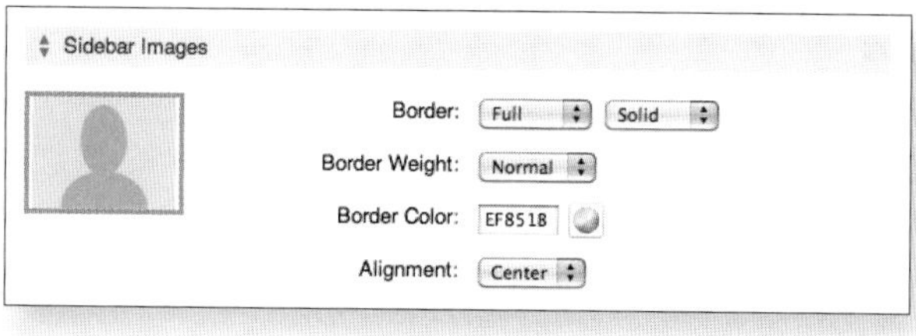

Figure 9.36 Sidebar images can have borders and can be aligned as you like them.

- **Sidebar Links.** You can make your sidebar links stand out by giving them different coloring from those in your posts.

Preview

When you've set everything in Theme Builder to your liking, click the Preview button to check out what your blog will look like with these settings (**Figure 9.37**, on the next page). Clearly, the theme I've designed won't win any awards, but it's unique.

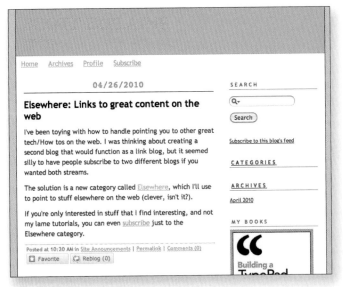

Figure 9.37 Here's a theme I built with Theme Builder. Did I mention that I'm not a designer?

Working with Advanced Templates

When you use one of TypePad's built-in themes or Theme Builder, you're shielded from having to deal directly with templates and tags. Modules and wizards allow you to change a theme without dealing with code; TypePad takes care of changing the code to reflect your changes.

If you're like the vast majority of TypePad users, the tweaks available for these two types of themes are all you need. Advanced Templates, however, are for those situations when you need total and complete access to the code.

What types of things can you do with Advanced Templates that just aren't possible any other way? I'm glad you asked:

- **Access the <head> section.** Web pages are coded in a language called HTML (for the most part). Many services allow you to add interesting bells and whistles to any Web page by using another programming language, called JavaScript. (Amazon.com has a service that automatically links book titles to Amazon product pages, for example.) Invariably, these services require you to place a snippet of code between the

<head> HTML tags at the top of your blog. Advanced Templates give you access to that code; the other theming options don't.

note Google Analytics is another example of a service that uses JavaScript in the head tag, though those clever people at TypePad will automatically handle this task for you. See Chapter 5 for details.

- **Integrate a TypePad blog into an existing Web site.** Let's say that you already have a robust Web site with a particular design. Wouldn't it be cool if your TypePad blog could have exactly the same design? You can make that happen with Advanced Templates.

tip Advanced Templates use a tag-based language. For more information about the available tags in TypePad, check out http://developer.typepad.com/tags. That page not only gives you a great idea of the scope of the available tags, but also includes some pointers on using them.

Getting to the Advanced Templates

OK, get ready to get your Advanced Templates on! To access this feature, follow these steps:

1. Click the Design tab in your blog's navigation bar to open the Design page (refer to Figure 9.2).

2. Click the Choose a Theme button to open the theme browser (refer to Figure 9.3).

3. Choose Customizable from the navigation menu.

   TypePad displays two icons in the body of the page: Theme Builder and Advanced Templates (refer to Figure 9.5).

4. Click the Advanced Templates icon.

   Much as you will with the default themes, you'll see some more information about Advanced Templates in the right column.

5. Click the green Choose button in the right column.

   Now you're looking at all the templates that TypePad thinks you should have available for your blog (**Figure 9.38**, on the next page).

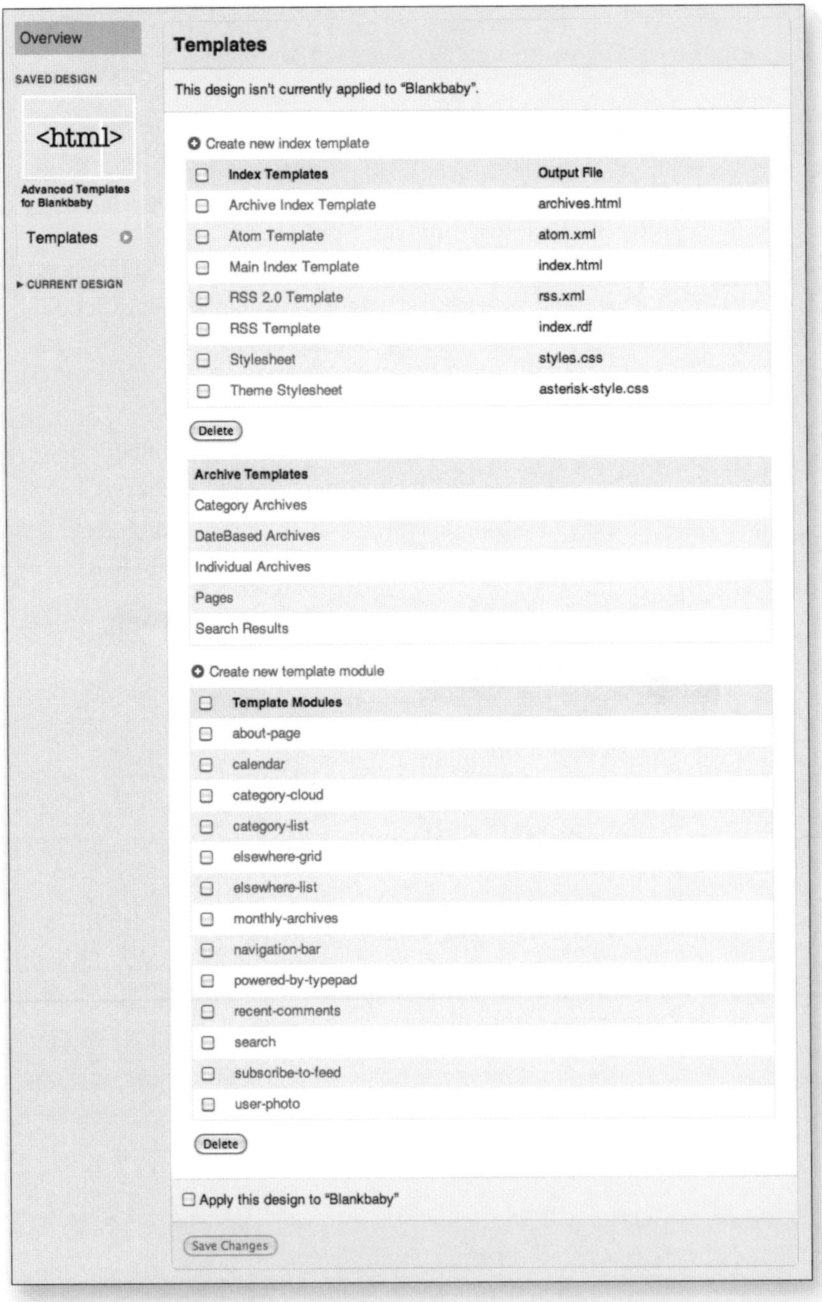

Figure 9.38 All the templates that are available to you when you use Advanced Templates.

The great thing about using Advanced Templates, though, is that you don't have to stick with the suggestions. In fact, you can delete every one of them and start from scratch, if you like.

Before I delve into what each template listed in Figure 9.38 does, I can tell you that you can apply this theme to your blog without any modification, and it would work (**Figure 9.39**).

Figure 9.39 A blog that has the default Advanced Template settings applied to it.

The templates are listed in three groups: Index Templates, Archive Templates, and Template Modules. I cover them all in the following sections.

Index Templates

Index templates control the appearance and contents of each index file in your blog. *Index files* include your main blog page (the one that lists your recent blog posts, for example) and the file that creates your blog's feed.

The table listing all the index templates in Figure 9.38 has two columns: Index Templates and Output File. In this case, these output files are—you guessed it—various index files in your blog.

Here are the default index templates and what they do:

- **Archive Index Template.** All your past posts make up your archives, which can be organized by date, category, or both. This template dictates how your archives appear.

- **Atom Template.** Several syndication formats allow people to subscribe to your blog; Atom is one of them. You can customize this template to create a custom syndication feed. If you want to include advertising in your feed, for example, you can add that here.

- **Main Index Template.** The *main index* is the page that folks get when they visit your URL. Usually, this page is a list of your recent posts or a static page (as I discuss in Chapter 7). Any modifications to this template will be applied to the main page of your blog.

- **RSS 2.0 Template** and **RSS Template.** RSS (*Really Simple Syndication*) is a syndication format that you can provide to your readers. The RSS 2.0 and RSS templates determine what items are included in your blog's feed. You can modify this template to include advertising, for example, or to limit the number of items that appear in your feed.

- **Stylesheet.** TypePad uses this template as a pointer to stylesheets that actually style your blog, which makes it easy to swap out stylesheets because you have to change only one file. You can use this template as your one and only stylesheet, though, if you like.

- **Theme Stylesheet.** By default, this template controls the way the theme looks. You can replace or modify this file to make the theme look any way you want, or you can select its check box and then click the Delete button to delete it.

Archive Templates

These templates can't be deleted, and you can't create new ones. What's the deal with that, hombre? These templates are required for your TypePad blog, so you can't get rid of them. You can customize them up the yin-yang, however.

The templates are

- **Category Archives.** This template is responsible for your category-based archives.

- **DateBased Archives.** If you want to change your date-based archives, this template is the one for you.

- **Individual Archives.** The name of this template is a little misleading, because it actually controls how each individual blog entry looks. Put another way, this template creates the page that's associated with an entry's permalink.

- **Pages.** This template controls the appearance of all your pages.

- **Search Results.** If you use TypePad's search widget (and I think you should), this template gives you control of the way the results look.

Template Modules

Template modules aren't full-blown templates, in that they aren't responsible for the layout and content of entire pages. Think of them as being snippets that you can use in other templates, much like the modules that you can drag and drop into TypePad's built-in themes (only without the dragging and dropping).

If you want to include one of these modules in one of the preceding templates (or in a module that you create yourself), just use this code, replacing `"module-name"` with the module you want to include:

```
<$MTInclude module="module-name"$>
```

The default modules are

- **about-page.** This module links to your About Me page.

- **calendar.** This module displays a calendar of your posts created in the current month. Each day on which you make a post is a link that points to the most recent post created on that date.

- **category-cloud.** This module displays a cluster of links to your category archives. The more posts you have in a particular category, the larger the text link is. Less-populated categories are displayed with smaller links.

- **category-list.** This module lists your categories in alphabetical order.

- **elsewhere-grid.** In this context, *elsewhere* means other accounts, which you should remember from setting up your TypePad account (see Chapter 2). This module displays a grid of your other accounts, using tiny icons from each service. It's a great way to link to lots of other accounts in a small amount of space.

- **elsewhere-list.** This module lists links to your other accounts.

- **monthly-archives.** This module creates a link to your archive page, as well as a list of links to the ten most recent monthly archive pages. You can have it list fewer or more months by changing the value of `lastn` in the code itself (the default is `10`).

- **navigation-bar.** This module is the stock navigation bar, which includes links to your home page, About Me page, archives, and feed (by default, Atom, though you can change this setting by editing the module).

- **powered-by-typepad.** Show your TypePad pride by using this module, which displays the phrase *Powered by TypePad* and links back to TypePad's Web site. (You could change it to read "I learned this by reading *Building a TypePad Blog People Want to Read*" and add a link that lets readers purchase a copy of this book. Just an idea.)

- **recent-comments.** This module lists links to the ten most recent comments left on your blog. As with the `monthly-archives` module, you can choose to display more or fewer links by modifying the value of `lastn`.

- **search.** This module displays a search box.

- **subscribe-to-feed.** This module displays a link to your blog's Atom feed.

- **user-photo.** This module displays the user image that you uploaded to your TypePad account.

To delete one of these modules, select its check box and click the Delete button.

Modifying Advanced Templates

Editing a template or template module is as simple as clicking the name of the template you want to modify to open the Edit Template page.

Figure 9.40 shows the edit page for the Main Index Template, which governs how the blog's main page looks.

Figure 9.40 Editing a template.

At the top of the page is the Switch Templates drop-down menu, which allows you to go from template to template, editing away to your heart's content.

Below that menu are the Template Name and (for index template files only) Output File fields, which you can change. If you plan to use a different page as your front page—perhaps a static page—you'd want to change this template's output file name to something other than index.html (because the index.html file is your blog's home page).

Managing Themes

As you've been experimenting with themes, TypePad has been helpfully saving the themes you've been changing. You can perform several actions on these themes, as well as on your active themes, as I explain in this section.

Viewing your designs

At the bottom of the Design page, you'll find the Your Designs section (**Figure 9.41**). This section lists all the designs that are currently being used in your blogs and themes that have been saved.

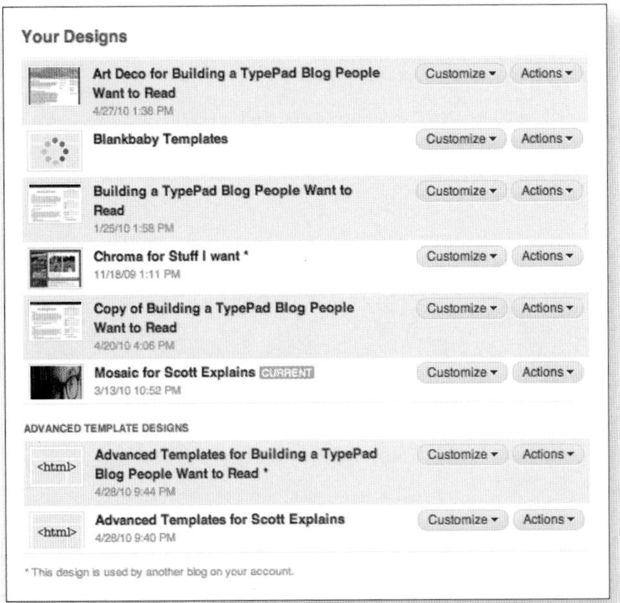

Figure 9.41 All your designs for all your blogs.

This section groups designs into two buckets. Designs based on stock themes and built with Theme Builder are listed together, and designs based on Advanced Templates are in a section called Advanced Template Designs.

Each entry represents a theme, starting with a thumbnail (notice in Figure 9.41 that the Theme Builder and Advanced Template themes use those features' icons as thumbnails), followed by the name of the theme and the date when it was saved. TypePad automatically comes up with a name for your theme by using the formula *Name of theme + name of your blog*.

The active design is denoted by an orange Current icon. Designs that are active for any other TypePad blogs associated with this account are denoted by an asterisk. Make sure that you don't delete these designs.

The final things to note in the Your Designs section are the Customize and Actions drop-down menus, which I cover separately in the following sections.

Customizing a design

The Customize drop-down menu allows you to jump directly to whatever section of the design you're allowed to customize. The Customize menu for the Mosaic theme, for example, includes Banner, Colors, Layouts, Content, and Custom CSS (**Figure 9.42**). The options vary depending on the theme.

Figure 9.42 The Customize menu gives you direct access to each section of the selected theme.

As you might guess, Advanced Templates have only one option in their Customize menu: Templates. This option takes you to the template's edit page, where you can customize all the Advanced Templates associated with the design in question.

Applying actions to a theme

The Actions drop-down menu contains the same options for all themes, Advanced and non-Advanced alike. Those options are

- **Apply.** This option applies the selected design to the active blog.

- **Preview.** This option allows you to see what a particular design would look like in this blog before you click the Apply button.

- **Rename.** TypePad automatically names designs for you, but the names lack a little something. You can rename any and all of your designs by choosing this option and entering a new name in the resulting dialog box. Make the name descriptive, and base it on the theme's distinctive features. (If you customized a design with a banner featuring a new logo, you could name it New Logo Design, for example.)

- **Duplicate.** Suppose that you have a cool idea for your blog's design, but you don't want to fiddle with the active design for fear that you'll screw it up somehow. Just choose this option to open a dialog box that lets you create a duplicate of the design (which won't be applied to your blog), and make all the changes you want. When you're happy with the way the design looks, click the Apply button. Your blog looks super-cool, and your readers are none the wiser that your new design took months of tinkering.

- **Delete.** As you use TypePad, you'll start to collect a large number of designs. TypePad is a little aggressive about saving designs, which is great because you'll never have to worry about losing one. The downside is that all those inactive designs clutter the Your Designs section. The Delete option removes the selected design.

 Make sure that you really want to delete the design, because there's no Undo option.

10

Checking out TypePad's Libraries

I've already covered most of the links in the TypePad global navigation bar, with one exception: Library. When you click Library, a drop-down menu offers you three choices: Photo Albums, TypeLists, and File Manager (**Figure 10.1**).

In this chapter, I cover all three libraries.

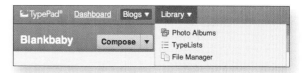

Figure 10.1 The libraries available in the Library drop-down menu.

Working with Photo Albums

TypePad's Photo Albums feature allows you to create a gallery of photos with links to each individual photo's page. You can list these galleries in a sidebar on a page of your blog, if you like, or just link to them. Each photo album has a permalink based on your TypePad URL. The only way to change this URL is to use domain mapping. (See Chapter 3 for everything you ever wanted to know about domain mapping.)

Before I delve into photo albums, however, I want to list a few of their shortcomings:

- **Restricted image sizes.** Photo albums allow you to display your photos only at certain set sizes; you can't display them at their original sizes.

- **No comments.** Photo albums don't support commenting on any of their pages (which is a little odd).

- **Not embeddable.** If you're posting your pictures to a TypePad photo album, I think it's safe to assume that you'll want to blog about the photos. Sadly, you can't actually embed a photo album in a blog post. Sure, you can link to photo albums, but they're separate entities from your blog.

- **No blog-matching designs.** You have several photo-album designs to choose among, but they aren't based on the themes that are available for your blog. If you want an album's design to match your blog's design, you're out of luck. (For more on TypePad themes and blog design, see Chapter 9.)

As an alternative, I suggest Flickr (www.flickr.com), which has many more social features, or Picasa (http://picasa.google.com), which is free and more flexible.

Given all these drawbacks, why would you want to use TypePad's photo albums? Well, they're included with your TypePad membership, so there's that.

Creating an album

To create a photo album, follow these steps:

1. Choose Photo Albums from the Library drop-down menu in TypePad's navigation bar (refer to Figure 10.1).

TypePad opens the Photo Albums page, which lists any albums that you've created in your account (**Figure 10.2**). (If you don't have any albums yet, nothing will be listed in this page.)

Click to create an album.

Click to upload photos.

Figure 10.2 The Photo Albums page.

2. Click the Add a Photo Album link to create your very first TypePad album.

   The Add a Photo Album page opens (**Figure 10.3**).

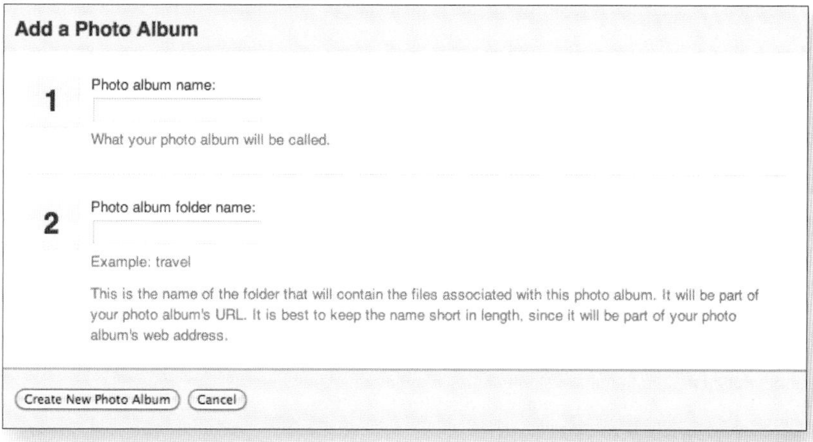

Figure 10.3 Add a photo album here.

3. Enter a name for your album in the top text field.

   TypePad will use this name as part of the album's URL, so try to keep it short (though you can edit the folder name separately).

4. Enter a folder name in the bottom text field.

5. Click the Create New Photo Album button.

   TypePad does just that.

Uploading photos to an album

note TypePad photo albums support only photos in GIF, JPEG, and PNG formats. Those three formats, though, should cover any photo you take with a consumer camera. (Photo geeks, note that you can't upload RAW images.)

To upload photos to a TypePad photo album, follow these steps:

1. Choose Photo Albums from the Library drop-down menu in the navigation bar to open the Photo Albums page (refer to Figure 10.2).

2. Click the yellow Upload Photos button.

   TypePad opens the Upload New Photos page (**Figure 10.4**).

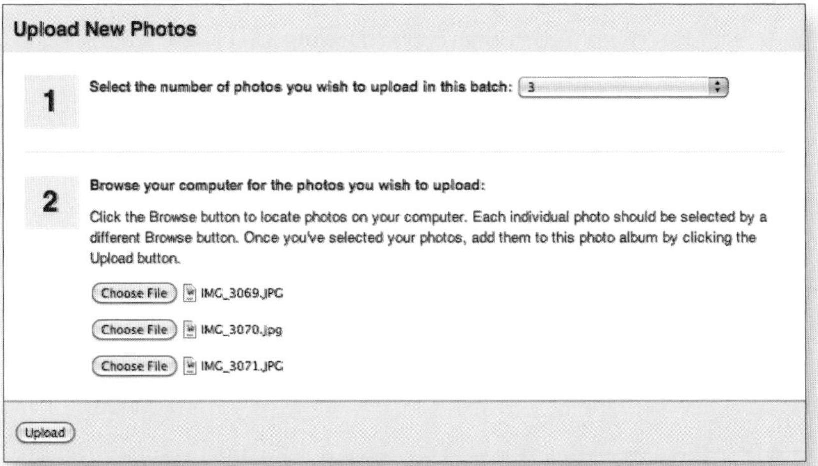

Upload New Photos

1   Select the number of photos you wish to upload in this batch: [3 ⬦]

2   Browse your computer for the photos you wish to upload:

Click the Browse button to locate photos on your computer. Each individual photo should be selected by a different Browse button. Once you've selected your photos, add them to this photo album by clicking the Upload button.

(Choose File) 🖻 IMG_3069.JPG

(Choose File) 🖻 IMG_3070.jpg

(Choose File) 🖻 IMG_3071.JPG

(Upload)

Figure 10.4 The Upload New Photos page lets you upload individual or zipped photos.

3. Tell TypePad how many pictures you want to upload by making one of the following choices from the drop-down menu at the top of the page:

   • **The number of pictures you want to upload.** TypePad allows you to upload as many as 15 pictures at the same time. But what if you want to upload more than 15 pictures or don't want to upload each one separately? Skip to the next item.

- **The option titled I'm Uploading a Zipped Folder.** This option (**Figure 10.5**) allows you to upload as many pictures as you want with one click. You need to do a little prep work to make this happen, though. First, gather all the pictures you want to upload into a folder; then compress that folder in .zip format. (Both Mac OS X and Windows 7 allow you to compress files without installing any other software.)

Figure 10.5 Choose this option to upload a .zip file full of photos.

 note   If you're a StuffIt fan, you're out of luck, as .zip is the only supported compression format.

4. Click the Upload button.

   TypePad starts uploading your photos (**Figure 10.6**). This process may take a few minutes.

Figure 10.6 Upload times depend on the number and size of photos and on the speed of your Internet connection.

Configuring a Photo Album

When your photos finish uploading (see the preceding section), TypePad creates your photo album and automatically takes you to the Photos tab of that photo album's management page (**Figure 10.7**, on the next page).

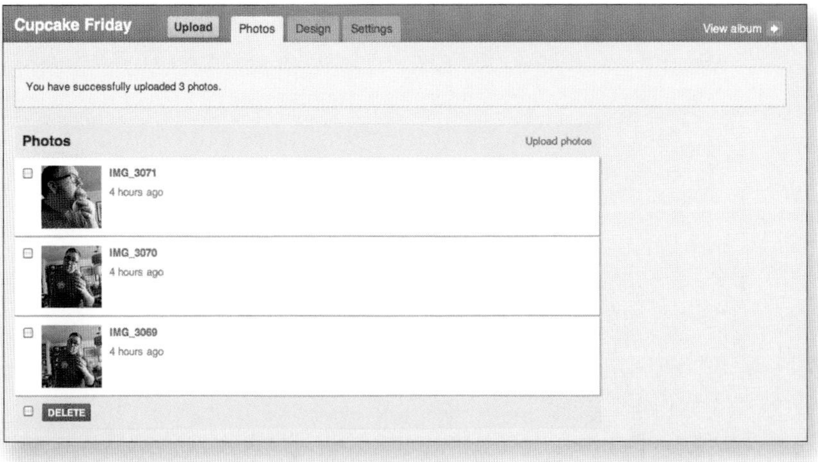

Figure 10.7 Success! My three photos have been uploaded into an album.

At the top of the page is the name of your photo album (in Figure 10.7, Cupcake Friday). Next to it is an Upload button that takes you to the upload page for this album. Finally, you see three tabs: Photos, Design, and Settings. I cover all these tabs in the following sections.

Working with the Photos tab

The Photos tab is all about adding photos to and removing photos from an album, as well as managing the pictures in the album. In this section, I show you how to do all that.

Adding and deleting photos

To delete photos from this album, select the appropriate check boxes (or select them all by clicking the bottom check box) and then click the Delete button. A confirmation dialog box pops up, asking you whether you're sure. Click OK, and whatever you want to delete is gone.

If you want to add a photo to this album, click the yellow Upload button or the Upload Photos link at the top of the page, either of which takes you to the Upload New Photos page (refer to Figure 10.4).

Editing photo details

If you want to edit a photo's name and caption, just click the photo itself in the Photos tab to open the Edit Photo page (**Figure 10.8**).

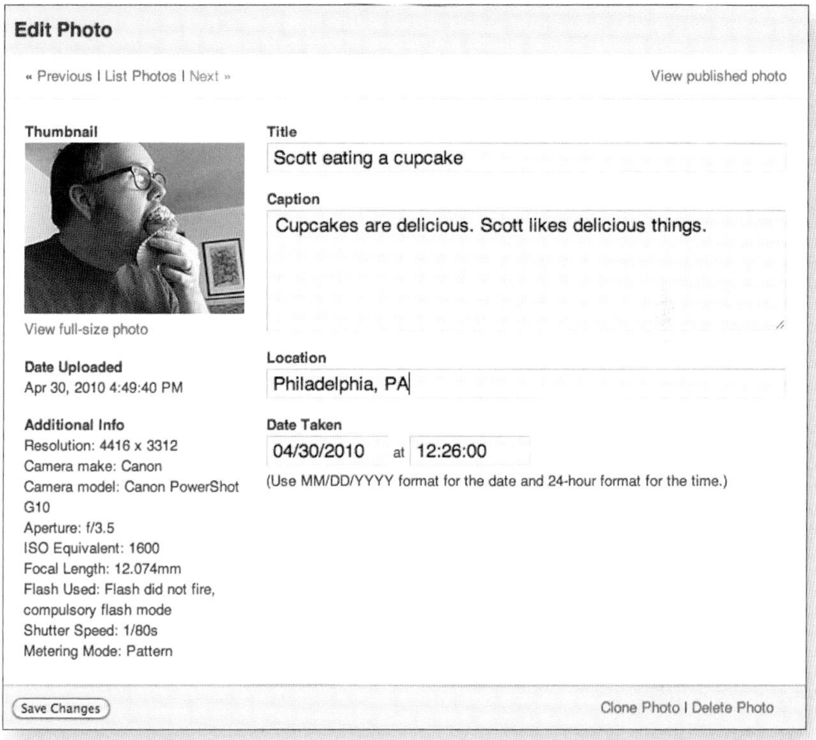

Edit Photo

« Previous I List Photos I Next »   View published photo

Thumbnail

View full-size photo

Date Uploaded
Apr 30, 2010 4:49:40 PM

Additional Info
Resolution: 4416 x 3312
Camera make: Canon
Camera model: Canon PowerShot G10
Aperture: f/3.5
ISO Equivalent: 1600
Focal Length: 12.074mm
Flash Used: Flash did not fire, compulsory flash mode
Shutter Speed: 1/80s
Metering Mode: Pattern

Title
Scott eating a cupcake

Caption
Cupcakes are delicious. Scott likes delicious things.

Location
Philadelphia, PA|

Date Taken
04/30/2010   at 12:26:00
(Use MM/DD/YYYY format for the date and 24-hour format for the time.)

(Save Changes)   Clone Photo I Delete Photo

Figure 10.8 You can edit the photo title, caption, location, and date taken here.

At the top of the Edit Photo page, you see a couple of navigation links. Previous and Next take you through the photos in your album (assuming that you have more than one photo in the album), and List Photos takes you to the photo list. You can also click the View Published Photo link to see the photo as it's displayed in the album.

In the top-left corner is a thumbnail of the photo, with a link to the full-size version right below it.

Right below the thumbnail are the date you uploaded the picture and an Additional Info list, containing information taken from the image file itself.

note The image shown in Figure 10.8 (am I not a handsome man?) was taken with a Canon G10, which embeds a host of information about the camera settings in each picture. Using a format called EXIF, TypePad can read this information and display it in the Edit Photo page. Depending on the camera you use, this page may list more or less information for your pictures than you see in the figure.

The rest of this page contains details that you can edit. Each picture has a Title, Caption, Location, and Date Taken field, and you can edit all these fields. Be sure to save your edits by clicking the Save Changes button.

Cloning photos

While you're looking at the bottom of the Edit Photo page, look to the right, and you'll see two links: Clone Photo and Delete Photo. The Delete Photo link deletes the photo, as you've probably figured out. Clone Photo creates a copy of the photo and inserts it into another photo album.

When you click the Clone Photo link, the Clone Photo dialog box opens, listing all your albums (**Figure 10.9**). Select the album(s) that you want this photo to appear in, and click OK. TypePad creates a copy of the photo (along with all the information associated with it) and inserts the copy into the selected album(s).

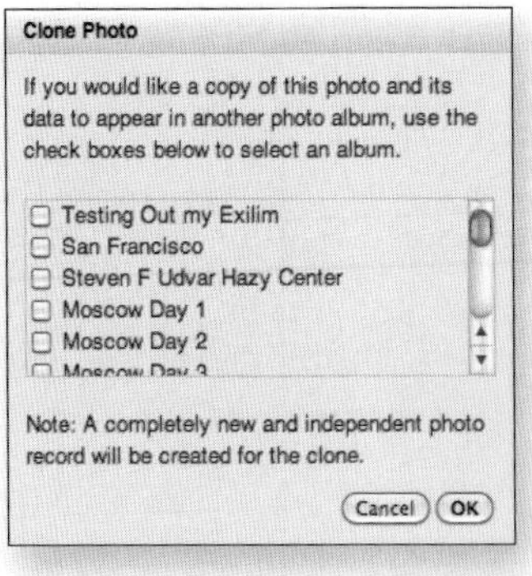

Clone Photo

If you would like a copy of this photo and its data to appear in another photo album, use the check boxes below to select an album.

- ☐ Testing Out my Exilim
- ☐ San Francisco
- ☐ Steven F Udvar Hazy Center
- ☐ Moscow Day 1
- ☐ Moscow Day 2
- ☐ Moscow Day 3

Note: A completely new and independent photo record will be created for the clone.

(Cancel) (OK)

Figure 10.9 Cloning a photo allows you to create a copy of the selected photo and place it in one or more other photo albums.

Working with the Design tab

Because photo albums are their own entities, your blog's design has no effect whatsoever on them. Each photo album has its own design settings and a special set of themes for you to choose among.

Much like your blog's Design page, the photo album Design tab has four sections: Overview, Layout, Content, and Style.

Overview

The Overview page (**Figure 10.10**) displays a thumbnail of your current design. If you have more than one album, you'll also see a section called Apply a Different Design. The drop-down menu in this section lists all your other albums. When you choose one and click Use This Album's Design, the album you're currently working with will use the design applied to the selected album.

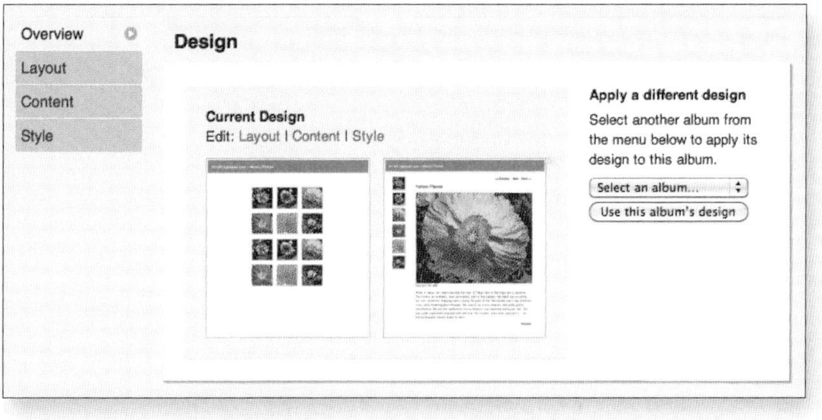

Figure 10.10 The Overview page.

Layout

The settings in the Layout page (**Figure 10.11**, on the next page) determine what the photo pages look like. The page is broken into two sections: Cover Page and Photo Pages. You can change the layout of each type of element independent of the other.

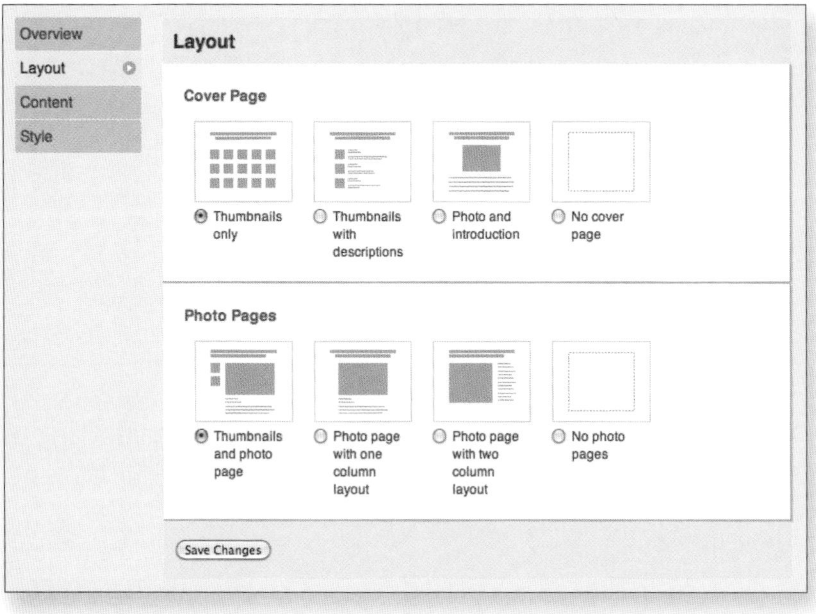

Figure 10.11 Just like blog themes, photo-album themes have several layout options.

You can think of the cover page as being the index page of your photo album. The four options control what people will see if they visit the album's URL directly:

- **Thumbnails Only** displays a list of your photo's thumbnails. Click a thumbnail to go to that photo's page.

- **Thumbnails with Descriptions** displays the thumbnails and their descriptions in a list.

- **Photo and Introduction** shows a single photo and the introduction that you can write for each photo album. (You set the introduction in the Settings tab, which I cover later in this chapter.)

- **No Cover Page** dispenses with the cover page and displays the first photo page.

The settings in the Photo Pages section determine how each individual photo is displayed. Once again, you have four options:

- **Thumbnails and Photo Page** displays a larger version of the selected photo along with thumbnails of the photos that appear before and after it in the album. Click the thumbnail to navigate the album.

- **Photo Page with One Column Layout** displays a large photo with the description and information listed below it.

- **Photo Page with Two Column Layout** displays the photo in one column and information about it in the column next to it.

- **No Photo Pages** transforms the album into a list of image files. This setting is useful if you just want to get a bunch of images from one place to another by using a Web page.

Content

The Content page (**Figure 10.12**) is where you control the information displayed in photo pages: photo title, caption, location, date taken, and EXIF data. (I discuss the EXIF format in "Editing photo details" earlier in this chapter.) This information is the same data that's available in the photo's Edit Photo page (refer to Figure 10.8).

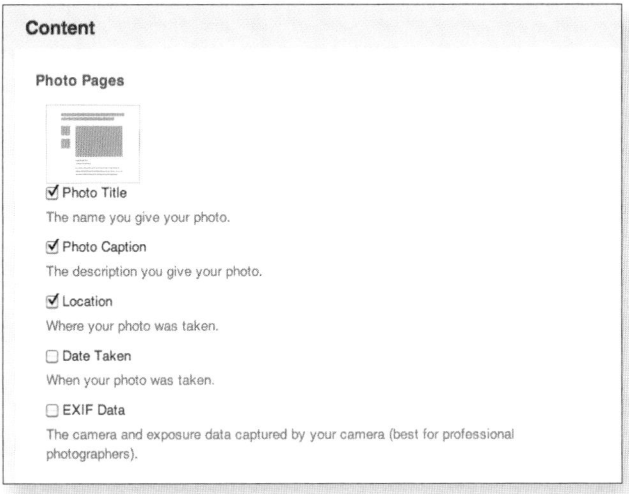

Figure 10.12 The Content page determines what information is displayed on each photo page.

Select the check box next to each piece of information you want to include in the photo page, and don't forget to click Save Changes (if you make any changes, of course!).

Style

The Style page (**Figure 10.13**) determines the appearance of your photo album. The drop-down menu lists all the available photo-album styles. Each time you choose a style, the two thumbnails on the right side of the page preview what the style will look like applied to your album.

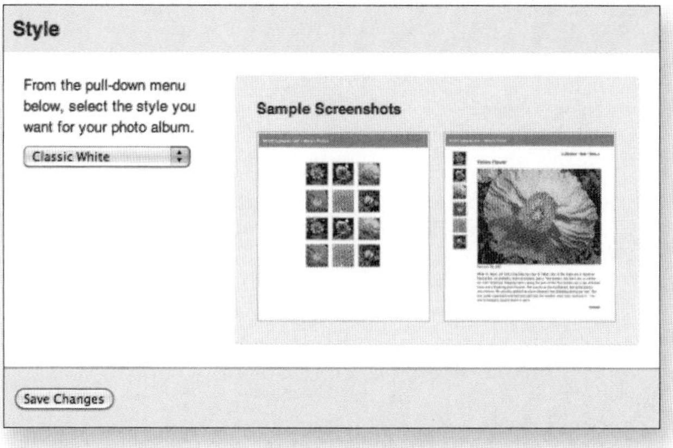

Figure 10.13 Several styles are available for your albums.

 note   There's no such thing as an Advanced Template (see Chapter 9) for photo albums. You must choose one of the built-in themes.

Click Save Changes when you've selected a winning theme.

Working with the Settings tab

The Settings tab is where you control the basic settings of your photo album. These settings apply only to the photo album you're currently viewing; they're not global settings.

TypePad offers two types of settings for photo albums: Basics and Advanced.

Basics

The Basics page (**Figure 10.14**) lets you enter the name of your photo album and a description, set a cover image, and make the album public (or not).

> **note** The description is optional, but if you're using a cover page that includes an intro, you write that intro here.

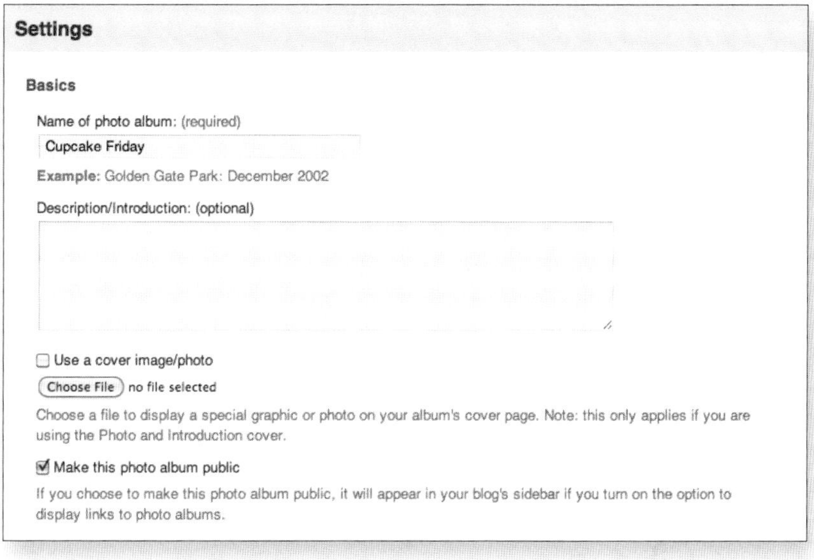

Figure 10.14 The Basics settings are the most commonly used.

To set a cover image, select the check box titled Use a Cover Image/Photo, click the Choose File button, browse your computer for the image you want to use, and select it. Interestingly, you can't just designate an image that's already in your photo album as the cover image; you have to upload a separate file.

If you want your album to be open to the public, select the bottom check box (Make This Photo Album Public). If you change your mind later, clear the check box.

Advanced

The settings in the Advanced page (**Figure 10.15**) give you a little more control of both your cover page (if you use one) and your photo pages.

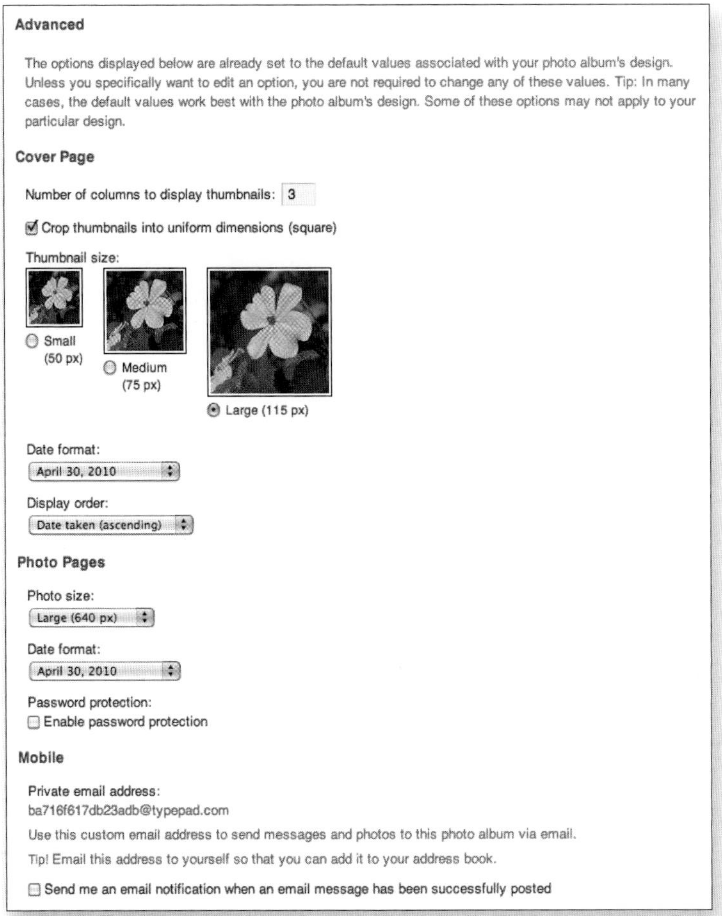

Figure 10.15 The Advanced settings.

You can set several options for the cover page:

- **Number of Columns to Display Thumbnails.** First, you can set how many columns of thumbnails should appear on your album's cover page. (The default is three.)

- **Crop Thumbnails into Uniform Dimensions (Square).** If you want your thumbnails to be cropped into squares, check this box. This setting makes the columns look more orderly, because all the thumbnails are the same size.

- **Thumbnail Size.** I like to use the largest of the three options, but pick whichever size appeals to you.

- **Date Format.** The Date Format drop-down menu offers ten formats for you to choose among.

- **Display Order.** Finally, you can decide how the thumbnails on the cover page should be arranged: in descending order based on the date taken, in ascending order based on the date taken, or alphabetically by title.

At the bottom of the page, you can set three options for your photo pages:

- **Photo Size.** Choose Small (350 pixels), Medium (500 pixels), or Large (640 pixels).

- **Date Format.** Again, the drop-down menu lets you pick one of ten options.

- **Password Protection.** If you want to password-protect your album, select the check box and then set a user name and password in the fields that appear when this option is checked.

Finally, the Mobile section lists the private email address associated with this photo album. This address is automatically generated by TypePad, and it's deliberately difficult to guess so that random people can't email pictures to your photo album. Any picture that's emailed to that address will be displayed in the album (and if you select the notification check box, TypePad will email you when a picture is posted successfully).

Managing Photo Albums

No matter where you are in TypePad, whenever you want to get back to the list of your current photo albums, choose Photo Albums from the Library drop-down menu in the top navigation bar (refer to Figure 10.1). The resulting Photo Albums page (**Figure 10.16**, on the next page) lists each album you have, along with the name of the album, its URL, how many photos are in the album, and links to the Design and Settings tabs.

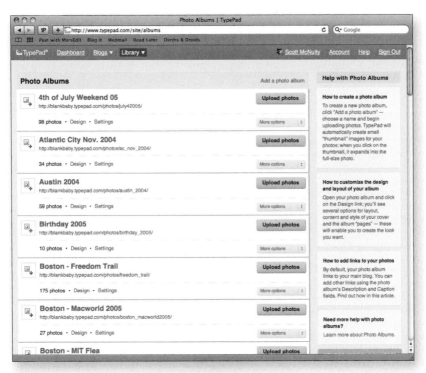

Figure 10.16 All your photo albums are listed alphabetically.

If you want to upload some new pictures to an album, click the icon to the left of the album's name (the small image with a plus sign on it) or the yellow Upload Photos button. Either action takes you to the Upload New Photos page for the selected album (refer to Figure 10.4).

You can delete a photo album right from this page by clicking the More Options button (**Figure 10.17**). When you do, TypePad displays one more option: Delete This Photo Album. Click that link to do just that.

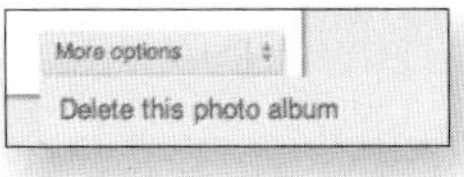

Figure 10.17 Deleting an album is just a click away.

Using TypeLists

What are TypeLists? Simply put, they're lists that you can display in your blog's sidebars (see Chapter 9).

TypeLists are global. You can create a TypeList that contains all your favorite Web sites, for example, and have it show up in all your blogs. Thereafter, whenever you fall in love with a new site, you just add it to your TypeList, and it will show up in multiple places.

Creating a TypeList

First things first—you have to start by creating a TypeList. (I assume that this one will be your first.) Follow these steps:

1. From the Library drop-down menu in TypePad's navigation bar (refer to Figure 10.1), choose TypeLists.

   TypePad opens the TypeLists page (**Figure 10.18**).

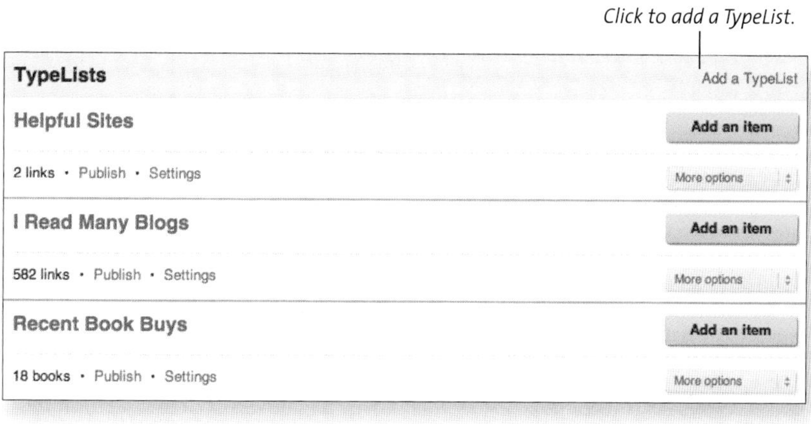

Click to add a TypeList.

Figure 10.18 A list of TypeLists.

2. Click the Add a TypeList link.

   The Add a TypeList page appears (**Figure 10.19**, on the next page).

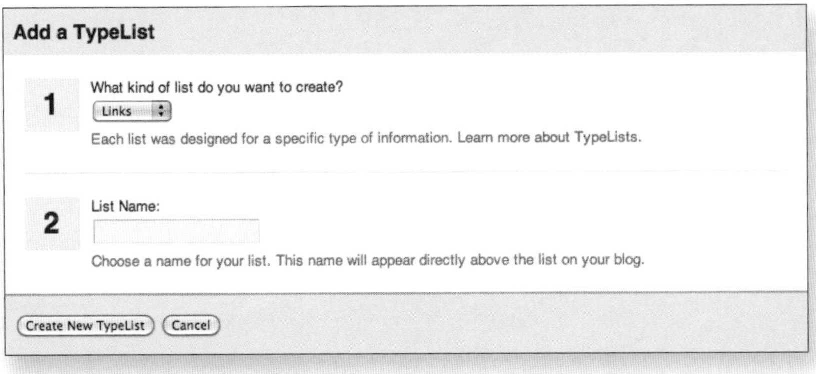

Figure 10.19 Add a TypeList here.

3. From the drop-down menu, choose the kind of TypeList you want to create: Links, Books, Albums, or Notes.

   I cover all four kinds later in this chapter.

4. Give the list a name.

5. Click the Create New TypeList button.

   TypePad creates your TypeList and takes you to the detail page of that TypeList, where you can add items.

Adding items to TypeLists

Now that you know how to create a TypeList, you need to populate it. A list that doesn't list anything won't be very interesting to your readers. The following sections cover how you add items to each type of TypeList.

Links TypeLists

A Links TypeList allows you to create a list of links to other sites of interest. You can maintain your *blogroll* (links to blogs that you enjoy reading), or any other set of links that you want to group, by using a Links TypeList.

Here's how to add links to one:

1. Complete the steps in "Creating a TypeList," selecting Links in step 3.

   When you click Create New TypeList, you're taken to the Add Link page (**Figure 10.20**).

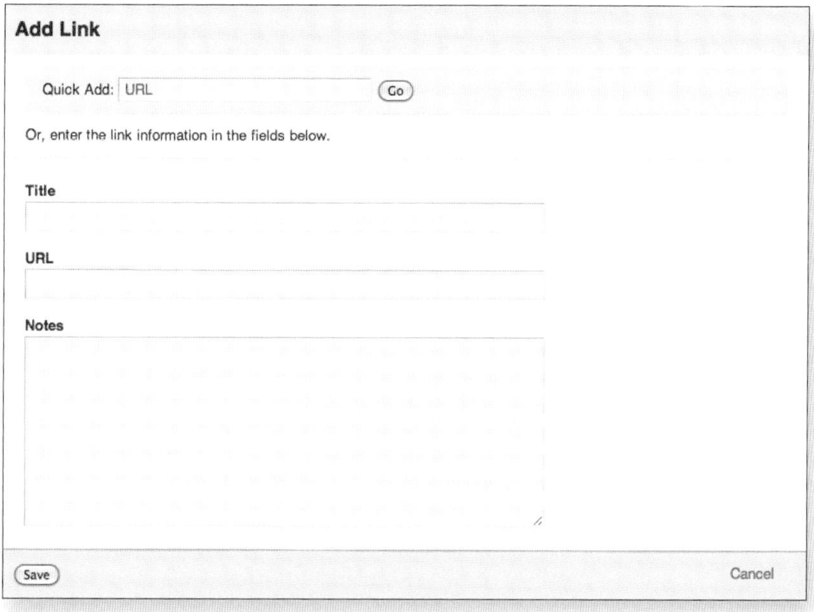

Add Link

Quick Add: URL   (Go)

Or, enter the link information in the fields below.

Title

URL

Notes

(Save)   Cancel

Figure 10.20 The Add Link page.

2. Add a link in either of these two ways:

   - **Quick Add.** To use the Quick Add feature, all you have to do is type the URL in the top text field and click the Go button. TypePad automatically fills in the title based on the title of the Web site; you must add notes manually.

   - **Manual entry.** In the text fields, enter the link's title, URL, and any notes you want to include.

3. Click the Save button.

   TypePad adds the link to your TypeList and takes you to the Items tab, where you can continue adding links.

note The Items tab works the same way for all four kinds of TypeLists, so I explain it once—in "Editing a TypeList" later in this chapter.

Books and Albums TypeLists

Books and Albums are different kinds of TypeLists, but they have a great many things in common. A Books TypeList displays a list of books, including images of the book covers, whereas an Albums TypeList displays a list of albums with the appropriate covers. **Figure 10.21** shows both kinds.

Figure 10.21 Books and Albums TypeLists in action in a blog's sidebar.

Adding an item to either kind of TypeList involves the same process as adding items to a Links TypeList (see the preceding section), with a few differences:

- The Quick Add function for books works on either keyword or ISBN (International Standard Book Number). Enter either item in the Add Book page's text box, and click the Go button (refer to Figure 10.20). TypePad queries Amazon.com and returns a list of matching books. Select the one you want.

- Quick Add works the same way for Album TypeLists, though it searches Amazon by using keyword search only.

- The details of the Items page are slightly different for these two kinds of TypeLists. Books have the following information associated with them: Title, Author, Notes, and Rating (one to five stars). Albums have Album Name, Artist, Song, Notes, and Rating (again, one to five stars).

Notes TypeLists

A Notes TypeList allows you to create a list made up of text. The text can be just that—text—or you can leverage this TypeList to display HTML code. Each note has two fields associated with it: Title and Body.

Suppose that you want to embed a series of YouTube movies in your blog's sidebar (**Figure 10.22**). One way to do that is to create a Notes TypeList, in which each item would have a title, and the body of the note would be the YouTube embed code.

Figure 10.22 You can use Notes TypeLists to add any text-based items to a sidebar, such as YouTube videos' embed code.

Notes TypeLists have only basic settings, so all you can change are the name of the list and the description.

Editing a TypeList

Nothing lasts forever, and most assuredly, you'll want to either edit or remove TypeList items. You do both things in the TypeList Items tab (**Figure 10.23**). To get there from the TypeList page (refer to Figure 10.18), click the name of the TypeList you want to edit.

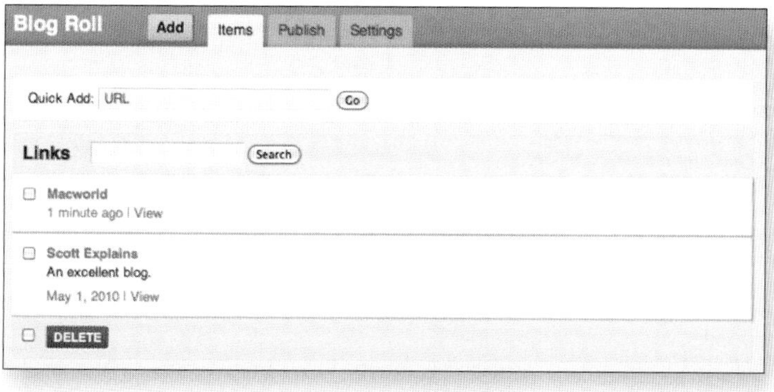

Figure 10.23 The Items tab for a Links TypeList.

To edit an item, just click it in the Items tab. TypePad takes you to the item's edit page, which contains the same fields that you used to add the item to the TypeList (see the preceding sections).

To delete an item, select its check box and then click Delete (**Figure 10.24**).

Figure 10.24 Deleting an item from a Links TypeList.

Publishing a TypeList

The Publish page controls where in your blog the TypeList shows up and is identical across all TypeList types. To access this page, click the list's Publish link in the TypePad page (refer to Figure 10.18). All your active blogs show up in the Publish page (**Figure 10.25**), with any blogs that use Advanced Templates listed in their own section. (For more info on Advanced Templates, see Chapter 9.)

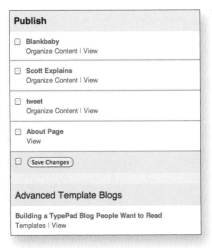

Figure 10.25 The Publish page.

Select the check box for each blog you want your TypeList to show up in, and click the Save Changes button. The TypeList is added to your blog's sidebar, placed at the bottom by default.

To move the newly added TypeList to the position you want it to be in, reopen the Publish page, select the blog, and click its Organize Content link. This link takes you to the design Overview page of the selected blog (refer to Figure 10.10). Click Content in the blue navigation menu, and your TypeList shows up in the Content page as a module. See Chapter 9 for a full discussion of how to alter your blog's appearance.

Each blog listed in the Publish page also has a View link that takes you directly to the blog (or page, in the case of the About Page entry) so you can check it out.

Configuring TypeList settings

The final tab of the TypeList page is Settings. To open the Settings page (**Figure 10.26**), click the list's Settings link in the TypePad page.

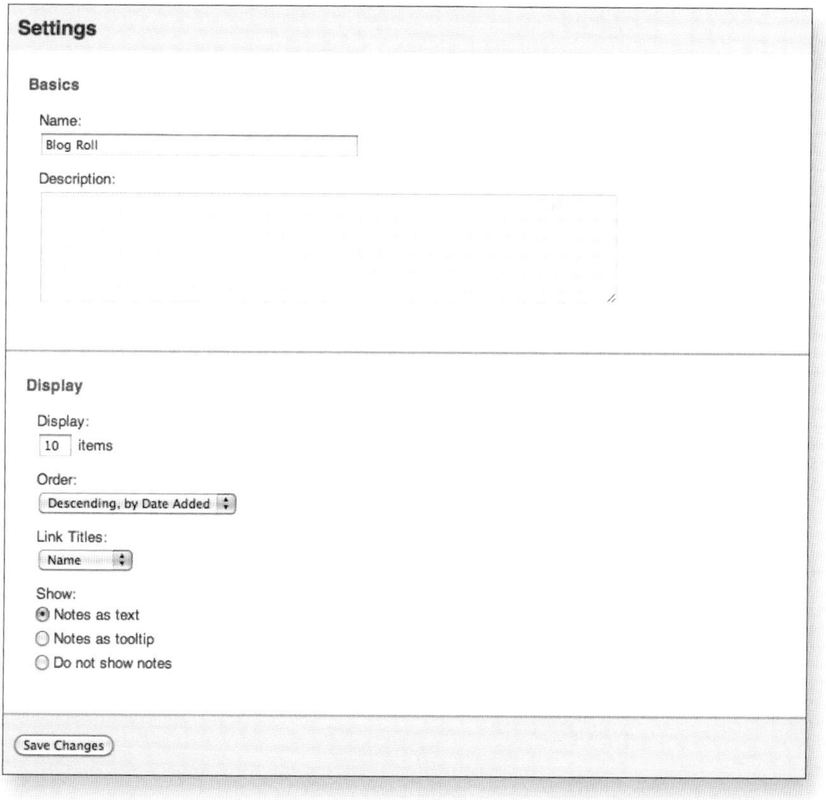

Figure 10.26 The settings for a Links TypeList.

All TypeLists have the same Basics settings: Name and Description. The name will show up when you display the TypeList in your blog, so be sure to enter a name that will make sense to your readers. The description is optional and is displayed only in the TypeList page (refer to Figure 10.18), so it's for your eyes only.

The Display settings control how your TypeList is displayed. In this section, you can set the following options:

- **Display x Items.** Enter a value in the text field. If you want to display all the links in this TypeList, set this value equal to or higher than the number of links you have in the list; otherwise, TypePad will display only the number of links you enter in the text field.

- **Order.** In this drop-down menu, you can set the order in which the links are listed.

- **Link Titles.** Choose one of the two options from this drop-down menu: Name or Site Name. They display the same information, so it doesn't really matter which you pick.

> **note** This option is available only for Links TypeLists.

- **Show.** Finally, you have to determine how the notes you've entered for each item are shown. They can be listed below the item as text, displayed as tool tips that appear only when someone hovers a mouse over the items, or not displayed at all.

The Display settings for Books and Albums TypeLists have a few more options than those for other TypeLists. In addition to setting the number of items to display and the display order, you can show artwork, ratings, and notes (**Figure 10.27**). Experiment with different combinations to find which display options please you most.

Make sure to click Save Changes when you're all set.

Figure 10.27 The Display settings for Books and Albums TypeLists are identical.

Working with File Manager

The final item in the Library drop-down menu (refer to Figure 10.1) is File Manager. I'm not going to lie to you—file management isn't the most exciting subject. That being said, it's a necessary evil. Choose File Manager from the menu to enter TypePad's File Manager page (**Figure 10.28**).

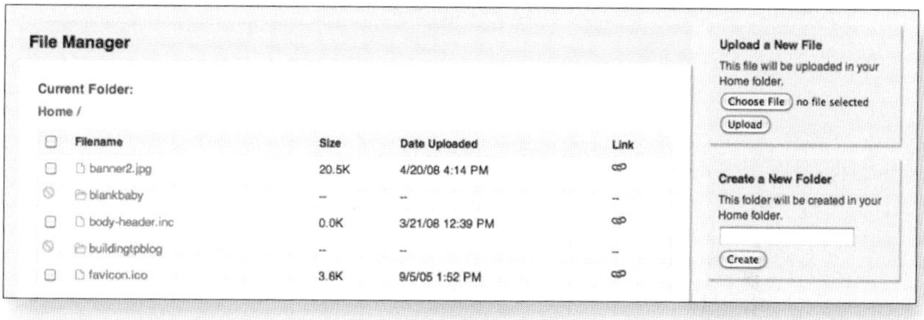

Figure 10.28 File Manager allows you to add and delete files hosted in TypePad.

Navigating File Manager

Way back in Chapter 5, when you picked a folder name for your blog, you may have wondered, "Why the heck am I doing this?" Well, check out all the files listed in File Manager; both folders and files are included. You should see at least one folder with a familiar name. That's right—each blog folder is listed here.

Most of this page is taken up by the list of folders and files. At the top of that list, you'll see the text *Current Folder,* which lets you know where you are in the file structure. Figure 10.28 (see the preceding section) shows the topmost folder of a TypePad account: the Home folder, which contains all the other folders (your blog folders) and files. When you delve into another folder by clicking its name in the list, the Current Folder display changes to reflect your current location (**Figure 10.29**).

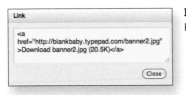

Figure 10.29 Your current location in your blog's file structure.

Now look at the list of files and folders in Figure 10.28 again. Each file has a check box next to it, whereas each folder has a slashed-circle icon next to it, which tells you that you can't delete folders. You can delete files by selecting the appropriate check boxes and then clicking the Delete button at the bottom of the page.

Each file entry displays some information about the file (**Figure 10.30**), starting with its name. (If you click the file name, the file opens in a new browser window.) Next are the size of the file, the date and time when it was uploaded, and a wacky link icon. When you click the link icon, a Link dialog box pops up, displaying the HTML code you need to create a text link to the file (**Figure 10.31**).

☐   ▢ prettybanner.jpg   16.1K   3/29/08 10:24 PM   ⬂

Figure 10.30 A file's details.

Link

```
<a
href="http://blankbaby.typepad.com/banner2.jpg"
>Download banner2.jpg (20.5K)</a>
```

(Close)

Figure 10.31 Click the link icon to see the HTML code that creates a link to that file.

Getting files into File Manager

How do you get files into File Manager in the first place? You have two ways to do this: by clicking the Insert File toolbar button in the New Post page (see Chapter 7) or by using the Upload a New File controls in File Manager (**Figure 10.32**). These controls work just like every other file browser that you've used so far in TypePad. Click the Choose File button, find the file on your computer, and click the Upload button.

Figure 10.32 You can upload files from File Manager.

Organizing files in File Manager

If you want to organize your files in folders, use the Create a New Folder controls (**Figure 10.33**). Enter a name for your folder in the text field (using only numbers, letters, dashes, and underscore characters), and click the Create button. Now you have a folder where you can store files (perhaps audio files, if you're hosting a podcast in TypePad).

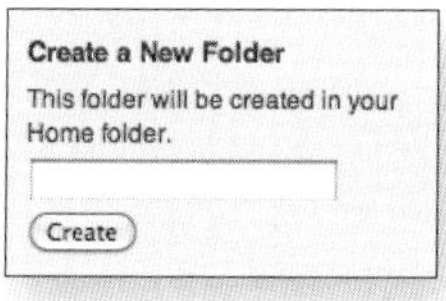

Figure 10.33 You can use folders to organize files.

note Think before you upload, though, because after you've uploaded a file to File Manager, you have no way to move it to a different folder.

11

TypePad Resources

At the beginning of this book, I mention one of the great things about TypePad: You don't have to worry about updating it. The TypePad team rolls out new features and bug fixes regularly, which is great for users because it means that they always have the latest and greatest of everything. For tech-book writers, though, this situation presents something of a challenge. I'm certain that by the time you read this book, TypePad will have some new features that aren't covered here. I couldn't cover them because they came out after I wrote the book. (I'm working on my time machine, but so far, I haven't met with much success.)

What's a person who's eager to stay on top of the latest TypePad news to do? Read blogs, of course! TypePad also has several resources to help you when you run into a problem or just want some professional help with any aspect of your blog.

TypePad Blogs

You really should check out a few blogs devoted to TypePad if you want to stay in the loop. Here are a few that I recommend:

- **The Official Everything TypePad Blog** (http://everything.typepad. com). This blog is where you'll find out about new features, interesting bloggers who use TypePad, and much more.

- **TypePad Dev Blog** (http://devblog.typepad.com). A whole team of people is working busily to make TypePad the best blogging platform out there. The TypePad Dev Blog chronicles that work, though I must admit that the blog is pretty geeky. (Personally, I like geeky.)

- **The TypePad Beta Blog** (http://beta.typepad.com). Six Apart rolls out new TypePad features to the beta team first. (In Chapter 2, I tell you how you can join this team.) This blog is devoted to all those new features that people "on the bleeding edge" are helping Six Apart test.

- **Blankbaby** (http://blog.blankbaby.com). This one is my personal blog. I can't promise you that it'll be all TypePad, all the time, but it's worth checking out. (I'm fascinating.).

TypePad Help

You may encounter an issue with your TypePad blog that isn't covered in this book. That's OK, because all of TypePad's paid plans include tech support as part of the price of admission. That's right—highly trained TypePad employees are standing by to help you with any and all problems you may have.

TypePad's global navigation bar includes a Help link (**Figure 11.1**). Clicking that link takes you to TypePad's Help Overview page (**Figure 11.2**).

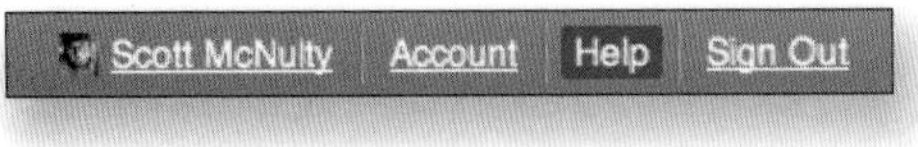

Figure 11.1 Help is just a click away.

The overview page gives you some links to other TypePad resources that you can check out, but the real power of TypePad's help system is the fact that it's ticket-based. To use this feature, click New Ticket in the blue navigation menu to reach the New Ticket page (**Figure 11.3**).

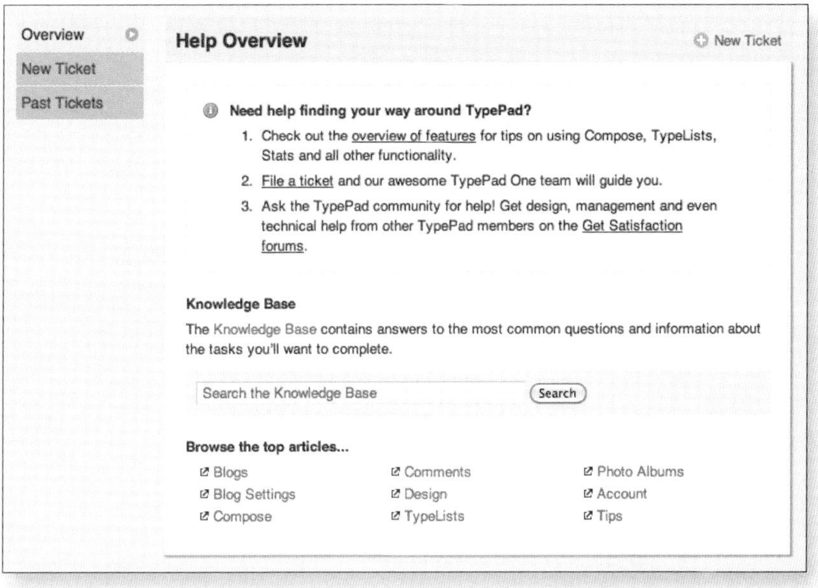

Figure 11.2 The help options that are available to TypePad users.

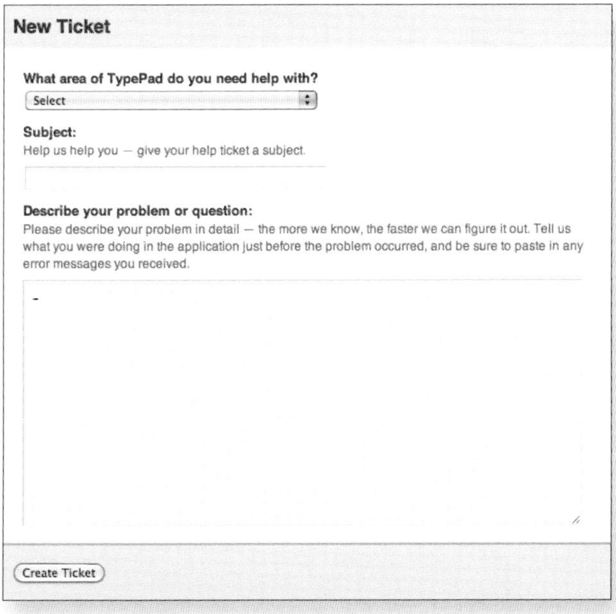

Figure 11.3 Filling out a TypePad ticket is easy, and the TypePad tech team is pretty responsive, in my experience.

Choose the area of TypePad for which you need help from the drop-down menu at the top of the page, enter a Subject line, and fill in the details of your error or problem in the text box. Then click the Create Ticket button to submit the ticket to the TypePad tech-support team, which will answer your question in the ticket itself. (The process is sort of like an email exchange.) You'll also be notified of any updates via email.

You can check the progress of a help ticket by clicking Past Tickets in the Help Overview page's navigation menu (refer to Figure 11.2). The resulting page lists all your open tickets and any tickets that have been resolved.

Help Yourself

If you don't want to fill out a ticket and would rather figure things out on your own, here are several help resources for you to check out:

- **TypePad Knowledge Base** (http://help.sixapart.com/tp/us). The TypePad Knowledge Base is without a doubt the best place to start any search for a solution to a TypePad–related problem. The site is searchable and features frequently searched-for articles to save you some time.

- **TypePad's Get Satisfaction page** (http://getsatisfaction.com/sixapart/ products/sixapart_typepad). Get Satisfaction is a Web site that many companies use to communicate with their customers about problems, bugs, and other aspects of their products. The TypePad Get Satisfaction forum is very active and a great way to find out whether the issue you're dealing with is really a bug or a feature.

- **TypePad Developer Resources** (http://developer.typepad.com). TypePad isn't just a product; it's also a platform. Clever developers can build applications on top of TypePad, and the Developer Resources site is there to help you build a fantastic app of your own.

- **TypePad Template Tags** (http://developer.typepad.com/tags). Chapter 9 is all about how your blog looks. If you're using Advanced Templates, which I cover in that chapter, you'll want to keep the Template Tags Web site handy.

- **Six Apart Status** (http://status.sixapart.com). TypePad is a hosted service, and sometimes, despite best efforts, services go down. The Six Apart Status Web site will let you know if TypePad is experiencing any systemwide issues.

TypePad One

Sometimes, you need just a little more help than you can get from a book (even this one!) or a Web site. TypePad One offers two different paid services—Tune-Up Service and Power Launch Service—that help you fine tune an existing blog or start a new one. Each service costs $249 per blog. You can find out more at www.typepad.com/one/typepad-services.html.

Blogging Terms 101

If you're an old hand at blogging, feel free to skip this appendix. If you're just wading into blogging, read on.

archives As you blog more and more, you'll have a pretty hefty number of posts before you know it. Your blog's archives page shows all your posts organized by date and category, making it the perfect place for a new reader to get an idea of what your blog is all about (and to help regular readers find that one post you did in October about cat sweaters).

blogroll *Blogroll* (which may be my favorite blogging term) means a list of links to the various blogs that you enjoy and want to share with your own readers.

tip   People often wonder how they can get their blogs a little more traffic. The answer: Link to other blogs, both in your posts and in your blogroll. This technique won't give you overnight success, but I can guarantee you that the bloggers you admire check their blogs' statistics as often as you check yours, and they'll notice your site coming up in their logs.

categories   Your blog is going to have a lot of posts about a variety of things. Some of those posts will be closely related, which is where categories come in. You define a list of categories and then assign those categories to your posts to group like posts with like posts.

comments   You aren't the only person who can post on your blog! Comments allow you to engage with your readers by giving them a space to express their opinions about whatever you post.

note   Comments are optional in TypePad, so you can enable or disable this feature as you see fit (see Chapter 5).

feed   A *feed* is a special file that allows people to subscribe to your blog via an application called a *feed reader*. (Where do people come up with these names?) Think of a blog as being like a magazine. You don't go down to the newsstand every day to check for the newest issue of your favorite mag; you buy yourself a subscription, and the latest issue finds its way into your mailbox without your having to do a thing. Your blog's feed allows people to subscribe to your blog and read your newest posts without having to refresh your blog over and over again.

header   A blog's header is the first thing you see when visiting. Typically, the *header* is a banner at the top of the page that includes the blog's name, an image (perhaps a logo or a photo), and links to various parts of the blog.

permalink   You're familiar with Web addresses like www.cnn.com, right? A *permalink* is the Web address of a particular post on your blog. As the name implies, this link should never change because you'll want it to work no matter who's linking to you or when. I discuss permalinks in more detail in Chapter 7.

post One of my pet peeves is the misuse of the word *blog*. I've heard time and time again that someone "wrote a blog" about this subject or that. The term *blog* (which is a shortened form of *Web log*) refers to the Web site, not to the parts of said site. You write posts for your blog; you don't post blogs. (Posts can also be called *entries*.)

tag Just as you can add categories to a post, you can tag a post. What's the difference? Tags are freeform, meaning that you don't have a list of predefined tags to choose among. That's about the only difference between tags and categories; you tag posts to provide more information about those posts to your readers. Perhaps you have a post about roses. You could tag it *flowers, red,* and *thorns* in addition to adding the category *roses*.

title Just like every good book (this one, perhaps), every blog post needs a title. The title should be short and related to the topic you're discussing; ideally, it includes a keyword or phrase that search engines will like (see Chapter 7).

trackback Whenever someone links to a post on your blog, that person's blog can send a trackback to your blog. A *trackback* is a method of notifying the blog that you're linking to of the fact that you've linked to its content. You can configure your blog to display a link back to the blog that linked to you. This feature is meant to help bloggers keep track of who is talking about their blogs and to help them discover one another. Sadly, the reality of trackbacks at the moment is that spammers are the people who use them most. I cover trackbacks, and show you how to disable them, in Chapter 8.

B

Alternative Ways to Post

Choices are good, right? Yes, they are. No one wants to be forced to do something one way and one way only. Fortunately, TypePad doesn't force you to post in any particular way; in fact, you can use several methods to post an entry to your TypePad blog.

In this appendix, I take a look at posting by using the Blog It bookmarklet, email, the TypePad mobile Web site, the TypePad iPhone app, and a couple of third-party applications.

Using Blog It

The Overview page of any of your TypePad blogs (see Chapter 5 for more info) contains a list called Other Ways to Post. The first entry is TypePad's bookmarklet, called Blog It (**Figure B.1**, on the next page), and for good reason. This bookmarklet—which is just a little piece of JavaScript that you can access the way you would a bookmark in your browser—makes it easy for you to quote some text or grab a picture from a Web site, add your own comment, and then post your creation to your blog.

Figure B.1 The Blog It bookmarklet makes blogging about Web sites that you've visited very easy.

To install the bookmarklet in your Web browser, just drag the Blog It button from the Other Ways to Post list to your browser's bookmark bar. The book-marklet is installed, and you'll see a new bookmark called Blog It (**Figure B.2**).

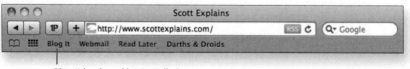

Blog It bookmarklet, installed

Figure B.2 Blog It, shown here in the bookmark bar of my browser of choice: Safari.

To use the bookmarklet, navigate to a Web site or blog that you want to post about, and click Blog It in the bookmark bar. A blog entry window over-lays the content of the Web page you're visiting (**Figure B.3**).

This window gives you several options to set:

- **Post Title.** Blog It automatically fills in the Post Title field with the title of the page you're visiting, but feel free to change that entry to what-ever you like.

- **Blog.** The Blog drop-down menu, to the right of the Post Title field, is set to your default blog by default, but it lists all the blogs associated with your TypePad account. If you want to post to a blog other than your default, just choose it from this menu.

- **Clipping.** When you click the Blog It bookmarklet while viewing a Web page, Blog It automatically grabs some text from that page and displays it in the Clipping text box. By default, it also displays the word *via* followed by a link to that content. This grabbed text, or *clipping*, is what will be posted to your blog, along with any notes you enter (covered later in this section).

Click the arrows to navigate clippings.

Reblog on TypePad

Post Title

Changing your iPad's email signature - Scott E>

Blog

Building a TypePad Blog |

Clipping   1 of 8 ——— *Blog It created this*
many clippings.

> You just got a brand new iPad, and you're excited about it! We all understand the
> excitement, but do you really want to remind everyone that you have an iPad every time
> you send them an email? Of course not! However, by default your iPad appends an email
> signature (basically some text that appears at the bottom of every email message) that
> says, "Sent from my iPad."
>
> via www.scottexplains.com

Your Notes

A great iPad tip

Share with

☐ **f** (blankbaby)
☐ ⌴ (blankbaby)
☐ ⌴ (scottexplains)

Publish Now   **Edit in TypePad...**

Figure B.3 The Blog It window. You can write an entire post
right from here (in HTML, if you want).

If you want to blog about something other than what Blog It grabbed
for you—say, a picture on the page, a different piece of text, or some
combination of both—you can cycle through all the images on the
page and some other text highlights by clicking the arrows on either
side of the Clipping box.

tip   **If you want to quote a particular section of the Web site that
Blog It doesn't list as a clipping, first highlight the text you want
to quote and then click Blog It in your browser's toolbar.**

Click the text in a clipping to edit it; Blog It displays that text's HTML
code in the Clipping box (**Figure B.4**, on the next page). You can edit
this code and then click OK to apply your changes or Cancel to
discard them.

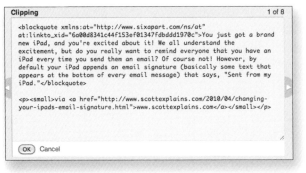

Figure B.4 Clicking text in the Clipping box allows you to edit that text directly.

- **Your Notes.** The Your Notes text box is where you enter your pithy thoughts about whatever you're linking to. The clipping will show up in your blog as a block quote so that people will know you're citing another site, and the text you enter in Your Notes will be displayed below that quote.

- **Share With.** The Share With section lists all the social-media accounts that you can post to from TypePad (see Chapter 2). Select the check box next to each network to which you want to post this entry.

- **Publish Now.** Click the green Publish Now button to post your entry immediately to whichever blog is selected in the Blog menu at the top of the window. When you click that button, a message appears, letting you know that your post has been posted and giving you a link you can use to go check it out (**Figure B.5**).

Figure B.5 Confirmation that your post has been published.

- **Edit in TypePad.** The other green button, Edit in TypePad, takes whatever clippings and notes you have in the Blog It window and transfers that material to TypePad's full-featured post editor, which I cover in Chapter 7. There, you can add tags and categories (features that the Blog It bookmarklet doesn't support), as well as more images.

  Figure B.6 shows the result of your efforts: a post created in Blog It.

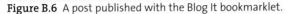

05/01/2010

Changing your iPad's email signature - Scott Explains

You just got a brand new iPad, and you're excited about it! We all understand the excitement, but do you really want to remind everyone that you have an iPad every time you send them an email? Of course not! However, by default your iPad appends an email signature (basically some text that appears at the bottom of every email message) that says, "Sent from my iPad."

via www.scottexplains.com

A great iPad tip

Figure B.6 A post published with the Blog It bookmarklet.

Posting via Email

I touch on this topic briefly in Chapter 5, but here's the full story. The idea is simple: Every blog and photo album that you host in TypePad has a unique email address associated with it. Things emailed to that address are automatically posted to your blog (or photo album). I use my blog's email address all the time to post pictures and files from my phone.

Images that you send by email are displayed in your blog just like any other images you post, and any file attached to the email is linked to from the post.

Keep a few things in mind when you blog via email:

- The title of the email will be the title of your post.

- The body of the email will make up the text of the post. Any email signature you may use will be included, so if you don't want the signature to show up in the post, make sure to delete the signature before you send the email.

- You can apply categories to posts sent via email. Before the text of your post, include a line that starts with the word *category* or *categories*, followed by a colon and a comma-separated list of categories. You can assign only existing categories to an email post.

Here's how it works. Suppose that I took a picture of a cupcake with my phone, and I want to post that picture to my blog with the title *Great cupcake*. I also want to make sure that the post appears in my blog's existing food and pictures categories. I'd write an email that looks like this:

To: My secret TypePad email address
From: Me
Title: Great cupcake
Body:
category: food, pictures
This cupcake was fantastic!

Then I'd attach the image to the email and (depending on the type of smartphone I'm using) press, tap, or click Send. That post would appear in my blog, and I'd get an email notification because I have TypePad set up to send email notifications (which I cover in Chapter 5).

Posting via TypePad's Mobile Web Site

If you have a smartphone with a compatible browser (iPhone, Palm Pre or Palm Pixi, or an Android phone), you can access TypePad's mobile Web site right on your phone. Just point your phone's browser to i.typepad.com, which forwards you to the mobile version of TypePad, and log in with your TypePad account credentials. You'll see a mobile version of the TypePad Dashboard (**Figure B.7**).

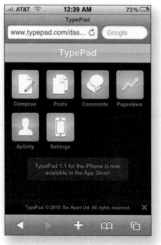

Figure B.7 TypePad's mobile Dashboard on an iPhone.

This mobile Dashboard lets you compose a post, manage posts and comments, see your blog's traffic, check out recent activity, and change some settings. I cover all these functions in the following sections.

Composing a post

Tap the Compose button on the mobile TypePad Dashboard to open the Compose page (**Figure B.8**), which allows you to do almost everything you can do in the full TypePad interface.

Figure B.8 Creating a post in TypePad's mobile interface.

The only things you can't do in the mobile version are upload files and insert pictures taken on your phone (though you can use HTML to embed existing online pictures in your post, if you like).

Managing posts and comments

The Posts and Comment buttons on the mobile Dashboard take you straight to the post and comment management pages, respectively. From those pages, you can approve comments or mark them as spam, as well as delete, edit, and unpublish posts.

Checking page views and activity

If you're out on the road and want to check in on your blog's statistics, the mobile Dashboard is there for you. Tap the Pageviews button, and you'll see the last 30 days' worth of traffic on your blog in a nice chart format (**Figure B.9**), with quick stats displayed at the bottom of the page. At the top of the page is a Referrers tab that takes you to the list of referrers.

Figure B.9   Traffic stats are easy to check on the go.

Tapping the Activity button shows you what the people you follow on TypePad are up to, much like the Recent Activity section of your blog's Dashboard. This section also shows you any new comments, trackbacks, reblogs, or favorites that your posts may have received.

Changing settings

Finally, the mobile Dashboard has a Settings button, which takes you to the Settings page (**Figure B.10**). This page lists your blog's secret email address, which you use to post via email (see Chapter 5), and lets you turn email notifications on or off. That's about it.

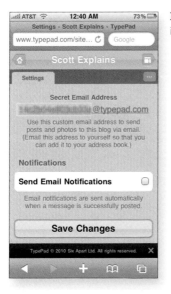

Figure B.10 Settings you can change in TypePad's mobile Dashboard.

Using the TypePad iPhone Application

iPhones are everywhere, so it seems, and if you have one, you can get a free TypePad app (**Figure B.11**) from Apple's App Store. The app is pretty basic, so I won't spend too much time on it. In fact, you can do a whole lot more on your iPhone by using the mobile version of TypePad, which I cover in the preceding section.

Figure B.11 The TypePad iPhone application allows you to upload images and videos.

Composing a post with the iPhone app is pretty easy. Launch the app, and tap Create a Post to bring up the Create a Post screen (**Figure B.12**). You can give a post a title, select the blog you want it to appear in, assign categories, and write the post itself, but you can't manage comments, see your blog's traffic, or change any blog settings.

The app does have one advantage over the mobile version, however: It lets you upload images. You can either take a new photo and upload it to TypePad via the app or upload any existing images you have in your iPhone's camera roll.

Figure B.12 Composing an entry in the iPhone app.

 note

If you have an iPad, you can access TypePad by using Safari. The Web site is very close to the full version, with one exception: It doesn't support file uploading.

Posting from Third-Party Blogging Applications

Lots of great third-party blogging applications for Windows and Mac OS X (and for various other operating systems, I'm sure) allow you to post entries to TypePad. The advantages of using one of these blogging tools instead of the Web version of TypePad are

- They can leverage all the robust features of the operating system. You can drag images into your posts, and maybe even search your Flickr stream for images.

- Drafts are stored locally, so even if you don't have an Internet connection, you can still write about that brilliant idea you had and post it when you have a connection again.

Because so many applications are available, I'm going to highlight my favorite Windows and Mac blogging apps in the following sections.

Windows Live Writer

Window Live Writer (**Figure B.13**) is a free, full-featured blogging tool from Microsoft. It supports creating and editing both posts and pages. It also has an inline spell checker and several plug-ins, and it makes embedding YouTube videos in your posts easy.

Figure B.13 The composition screen of Windows Live Writer.

Download Windows Live Writer at http://download.live.com/writer.

MarsEdit

I've been using the Mac application MarsEdit (**Figure B.14**), from Red Sweater software, for many years now. It has lots of rich media-handling capabilities that make getting images from iPhoto and Flickr into your posts a breeze. It also includes its very own bookmarklet, which allows you to start a post from any Web page by clicking a button.

Figure B.14 The composition screen of MarsEdit.

MarsEdit costs $29.95 and is available at www.red-sweater.com/marsedit.

Index